ALSO BY EVE GOLDEN:

Platinum Girl: The Life and Legends of Jean Harlow (1991)

Vamp: The Rise and Fall of Theda Bara (1996)

Anna Held and the Birth of Ziegfeld's Broadway (2000)

Golden Images (2001)

The Brief, Madcap Life of Kay Kendall (2002)

Vernon and Irene Castle's Ragtime Revolution (2007)

Table of Contents

Bride of Golden Images

42 ESSAYS ON FILM STARS OF THE 1930s–60s ORIGINALLY PUBLISHED IN CLASSIC IMAGES AND FILMS OF THE GOLDEN AGE

by Eve Golden

WITH 100 PHOTOS FROM THE EVERETT COLLECTION

BRIDE OF "GOLDEN IMAGES"

42 ESSAYS ON FILM STARS OF THE 1930s–60s

ORIGINALLY PUBLISHED IN *CLASSIC IMAGES* AND *FILMS OF THE GOLDEN AGE*

©2009 EVE GOLDEN

WITH 100 PHOTOS FROM THE EVERETT COLLECTION

Published in the USA by:

BEARMANOR MEDIA
P.O. BOX 71426
ALBANY, GEORGIA 31708
www.BearManorMedia.com

ISBN-10: 1-59393-462-9 (alk. paper)

BOOK DESIGN AND LAYOUT BY VALERIE THOMPSON

To Sharon Donovan
"Oh, lock the portal as you go,
And see its bolts be double. . . .
Come back in half an hour or so,
And I will be in trouble."
— ***Dorothy Parker***

Introduction

Back in 2001, I put together *Golden Images*, a collection of silent movie star articles originally published in *Classic Images* and *Films of the Golden Age*. It's taken me nearly ten years—oh, I keep busy—but here is the sequel, *Bride of Golden Images* (if Abbott and Costello were in this book, yes, it would have been called *Abbott and Costello Meet Golden Images*).

As in the first book, these articles have all been seen in *CI* and *FGA*. But, also as in *Golden Images*, I have gone over them with a fine-toothed comb: rewriting, doing additional research, and handing it over to my fabulous editor, Richard Kukan, so that clunky phrasing and just plain bad writing can be fixed.

I loved writing for *CI* and *FGA* (I basically ran out of subjects, so only do an occasional piece for them now, such as a recent tribute to the late Anita Page). What other publication will happily print pieces on the Duncan Sisters? Judy Tyler? Jimmy Durante? The research and writing were *fun* for me, and I hope that comes through in these articles. It was an additional kick for me to be able to illustrate this book with photos from The Everett Collection, where I work as an archivist.

Bride of Golden Images covers the talkie years, from the late 1920s through the 1960s. It's an eclectic collection of superstars, second bananas, character actors, and stage stars dipping their toes into the movies. Some of them immortal (Garbo, Dietrich, Crawford, Monroe). Some fondly remembered mostly by movie and pop-culture buffs (Carmen Miranda, Edward Everett Horton, Betty Grable, Inger Stevens, Constance Bennett). And then, those whose stories are known only to us few real fanatics: Lyda Roberti, the

Hilton sisters, Helen Kane, Renate Müller, Phillips Holmes. If I can bring those people back to life for just a few moments, I will be, as the saying goes, "the happiest little girl in all of Toyland."

EVE GOLDEN
NEW YORK, 2009

Foreword

For the longest time I hated Eve Golden. That's right, actually despised the lady.

It wasn't entirely my fault. When I started writing for *Classic Images* in 1995, Eve was already (since 1991) established as one of *the* most popular writers in the magazine's history—and one of the best. So, of course, our editor Bob King, rightfully, favored Eve, and would constantly talk about how wonderful she was. "Why can't *you* write more like Eve Golden?" he would ask me. So, I resented her, skipping her articles with a vindictive vengeance. I'll show *her!*

Then, one day, I noticed her Marilyn Monroe article. Ordinarily, I don't like to read about Marilyn; so much has been written already about her, much of it the same old-same old. But, despite my initial misgivings, I read on. I was simply knocked-out at how Eve had the ability to make it seem that she was the first to ever write about Marilyn—her take on Monroe was fresh, interesting, provocative, not corrupted by outside forces; Eve had opinions of her own.

After I was finished, I was thoroughly ashamed of myself. Because, you see, Eve Golden wasn't just one of the best: she was and *is* the best *Classic Images* has ever had to offer. I started examining her articles, dissecting them, trying to figure out how she could make her subjects—many of them more than 50 years away from their heyday—sound as fresh and exciting as when they started. But, alas for us fellow writers, it's all Eve. No one has her style, the grace, the elegance she possesses. Her articles float along, much like a graceful Astaire dance step. She glides around the page, effortlessly taking her reader into a different era. It's marvelous, it's exhilarating, and it's damn annoying that it can't be bottled! Eve Golden is one of only three writers in this world that I truly aspire to emulate (the other two are Doug McClelland and Tom Weaver). She takes her knowledge, adds a bit of zany humor, mixes a firm grasp of the movies and the personalities and out comes a soufflé of pure, tasty magic.

I also admire her brevity, something I've *never* learned. She can say so much in so few words, capturing the essence of her subject brilliantly. Take this terrific quote about Jean Arthur: "Talking films revealed her quirky, remarkable voice: nasal, raspy, querulous—an odd, expressive voice which somehow fit her intense, funny and very smart screen persona."

When I became *Classic Images'* book reviewer in 2001, I had to review a lot of dismal books on film (and still do). I probably would have lost my mind if not for the work of Eve Golden. Her biographies, on Jean Harlow, Theda Bara, Anna Held, Kay Kendall, Vernon and Irene Castle, not to mention *Golden Images: 41 Essays on Silent Film Stars*, are glimmering beacons in a sea of truly awful, poorly-researched tomes that I've had to endure.

As you will notice as you addictively read through these pages, Eve engages the reader with an irresistible force that moves him through every sentence of every article she writes. Combining this with a thorough knowledge of her subjects in particular, and a thorough knowledge of film history in general, has always made her a standout. Her careful attention to detail is the icing on the cake.

Now more of her *CI* articles have been combined into this book. Despite her scholarly attention to accuracy, there is not even the faintest whiff of the dry and dusty pedantry or smug superiority of some film historians (one of whom, a lesser writer of silent cinema, remains insanely jealous of Eve). Her smart, insightful observations ring just as true today as they did when first published. If that isn't enough for you—her writing is just plain fun. And it's fun because Eve has a real passion for classic films and for the people who made them.

A book by Eve Golden is like taking a course in film history. Your eyes will be opened. Your knowledge will grow. Your mind will expand. Come to think of it, those things don't always happen in film history courses, so allow me to correct myself. . . A book by Eve Golden is what a course in film history *should be*. Ah, if only school had been this much fun.

LAURA WAGNER
CLASSIC IMAGES

Jean Arthur

Many stars labored for years on the outskirts of success before hitting the big time: John Wayne, Jack Nicholson, Myrna Loy, Betty Grable. Jean Arthur was one of these steady, slogging workers; she was a "promising starlet" for more than a dozen years before getting her name at the top of the bill. And after a few years of stardom, she up and walked away from it all.

Gladys Georgianna Greene was born on October 17, 1900, in upstate New York, and spent her childhood in upper Manhattan (her birthdate was later pushed to 1905 and then 1908 to disguise her late-won success). Her father was a photographer, and Gladys was quickly comfortable in front of the camera. By the early 1920s, she was working as a photographer's and artist's model. It wasn't long before she was applying for work at film studios; in 1923 Fox signed her for a supporting role in John Ford's *Cameo Kirby*, costarring John Gilbert. Her name was changed to Jean Arthur (in tribute to Jeanne d'Arc and King Arthur, according to the fan magazines).

Jean had a great look for the movies: apple-cheeked, big-eyed, with a tiny mouth and a short-cropped flapper hairdo. For the next few years, Jean bounced from studio to studio (including many poverty-row houses like Tiffany and FBO), appearing in two-reel comedies with Charley Chase (*Bigger and Better Blondes*), Slim Summerville (*Case Dismissed*), and Monty Banks (*Flying Luck, Horse Shoes*), and in Buster Keaton's *Seven Chances*. But much of her time was spent in Westerns: Jean made 13 of them with Action Pictures beginning in 1924, four of them costarring Buffalo Bill, Jr.

Jean Arthur in the mid-1930s.

She rode back and forth to other studios as well, appearing in cheap, popular and long-forgotten horse operas with Bill Cody, Franklyn Farnum, and Lefty Flynn, and in six films with Wally Wales in 1925 and '26.

A good part in the college comedy *The Poor Nut* (1927) prompted

Paramount to sign Jean. Several decent films followed, including three in 1929: *Sins of the Fathers* (as Emil Jannings' daughter), *The Canary Murder Case* (her first talkie), and *The Saturday Night Kid* (as Clara Bow's rotten, thieving sister). Talking films revealed her quirky, remarkable voice: nasal, raspy, querulous—an odd, expressive voice which somehow fit her intense, funny and very smart screen persona.

She continued to work steadily, but in the early 1930s she still had not progressed any further than such starlets as Dorothy Sebastian, Sharon Lynn, Peggy Shannon, Barbara Kent—charming, talented flashes in the pan. Jean appeared with William Powell in the melodrama *Street of Chance*, with struggling silent stars Blanche Sweet and Evelyn Brent in *The Silver Horde*, and in two 1931 Universal comedies, *The Virtuous Husband* and *Ex-Bad Boy*. She'd had enough. Jean returned to New York to try and find stage work.

From 1932-34, Jean appeared in five Broadway shows, none of them running for more than a month or two (some were for the respected Theater Guild, however, and were intended for limited runs). She was in *Foreign Affairs* with Dorothy Gish; *The Man Who Reclaimed His Head* with Claude Rains; *The Bride of Torozko* with Sam Jaffe and Van Heflin. Not much money and no national recognition, but this all gave Jean great experience and self-confidence.

By December 1932 she was back in movies while still dabbling in theater; after a handful of unremarkable films, she finally signed a 1934 contract with Columbia and was off and running with the John Ford comedy *The Whole Town's Talking*: "It may be handsomely recommended as the best of the new year's screen comedies," said the *New York Times*. Jean burst forth as a modern, fast-talking screwball comedienne, and her career was finally in high gear. None too soon—Jean was nearly 35 years old.

Jean had negotiated a contract giving her unusual freedom in choice of projects, including script and director approval. If Columbia's Harry Cohn expected her to be a good little girl and accept what was given her, he was in for a bad shock (perhaps she overheard his remark about her face: "Half of it's angel, and the other half horse"). Like Bette Davis at Warners, Jean demanded only the best, and was not shy about putting her foot down and speaking plainly: "I just *couldn't* act in a bad picture," she flatly stated, despite the fact that even Garbo, Shearer, Cagney and Tracy had to swallow their pride and accept a few stinkers.

Like other stars, Jean appeared in fan magazines, fashion spreads, at red-carpet events; but she managed to keep her private life fairly private. After a brief 1928 marriage to Julian Ancker ("Julian nor I had enough income to make it possible for us to live together, so our marriage lasted one day"), she wed film producer Frank Ross in 1932; the two divorced in 1949 and Jean's other romantic liaisons—if any—remained safely hidden as she quietly did her work, socialized with friends, and went home with no scandals and no children to write tell-alls.

Jean appeared in a dozen films in 1935 and '36, some on loan-out from Columbia (*Public Hero No. 1* at MGM, *Diamond Jim* at Universal). Her first really great role, the one that cemented the "Jean Arthur character," was as the wisecracking big-city reporter who eventually melts for country rube Gary Cooper in Frank Capra's *Mr. Deeds Goes to Town* (1936). It was the first of three terrific films for Capra: Jean played the down-to-earth daughter of an annoyingly wacky family in Capra's rendition of Kaufman and Hart's *You Can't Take It With You* (1938), and she was another hard-boiled city gal won over by a starry-eyed yokel in *Mr. Smith Goes to Washington* (1939). "Jean Arthur is my favorite actress," said Capra, who had successfully worked with Stanwyck, Colbert and Hepburn. ". . . push that neurotic girl . . . in front of the camera . . . and that whining mop would magically blossom into a warm, lovely, poised and confident actress." Capra obviously recognized that Jean was often frustrated in her career choice. "I guess I became an actress because I didn't want to be myself," she later conjectured.

Jean had little to complain about as the 1930s wore on. *Easy Living* (1937) was a marvelous, classic screwballer, with a Preston Sturges script; she played Calamity Jane in *The Plainsman* and costarred with William Powell for the fourth and last time in *The Ex-Mrs. Bradford* (both 1936); she played opposite Charles Boyer and a dying Colin Clive in the shipboard drama *History is Made at Night* (1937); for Howard Hawks, she was in the aviation adventure

Only Angels Have Wings, with Cary Grant and Columbia newcomer Rita Hayworth (1939). The 1940s started off well with three rollicking good comedies: *The Devil and Miss Jones* (as a department-store unionizer, with Joel McCrea), *The Talk of the Town* (unwittingly harboring escaped political activist Cary Grant), and *The More the Merrier* (a World War II housing-shortage farce, with McCrea again).

In 1944 Jean's Columbia contract ran out, and so did she (Hollywood lore has her running down the streets screaming, "I'm free! I'm free!"). She enrolled in Stephens College in Missouri and Bennington College in Vermont, where she studied philosophy, anthropology and sociology. But she dropped out when she was offered a film she couldn't refuse, Billy Wilder's dark post-war comedy *A Foreign Affair* (1948). As a prim congresswoman investigating America's occupation of Germany, Jean battled with ultra-glamorous Marlene Dietrich for John Lund (both actresses were pushing fifty and both looked great).

Jean returned to Broadway (she had briefly appeared in a wartime revue, *Count Me In*) for a 1950 revival of *Peter Pan*, which proved immensely successful, but it was her last hurrah onstage. Illness (or, some said, emotional distress) caused her to drop out of the 1946 hit *Born Yesterday*, handing Judy Holliday the role of her lifetime. Her other theatrical ventures were a ghastly "mod" play, *The Freaking Out of Stephanie Blake*, which mercifully closed during previews in 1967, and *The First Monday in October*, which she dropped out of during its 1975 pre-Broadway run.

Shane (1953) was Jean's last movie—a great film to go out on, especially after her many 1920s Westerns. The cult drama, directed by George Stevens, starred Alan Ladd as a weary old gunfighter and Jean as a rancher's wife whose life he disrupts. Jean, unlike many of her contemporaries, never really dived into TV. She appeared on *Gunsmoke* in 1965, and her friend Lucille Ball convinced her to try her own series, *The Jean Arthur Show*, which ran briefly in 1966 (Jean played a chic, bubbly defense attorney). "The pilot is always good," Jean sighed about this last project, "and you think it's a possibility to get better and better. It never does. They don't do anything about it, they don't want to."

Jean retreated to her beloved home in Carmel, California. "I first

Jean Arthur with a wire-haired terrier (though not the famous Asta) in 1939.

saw the house in 1937 when I was going to murder a movie producer and my husband had to get me out of town." She cared for her dying mother in Carmel and avoided the press assiduously, gaining a somewhat unfair reputation for being a recluse. "I was ready and willing to work," she insisted, "but the roles I was offered were depressing or just old-maid parts." She spent her free time reading, cooking, gardening, and playing with her five cats. Jean also taught acting classes at Vassar between 1959 and 1972, as well as at North Carolina School of the Arts. "I have a very good life," she said, "with some good friends, a brood of cats and the sea on three sides of me."

Jean Arthur died of heart failure at the Carmel Convalescent Hospital on June 19, 1991, at the age of 90. Her ashes were scattered to the sea near her home. Happy and content in her later years, Jean did not look back on her film career with any great nostalgia. "I bumped into every kind of disappointment, and was frustrated at every turn. Roles promised me were given to other players, pictures that offered me a chance were shelved, no one was particularly interested in me, and I had not developed a strength of personality to make anyone believe I had special talents. I wanted so desperately to succeed that I drove myself relentlessly, taking no time off for pleasures, or for friendships."

Warner Baxter

When one thinks of the Golden Age sex gods, the names Gable, Valentino and Gilbert come to mind. But a few men—a little older and perhaps stuffier than those other gentlemen—had hearts fluttering as well. Women of a more mature and intellectual bent have long found pin-up boys in William Powell, Walter Pidgeon, and Warner Baxter.

The Oscar-winning actor was born in Columbus, Ohio, on March 23, 1889 (though, as usual, sources vary by as much as five years). The Baxters moved to San Francisco just in time to lose their home in the earthquake and fire of 1906. Though theatrically inclined as early as high school, Warner followed his parents' wishes and became a farm-implement salesman back in the Midwest. He was working in Louisville when his first break came. A local vaudeville company had an emergency: their juvenile was sick and the company needed a replacement. Warner jumped at the chance and toured for months before his appalled parents made him come home.

Show business was put on hold. The frustrated actor entered the insurance field, and within a couple of years was manager of the Travelers Insurance Company in Philadelphia (so says his résumé—though he was only about 25 at the time). Still searching for career satisfaction, he invested in an Oklahoma garage and was soon flat broke again. He realized that he'd only be happy acting, and in 1914 joined a Dallas stock company. He never looked back.

Warner Baxter—unlike many stage actors—*wanted* to get into films, and his first attempt was the Mae Marsh starrer *All Woman* (1918). It led to nothing, and he went back to the stage, where he had a huge hit in *Lombardi, Ltd.* (1918-20). He toured in that show for two years—which also made him a much more appealing bet to Hollywood. It also led to love (an early marriage, to Viola Caldwell, had fizzled out quickly). While touring in *Lombardi, Ltd.*, Warner and costar Winifred Bryson married; they stayed wed till Warner's death.

Warner Baxter's film career began in earnest in 1921, with supporting roles in *Sheltered Daughters*, *The Love Charm*, and *Cheated Hearts*. He bounced from studio to studio over the next three years, appearing in larger roles and learning his craft. He was by no means a star yet, but audiences began to recognize his name and his face. He costarred with Ethel Clayton in *Her Own Money* and *If I Were Queen* (both 1922) and had a good dramatic role in *Blow Your Own Horn* (1923), but was fired from Ernst Lubitsch's *The Marriage Circle* (1924) after only a few days' work. Warner bounced right back, appearing in several First National films with Florence Vidor and Agnes Ayres.

Paramount signed him in 1924 for *The Female*, and kept him on for 16 films (including two loan-outs). It took Warner two years to get his big break, during which time he made such films as Cecil B. DeMille's extravagant, naughty *The Golden Bed* (1925), the Fannie Hurst story *Mannequin* (1925), with Alice Joyce and Dolores Costello, and *Miss Brewster's Millions* (1925), a Bebe Daniels version of the frequently remade *Brewster's Millions* farce. But his first major hit for Paramount was *Aloma of the South Seas* (1926). This island film gave Warner the opportunity to display generous portions of his physique; ladies swooned, and his star was on the rise. That same year he was the first actor to portray *The Great Gatsby* (on film—James Rennie had already played the Broadway Gatsby).

Warner left Paramount and began freelancing in 1927, making eight more films before the talkie revolution hit. Most of his late silents were pleasant but forgettable films like *Three Sinners* and *Craig's Wife* (both 1928). But a huge hit was handed to Warner with *Ramona* (1928), costarring Dolores Del Rio. Director Edwin Carewe rather stiffly told the press that he'd interviewed 60 actors, but that "Baxter's . . . natural qualifications make him peculiarly fitted for the role of Alessandro. And I feel confident that this great

The dashing and handsome Warner Baxter in 1932.

romantic part will afford him an opportunity to register his finest characterization." Carewe was right, and both stars scored great popular hits in the movie. Warner went on to costar with Lon Chaney, Lionel Barrymore and poor tragic Ziegfeld Girl Mary Nolan in the tropical thriller *West of Zanzibar* (1928). Playing a debauched and disgraced doctor who finds redemption with Nolan, Warner was unrecognizable to fans who came to know his later, quieter roles.

Warner Baxter's star-making talkie role was that of The Cisco Kid, in Fox's 1928 all-talking *In Old Arizona*. He got the role by a fluke: actor/director Raoul Walsh was set for the lead when he lost an eye in an auto accident (Walsh never acted again, though of course his directing career was not affected). The role of the romantic Mexican bandit was out of the ordinary for the staid, Midwestern Warner Baxter, but—with a pencil moustache and curly black toupee—he made it his own. He won an Academy Award for the role (the film won Best Picture as well), and he played Cisco again in *The Cisco Kid* (1931), the comedy short *The Slippery Pearls* (1931), and *The Return of the Cisco Kid* (1939).

After his great success for Fox, that studio signed him to a long-term contract; Warner stayed with that studio (barring occasional loan-outs) through 1940. After a spate of indifferent early talkies in 1929 and '30, things picked up with *Doctors' Wives*, a 1931 romantic melodrama with Joan Bennett, and *Daddy Long Legs* (1931), with Janet Gaynor, his second of four films with her. He starred with Lupe Velez in the third version of *The Squaw Man* (1931). In all, he made 20 films between 1931 and 1934.

The role Warner Baxter is best known for today is that of harried Broadway producer Julian Marsh in Lloyd Bacon and Busby Berkeley's classic *42nd Street* (1933, on loan-out to Warner Brothers). Warner is the mature heart of the film, bullying and nurturing young performers Ruby Keeler, Joan Blondell, Dick Powell and Ginger Rogers through their paces. Much darker than the campy Broadway musical it inspired, *42nd Street* also gave Warner the honor of uttering the classic line, "You're going out there a youngster—but you've *got* to come back a star!"

Penthouse (1933) was another high point, a classy soap opera with Myrna Loy; and *Stand Up and Cheer!* (1934) was a delightfully loopy political musical costarring Madge Evans and a tiny Shirley Temple in her breakthrough role. Warner played a comic version of Julian Marsh, appointed by FDR to cheer the country out of the Depression with tap-dancers, hillbillies and a penguin that talked like Jimmy Durante. That same year he was in *Broadway Bill*, Frank Capra's horse-racing comedy, with Myrna Loy (and a young Lucille Ball in a bit part).

By this point, Warner Baxter was too old, in the latter half of his forties, to be on a par with Clark Gable or Cary Grant for young romantic leads. He wasn't yet to the character-actor stage, but he had a good ten years on the younger set. Still, some did appreciate his sex appeal: in 1936 *Picturegoer* called him "a Valentino without a horse . . . the chap the lonely woman on the prairie sees when she looks at the men's ready-to-wear catalogue . . ." That year, Warner Baxter earned $284,000, becoming one of the highest-paid actors in the country. He also gave what is generally thought of as his best performance in 1936, as the still-controversial Dr. Mudd in *Prisoner of Shark Island*. Starring as the man jailed for setting John Wilkes Booth's broken leg, Warner gave a typically quiet, restrained performance in what might otherwise have become an overblown action/adventure film.

Offscreen, Warner Baxter was athletic and outdoorsy, enjoying hunting, deep-sea fishing and tennis; his expertise on horseback came in handy in several films. At least one horse turned on him: while filming *Under the Pampas Moon* (1935), his mount grabbed his "Mexican" hairpiece and made off with it, along with a bit of the actor's scalp and ear. The film was more notable for being the speaking debut of Rita Cansino, still two years away from being renamed Hayworth.

Warner finished out the 1930s with a handful of pleasant films, including *The Road to Glory* (1936, with Fredric March), *Vogues of 1938*, two comedy/dramas with Loretta Young, *Wife, Doctor and Nurse* (1938) and *Wife, Husband and Friend* (1939), and Alice Faye's non-musical *Barricade* (1939). His biggest hit during this period was the adventure *Kidnapped* (1938), with Freddie Bartholomew. He then left Fox (by now, 20th Century-Fox) and moved to Columbia, where he made *Adam Had Four Sons* (1941, with Ingrid Bergman). Then, Warner Baxter vanished from the screen.

Warner Baxter at home with his wife, Winifred Bryson, in the early 1930s.

When he returned two years later, he freely admitted that he'd suffered a nervous breakdown. "I had to leave the screen," he said in an unusually frank interview. "It was frightening, that crack-up, the result of 22 years of competitive picture-making . . . It's bound to catch up with you eventually because it's so hard and nerve-wracking!" He spoke at length of his unsettling symptoms: "My mind was telegraphing the wrong messages. I wasn't getting the right responses. I'd start to say or do something, and before I even began, I'd forget what it was." Happily, Warner recovered. Not only did his career pick back up, but he was clever enough to diversify his interests, getting involved in real estate and politics (he was eventually elected mayor of Malibu).

At this time, Warner embarked on his second film series, though not as high-profile as *The Cisco Kid*. He appeared as Dr. Ordway in six *Crime Doctor* films for Columbia, from 1943 (*Crime Doctor*) through 1949 (*The Crime Doctor's Diary*). These films weren't much more than B walk-throughs, but they did add to the Baxter bank account and kept him in front of audiences. By the mid-1940s, he was well into middle age, inevitably crossing the line from leading man to character actor. "There are two courses open to a player at my stage of a career," he said. "He may continue on with romantic leads, until there comes that awful day when he finds roles no longer available. Or he may anticipate that event by several years and seek other forms of dramatic expression in which to mold a new career against the day when his earlier type of role no longer is open to him."

Warner next made *Lady in the Dark* (1944), a film that damn near finished Ginger Rogers' career as an A star. A loud, dull and overstuffed musical, it had bombed onstage with Gertrude Lawrence, and the film was one of the most expensive disasters of the war years. Ginger wasn't the only one hurt by *Lady in the Dark*; Warner Baxter never had another hit film. He made another eleven films after that (including four Crime Doctors). But none were worthwhile: *Just Before Dawn* (1946), *The Millerson Case* (1947), *A Gentleman from Nowhere* (1948), *The Devil's Henchman* (1949). Politics and real estate took up much of his time, along with his wife (he and Bryson had had no children).

By the late 1940s, Warner was suffering from degenerative arthritis; there was little doctors could do. When he made his last film, the dreary *State Penitentiary* (1950), he was in constant pain and finding it difficult to eat. Warner's malnutrition led his doctor, Richard Barton, to hospitalize him in April 1951; that month a lobotomy was performed to relieve his pain (lobotomies were all the rage among certain segments of the medical community in the post-war years). Nothing more could be done, and Warner was sent home, where he quickly developed bronchial pneumonia. He died at home on May 7, 1951. Although he is best remembered today for his roles in *42nd Street* and *Prisoner of Shark Island*, at the time every one of his obituaries depicted him as the now-forgotten Cisco Kid.

Constance Bennett

Few stars achieved the sheer force of glamour that Constance Bennett did in her long career on film, stage, TV and radio. She made her first appearance at eleven in one of her father's films, and her last film opened after her death. In all, Constance (never "Connie") appeared in 57 movies, two of which, *What Price Hollywood?* and *Topper*, became genuine classics. But who was Constance Bennett? Her sister Joan depicted her as a lovable steamroller in her 1970 book *The Bennett Playbill*. An interview with her son Peter Plant in 1997 shed some light on her personal life and her career as well.

She was born on October 22, 1904 (not 1905, as she herself insisted), the eldest of three daughters of Richard Bennett and Adrienne Morrison, both stage players. The Morrisons had been on the stage for generations, while Richard Bennett was a newcomer. But it was Richard who became the family star, while his wife more or less retired to raise their daughters. Richard Bennett was an old-fashioned trouper: opinionated, intelligent, hard-working and often impossible. He starred in dozens of Broadway shows, including *The Lion and the Mouse* (1905), the "social disease" drama *Damaged Goods* (1912), *He Who Gets Slapped* (1922), *They Knew What They Wanted* (1924) and *Winterset* (1935). All three Bennett girls were brought up in the theatrical tradition and it was no surprise when all of them took up the family trade. Joan, of course, had an impressive career of her own, while Barbara appeared in a handful of movies.

"I don't think she had any great interest in the history of the family," said Peter Plant of his mother. "Neither do I. But I will say

The height of soigné sophistication: Constance Bennett in 1934.

that having a thespian background was a big asset in business for me—the skills of communicating, having poise and presence, were developed in me as a child. I was taught how to walk in and out of a room, how to light a lady's cigarette. I would stand and look an adult in the eye when I was six or seven years of age. She gave me a very strong self-image at an early age. That's the whole thing about having a decent self-image, as I would put it. That image enabled me to play from strength."

Constance grew up a spoiled, headstrong girl, attending the best schools and affectionately bullying her kid sisters. She made her first appearance before the camera as a nymph in her father's film *The Valley of Decision* (1915), and thereafter returned to school. She briefly wed one Chester Moorhead in 1921, but that was quickly annulled. At 18, Constance embarked in earnest on her film career, making brief appearances in Select Studio's *Reckless Youth* and *Evidence* (both 1922). She worked her way slowly up the cast lists, playing supporting roles in such films as *Into the Net* (a Pathé serial of 1924), *Cytherea* (also 1924), *The Pinch Hitter* (with Glenn Hunter, 1925), and *My Son* (with Alla Nazimova and Jack Pickford, also 1925).

By mid-1925, Constance began getting starring roles. She looked a lot like her father: square face with a strong jaw and good, high cheekbones, remarkably large blue eyes and an air of importance. One of her first hits, *Sally, Irene and Mary* (1925), showed her unusual star quality. A mere 21 years old, she looks and holds the screen like a veteran of 35. Sharing the film with such competition as Joan Crawford and William Haines, Constance steals it in a walk. She not only turned in a bright and well thought-out performance as a self-destructive chorine, but she knew how to enter and exit, how to catch the right light, and how to move (or not move) in order to become the center of attention.

Constance Bennett appeared in an impressive nine films in 1925 and signed an MGM contract late in the year before suddenly giving it all up for Philip Plant, whom she married that same year (son Peter was born in 1929). Constance lived the life of a wealthy society matron until the marriage ended in 1929 and she returned to films (and blithely ignored an annoyed MGM, whom she'd walked out on four years earlier). She was back, rested and quite ready to resume her career. She signed with Pathé and stayed with that studio through the early 1930s, though often on loan-out. She reentered the film world with the society drama *Rich People* and the comedy *This Thing Called Love* (both 1929). In 1930 and '31, Constance found her forte in glamorous dramas like *Common Clay* (as a seduced housemaid) and as discontented kept women in *The Easiest Way*, *Bought*, and *The Common Law*.

When Pathé was bought out by RKO in 1931, she made six films for that studio, most of them racy, sophisticated "women's pictures" with such costars as Ben Lyon (*Lady with a Past*, 1932), future husband Gilbert Roland (*Our Betters* and *After Tonight*, both 1933) and Joel McCrea (*The Common Law*, 1931, *Rockabye*, 1932, and *Bed of Roses*, 1933). Constance always seemed to be gowned in satin, looking beautifully distraught in art-deco penthouses. She loved, she suffered, she paid the price, and she had loyal housewives and shopgirls flocking to her movies.

She also lived the life of a movie star, with an elegant home, fashionable clothes, and hordes of men paying her court. In 1932 she married Gloria Swanson's ex, the handsome and charming Marquis de la Falaise de la Coudray. When that marriage broke up after eight years, she took up with her former costar Gilbert Roland. She and Roland created something of a scandal in the late 1930s when a fan magazine article called "Hollywood's Unmarried Husbands and Wives" outed them (as well as Clark Gable and Carole Lombard, and Charles Chaplin and Paulette Goddard). Constance and Roland did marry, from 1941 through 1945, and had two daughters, Lorinda and Christina ("Gyl").

Much of Constance's socializing, said Peter Plant, was "with industry people, but mostly people in production. The people that came to our home were Lewis Milestone, Mervyn LeRoy, the Goetzes, the Zanucks, the Selznicks. She was good friends with Jack Warner and his wife. We used to go and visit their home a lot, also [Paramount production head] Henry Ginsberg." Plant recalled that most of his mother's parties were small dinners for friends (Marlene Dietrich, Kay Francis, the Thalbergs, Douglas Fairbanks). "I do recall one large party," he added, "with Glenn Miller's orchestra. However, acting was her main interest, and to her last days she never wavered in her commitment to her work."

In the early 1930s, RKO loaned Constance out for a handful of films, few of which amounted to much. But one at her home studio brought her to the top of the heap: the wonderful *What Price Hollywood?* (1932), in many ways superior to the many versions of *A Star is Born* which it inspired. Directed by George Cukor, Constance played an ambitious Brown Derby waitress discovered by a washed-up director (Lowell Sherman, in one of the best performances of the year). The movie's love angle is played down, as society husband Neil Hamilton is a secondary character—the platonic friendship between the actress and her discoverer is what matters here. A dark, funny and scathing film, *What Price Hollywood?* remains a very modern classic.

Constance Bennett took her acting very seriously from both monetary and artistic standpoints. "Money was very important to her," said her son, "but people who come from a stage background are often more serious about their responsibilities to their craft, their art, and to the people they're working with—and to the public, also. When you just work in front of the camera, there's not the contact with the public, and the discipline of knowing the entire script just isn't there. I remember when I was a little boy and I discovered another little boy was getting more for doing his chores than I was, I decided to bring this up to my mother, and she said, 'I'm going to ask you a question: has your friend a pony? Has he a swimming pool?' She said, further, 'Bear in mind, all the things we have come from the people who see my films, so you must always be polite to fans who approach us. They are trying to thank us for what we have given them, so we have to be gracious.'"

Hit films were few and far between for Constance as the decade wore on. She left RKO in 1934 for 20th Century-Fox, where she made the agreeable *Moulin Rouge* and *The Affairs of Cellini*. Then it was on to MGM for the drama *Outcast Lady* (1934) and the slight, enjoyable Clark Gable comedy *After Office Hours* (1935). But her star was waning a bit by then. She made a British drama, *Everything is Thunder* (1936), and came back to the US for *Ladies in Love*, where she played second fiddle to Loretta Young and Janet Gaynor. She had another run-in with MGM, when she sued over the financial beating she took over loan-outs.

Constance was in her early thirties by then, and things were not looking promising. But rescue came from Hal Roach, who starred her in a brilliant screwball comedy, playing up her ability to appear utterly chic and scatterbrained at the same time. She was assigned to play Marion Kerby in *Topper* (1937) when Jean Harlow, originally slated for the role, died. She and Cary Grant, as her husband, were a gorgeous, clever pair and played off each other brilliantly (they both seem to be having genuine fun with their roles). *Topper*

"Luxury is out of date in wartime," says Constance in 1944.

followed the lives and afterlives of the Kerbys, who—after being killed in a car accident—try to help their friend Cosmo Topper (Roland Young, in a role originally planned for W.C. Fields) and his wife (the always-wonderful Billie Burke). Constance also appeared in one of the sequels, *Topper Takes a Trip* (1939) which, lacking Cary Grant, was less satisfying.

Roach also starred Constance in the comedy *Merrily We Live* (1938), a shameless copy of *My Man Godfrey*. Despite the script's lack of originality, she was delightful—really, as good as Carole Lombard—playing the scatterbrained heiress who adopts a hobo (a very sexy Brian Aherne) as her butler—also featured in the film are two memorable sheepdogs, named "Get off the rug" and "You, too."

As brisk and confident as she appeared onscreen, Constance was not a clever businesswoman, and got involved in at least two disastrous ventures. In the mid-1930s she developed her own line of cosmetics. As her son recalled, "The cosmetics were a good, quality product, but at some point she gave someone a license of franchise for it, and he ended up putting nothing but lanoline in the jars, and it ruined the product." All that remains is a delirious promotional short she made, which was released as *Constance Bennett's Daily Beauty Rituals*—it turns up on TV and on the Internet, and is well worth searching out ("wishing you loads and loads of loveliness"). Constance also became involved in Fashion Frocks, "a dress line from the Midwest on which she put her name—mail-order dresses in women's magazines." That, too, failed. One of her drawbacks was that "she was very smart, but would not take advice—she had a number of advisors, but she had the idea that she was capable of doing things where she was in over her head."

Constance made only eleven films in the 1940s, the best of which were *Two-Faced Woman* (MGM, 1941) and *Centennial Summer* (20th Century-Fox, 1946). The former is noted as a legendary flop, but it suffered mostly from Greta Garbo's lack of comedic training. Constance herself, as Garbo's brittle rival in love, is a delight. One scene—wherein she drifts elegantly into a ladies' room, shrieks wildly into the mirror and drifts elegantly out again—is a moment of sheer joy. Constance played Dorothy Gish's glamorous sister in *Centennial Summer*, an unusually sweet and nostalgic vehicle for her.

The rest of her 1940s credits passed without much notice. She broke *The Law of the Tropics* (1941), looked on as *Wild Bill Hickok Rides* (1942), joined Gracie Fields in the *Paris Underground* (which she also produced, 1945), was a *Smart Woman* and an *Angel in the*

Amazon (both 1948). Constance also threw herself into the war effort in the 1940s, working on the "Bundles for Britain" charity and traveling to entertain the troops. By the time the 1950s dawned, the still elegant, now middle-aged Constance was ready for a change of pace, which arrived with the new popularity of television.

She had already appeared on radio, and jumped into this new medium with alacrity. Anthologies were big in the 1950s, offering stars the chance to play varied roles without having to sign on for a whole series. Constance made appearances on such shows as *Suspense, Cameo Theater, Robert Montgomery Presents, Teller of Tales* and *Faith Baldwin's Theater of Romance*. She also picked up paychecks as a panelist on the game shows *The Big Payoff* and *It's News to Me.*

She never tired of acting, said Peter Plant. "She liked it, she enjoyed it, and she worked very hard at it. When she was making a film, she would really be busy preparing for the next day's scenes. I would visit her for half an hour, and then she would go back to her script. She had what her father had, a photographic memory. Richard Bennett, I understand, could read a play through once, and he knew the whole play, *and* everyone else's cues. I have the good fortune to have inherited that, and it's made many people think me more intelligent than I am." Constance turned to the stage with such shows as *Without Love* (a 1940s tour), *Auntie Mame* (brilliantly cast, in 1958), and *Toys in the Attic* (1961). In the early 1960s she and her daughter Gyl played *Hay Fever* in Chicago. "I think she preferred the stage," said her son. "She preferred being before the live audience. To keep working you have to be flexible, and she was flexible. She did radio—*Kraft Radio Theater, Lux Theater, Chesterfield*. I know this not because I heard them, but because periodically there would be these huge baskets of Kraft cheese, large boxes of Lux Soap, cases of Chesterfield cigarettes."

Constance found lasting personal happiness with Brigadier General John Coulter, whom she married in 1946. Her career slowed down, for several reasons: age, her new marriage, and another factor, which her son pointed out. "After World War II, when the unions came into the studios, you couldn't do fifty takes anymore, and all the major studios were doing what is now called downsizing.

She was used to working with directors who made sure the thing was done *right*, no matter how long it took—until the studio heads noticed the dollars slipping away and put the brakes on."

In 1965, Constance had her first real film role in more than a decade, as Lana Turner's rich-bitch mother-in-law in the high-camp *Madame X* (released in 1966). She looked unrecognizable: chic and elegant but frighteningly thin, due to the cancer which no one but her immediate family knew about. Constance wiped up the floor with Lana, memorably snapping, "You're still a little shopgirl from Phoenix—you should have stayed on the other side of the counter!" "It was a grueling production experience," recalled Peter Plant. "But my mother, knowing she would soon be gone, but being true to her profession, got through it fine."

It was during the last years of her life that she became closer to her sister, Joan (Barbara, wife of tenor Morton Downey and mother of future talk-show host Morton Downey, Jr., had died in 1958). "Aunt Joan was fearful of Constance," said Plant, "and was intimidated by her, felt inferior to her. But in the last years of my mother's life, she and Joan were very close and very friendly. Joan spent a lot of time with her when she was ill in New York."

Constance Bennett died on July 24, 1965, in the Watson Army Hospital in Fort Dix, New Jersey. "I'm sure her cancer was caused by smoking too bloody many Chesterfield cigarettes for too many years," said Plant, "and also due to taking massive injections of hormones in the 1950s to preserve her figure and make her appear younger than she was. I could name several of her female star peers who met the same fate pursuing youthfulness."

By that time, Joan had surpassed her sister in reputation as an actress; Constance was recalled in her obituaries as more of a glamour girl. Not long before she died, she said of her professional longevity, "If there's a secret to it, it's working like a beaver to be happy. What I mean is, I've always been interested in everything I did. When you're interested in anything, you're happy."

Joan Blondell

Joan Blondell had it all: looks, talent, energy, humor. If she never became a top-flight superstar, the fault lies mostly with Warner Brothers. At MGM, Joan could have easily had Jean Harlow's career; at Paramount, Claudette Colbert's or Carole Lombard's; at Fox, Loretta Young's; at RKO, Ginger Rogers'. Some of the fault lies, too, with Blondell herself, who later admitted, "The instant they said 'cut!' I was whammo out of that studio and into the car . . . In order to be a top star and remain a top star and to get all the fantastic roles that you yearned for, you've got to fight for it and you've got to devote your twenty-four hours to just that; you've got to think of yourself as a star, operate as a star; do all the press that is necessary . . . What meant most to me was getting home, and that's the truth."

But if Joan Blondell got slightly lost in the shuffle at Warners, she still managed to turn in some delightfully snappy performances and typify the warm-hearted, wisecracking Depression dame. And when she aged, she did so with grace and humor.

Rose Joan Blondell was born in New York City on August 30, 1906. Her parents were vaudevillians who took their family (Joan and her siblings, Gloria and Edward) on tour through the US and to Australia and China. She spent her early teen years living the life of a roustabout, which may explain her hard-bitten wisdom and her later longing for home and family.

At 17, Joan won $2,000 in a beauty contest and headed back to her hometown. Department store and library clerking paid the rent while she sought acting work. In the late 1920s Joan appeared in Greenwich Village revues, touring shows, and possibly as a *Ziegfeld*

Follies girl (probably as a dancer, not a showgirl). She also appeared in small supporting roles in three Broadway shows: the hit melodrama *The Trial of Mary Dugan* (1927), the comedy *Maggie the Magnificent* (1929) and the crime drama *Penny Arcade* (1930). Those last two shows also featured a hot young fireplug, also from New York, named James Cagney. He and Joan became lifelong friends and wound up heading West to Warner Brothers together, costarring in seven films between 1930 and '34.

After appearing in a few Vitaphone musical shorts in New York, Joan signed with Warner Brothers and joined the great migration of stage artists into the talkies. She and Cagney filmed their stage show *Penny Arcade*, retitled *Sinners' Holiday* (1930), and both were off and running. The hard-working, uncomplaining actress was Warners' dream come true, and they worked her to the bone for the next nine years, making some 45 features for them and another seven on loan-out. In 1931 alone she appeared in ten films, sometimes working on two at once: some good, some awful, no starring roles. But Joan Blondell was nearly always the high point of the films (with the exception of *The Public Enemy*, in which she had an oddly colorless role). "We worked so hard," she said, "and hardly ever had a day off . . . Saturday was a working day and we usually worked right into Sunday morning."

Joan's good nature may have worked against her in the long run. While fellow Warner Brothers workers Bette Davis, James Cagney, Olivia de Havilland and Humphrey Bogart fought like lions for better roles and more creative input, Joan took things in stride, at least through the early 1930s. "I just sailed through things, took the scripts I was given, did what I was told. I couldn't afford to go on suspension—my family needed what I could make."

Joan's light brown hair was bleached and fluffed, her eyebrows thinned. She had a cute, curvy little figure when she arrived in Hollywood, and it was frequently shown off in bathing suits and lingerie. "I just showed my big boobs and tiny waist and acted glib and flirty," she said in later years. "I was the fizz on the soda."

Many of her early films show up on TV and are available on DVD, and Joan is always bright and delightful in them. In the racy *Millie* (1931) she shared a bed with Lilyan Tashman, she was Barbara Stanwyck's smart-mouthed pal in *Night Nurse* (1931), and

The hardest-working tootsie at Warner Brothers: Joan Blondell, early 1930s.

moved up to her first costarring role in *Blonde Crazy* (1931, with Cagney). Things improved steadily through 1932, with *The Greeks Had a Word for Them*, a gold-digging comedy costarring Madge Evans and Ina Claire. She was one of *Three On a Match* (with Ann Dvorak and Bette Davis in a very tough melodrama), William Powell's adoring secretary in *Lawyer Man*, and a gangster in *Blondie Johnson*.

In 1933 and '34, she was cast in three films that would insure her posterity: *Gold Diggers of 1933, Footlight Parade* and *Dames*, Busby Berkeley musicals (directed, respectively, by Mervyn LeRoy, Lloyd Bacon and Ray Enright) which, along with *42nd Street* and *Gold Diggers of 1935*, have been constantly revived and praised since their "rediscovery" in the late 1960s. Playing supporting roles, Joan couldn't match the singing and dancing skills of costars Dick Powell, Ruby Keeler, Ginger Rogers or James Cagney, but she sparkled and snapped and managed to talk/sing her way through such numbers as "Forgotten Man" and "The Girl at the Ironing Board." Sadly, Joan's later musicals (*Broadway Gondolier, Colleen, Gold Diggers of 1937*) were pale, post-Code imitations and the series spun itself out.

It's a testament to Joan's talent that she is so fondly remembered even though so few of her films were even adequate. Her Warners cohorts were given classics while Joan remained the reliable backup in unremarkable films badly needing her gifts. She teamed with similarly smart, tart actress Glenda Farrell in seven films in the mid-1930s, none of them worthy of their talents (*Traveling Saleslady, Miss Pacific Fleet, Havana Widows*, among others). Her biographer, Matthew Kennedy, quotes her as admitting, "If I had taken myself more seriously . . . if I had fought for better roles as, say, Bette Davis did . . . I think I might have been a damned good dramatic actress. But it was just my way; I don't think I ever had the security of feeling confident in myself, really, ever. I used to think, 'I'm just lucky to be here!'"

Joan not only worked hard at Warner Brothers, she socialized, too, marrying cinematographer George Barnes (*Rebecca, Meet John Doe, Spellbound*) in 1932. Their son Norman (later a production manager, producer and director in films and TV) was born in 1935, and the couple split up the following year. By then she was friendly with occasional costar Dick Powell, and the two wed in 1936; their daughter Ellen (later a film and TV hairstylist) was born in 1938.

By the time Joan's contract came up for renewal, she was more than ready to jump ship. She grew more frustrated by the sameness of her roles, and in 1935 even Joan's easygoing temper broke. She wrote to Warner Brothers' executive producer Hal Wallis, "Imagine

Husband and wife Dick Powell and Joan Blondell in *Gold Diggers* of 1937.

yourself eating the same meal over and over again, accompanied by the same people and the same small talk calling for the same small answers from yourself. After about the sixth meal you would become pretty weary and your answers would cease to have any life to them whatsoever. That is pretty much the position I am in." Of her later Warners films, only a few stand out: the comedies *Stage Struck* and *Three Men on a Horse* (both 1936), *Stand-In* (1937), and the delightful *The Perfect Specimen* (1937), in which Errol Flynn proved Joan's equal at light screwball comedy.

After fleeing Warner Brothers, Joan busily freelanced through the early 1940s: *Topper Returns* (United Artists, 1941), the excellent all-female war drama *Cry 'Havoc'* (MGM, 1943), and her best mid-career role, as blowsy Aunt Sissy in Elia Kazan's coming-of-age drama *A Tree Grows in Brooklyn* (20th Century-Fox, 1945), "which let me have a moment or two of tenderness, of maturity, that no one had ever given me before." She was the only bright spot in the Clark Gable comeback film *Adventure* (1945), memorable only for the ubiquitous tagline, "Gable's back, and Garson's got him!" It was one quick leap from ingénue to character actress. Joan herself admitted that she may have jumped the gun a bit. "I could have had some extra gauzes put on the cameras instead of going from young girl to old girl roles in one leap" (she was, at the time, 39—old by current Hollywood standards).

It was Joan Blondell's good fortune—and good sense—to develop a screen character that aged well. When middle age and increasing weight took their toll, she was able to segue into playing wry, wisecracking old dames. Many of her contemporaries fell by the wayside, but Joan stayed busy. She didn't maintain the high-profile popularity she'd had in the early 1930s, but she kept working, to critical acclaim.

The Powells divorced in 1944, and in 1947 Joan embarked on a stormy, brief (three-year) marriage to mercurial producer Michael Todd, who had starred her in the disastrous Broadway show *The Naked Genius* (written by Gypsy Rose Lee, 1943). She emerged from that marriage broke and exhausted, and remained single for the rest of her life. All she ever wanted, she lamented, was "one husband and one house and one garden and a lot of children . . . The only time I'd ever marry again is if someone beat on my door . . . and said, 'I have $27 million and I'll live elsewhere.'"

Joan continued settling into a plump and happy middle age. She played a carnival worker in the excellent film noir *Nightmare Alley* (with Tyrone Power, 1947) and got a Best Supporting Actress Oscar nomination for *The Blue Veil* (1951), as Natalie Wood's mother. She also returned to the stage from time to time, including runs in *Come Back, Little Sheba, The Rope Dancers, Crazy October* (with Tallulah Bankhead) and, in 1971, the absurdist comedy *The Effect of Gamma Rays on Man-in-the-Moon Marigolds.*

Joan in one of her last roles, in TV's *Banyon*, 1972.

Beginning in 1951 and for the rest of her career, Joan's most reliable paychecks (if not her best roles) came from television. She appeared on most of the Golden Age anthologies: *Suspense, Schlitz Playhouse of Stars, General Electric Theater, Studio One, Playhouse 90*, even her ex's *Dick Powell Theater*, in 1962. She didn't get her own series, despite filming numerous pilots, but she guest-starred on *The Untouchables, Wagon Train, My Three Sons, The Man from U.N.C.L.E., Medical Center, The Love Boat, Fantasy Island*.

Joan also worked steadily, though at a slower rate, in films. She was Jayne Mansfield's long-suffering secretary in *Will Success Spoil Rock Hunter?*, and costarred in the middling Tracy/Hepburn comedy *Desk Set*, and the dark psychological drama *Lizzie* (all 1957). As her weight increased and her health failed (arthritis, heart problems and, eventually, leukemia) she appeared in such films as Steve McQueen's *The Cincinnati Kid* (1965), the legendary all-star flop *The Phynx* (1970), the James Garner comedy *Support Your Local Gunfighter* (1971), the John Cassavetes indie *Opening Night* (1977) and the hit musical *Grease* (1978).

Joan's last big breakthrough was her hit TV series *Here Come the Brides* (ABC, 1968-70), costarring teen idols Bobby Sherman and David Soul. Loosely based on *Seven Brides for Seven Brothers*, the show featured Joan as Lottie, a warm-hearted, tough-talking saloon keeper in 1870s Seattle. She continued to receive offers right up to the end, but regarded most of these "alleged scripts" with disdain. "I'd rather work in Macy's basement: there's more dignity to that."

She was living in Santa Monica when she died of complications from leukemia on December 25, 1979, her sister and her children at her bedside. The obituaries showed a genuine sadness and affection for the actress which was often missing from tributes to bigger and better-known stars.

Jack Buchanan

Jack Buchanan is often referred to as "The English Fred Astaire." This is inaccurate on several counts. For one thing, song-and-dance man Buchanan was born in Helensburgh, Scotland. For another, he was more akin to Cary Grant than the doe-like Astaire. Had he been born ten years later, he might have become the first great musical star of films, but Jack was already fortyish when Hollywood discovered him. He was born Walter Jack Buchanan on April 28, 1890 (some sources say 1891), the son of a well-to-do auctioneer. By the time he'd reached his teens, though, the family fortune had fallen to such an extent that they were taking in boarders. By the time he'd left Glasgow Academy, Jack had decided on the stage as a career. He was tall (6' 2") and handsome, but had not a minute's training as an actor, singer or dancer.

After some amateur plays, Jack began climbing his way up the ladder in professional companies: tiny roles, touring companies, and several notable flops. His loyal mother and sister followed him to London in 1912, where he had a walk-on in *The Grass Widow*. He was discovered by Ivor Novello (who always had an eye for a handsome young actor), for a touring production of the light comedy *Tonight's the Night* (1915-17). This show was to be Jack's real school, and he emerged ready for stardom.

Producer André Charlot cast Jack in *Bubbly* (1917), and then in the revue *A to Z* (1921). Here he worked alongside fellow newcomers Beatrice Lillie and Gertrude Lawrence ("Charlot's Harlots" as they dubbed themselves). In 1923 he had his first real hit, both starring in and producing the farce *Battling Butler*, at the

New Oxford Theatre in London—that show also provided Jack with his Broadway debut, in 1923-24. Jack, Bea and Gertie teamed up for *Charlot's Revue of 1924* and *'25*, both on London's West End and on Broadway, and the high-spirited, nonsensical shows made the trio international stars. Jack's rather high, reedy singing voice and bubbly giggle contrasted charmingly with his athlete's build and untrained but graceful dancing style. And, as Bea Lillie noted, no one could wear white tie and tails like "Johnnie B." He had to leave New York to star in *Toni* (1924) in England, which was followed by the British version of Ziegfeld's *Sunny* (1927) and *That's a Good Girl* (1928).

In the meantime, while Jack's stage career was flourishing, his film career was chugging slowly along as well. He'd made his film debut in 1917 with *Auld Lang Syne*, but had a hard time catching on in silents: he was good looking, but so much of his charm was vocal. He starred in a handful of British silents, none of them terribly successful: *Her Heritage* (with the great Phyllis Monkman, 1919); *The Audacious Mr. Squire* (1923); four films in 1925, including a Bulldog Drummond mystery; and two more in 1927 (*Toni* and *Confetti*). But it took talkies to really allow Jack's film career to flourish, if only for a brief time in the early- to mid-1930s.

The British film industry was not up to much in the early talkie years, so Jack made his debut in First National's risqué comedy *Paris* (1929), costarring cooing French songstress Irene Bordoni. The film was a big enough hit for Jack to sign on to Paramount for another film, the delightfully silly *Monte Carlo* (1930), costarring Jeanette MacDonald and directed by Ernst Lubitsch. The plot was an old one: wealthy Jack masquerades as a barber to win over haughty Countess Jeanette. But the naughty dialogue, the wonderful songs (including "Beyond the Blue Horizon") make this one of the most charming musicals of the early talkie era.

Jack called Lubitsch "one of the most sympathetic and understanding directors anyone could wish to meet . . . He realizes that an actor has ideas of his own, even if they don't happen to coincide with the scenario, and he is always willing to discuss each little point that arises in connection with a scene or incident. That's why he gets such amazing results. Some directors seem to think that shouting at the top of their voices and bullying the players will

The dashing Jack Buchanan, ca. 1929.

achieve the best work. Lubitsch usually gets his own way, but by tactful means."

Despite his early successes, Jack did not become a Hollywood star. After taking time off for the Cole Porter Broadway musical *Wake Up and Dream* (1929-30), he returned to England, where he financed the Leicester Square Theatre and starred in the stage show *Stand Up and Sing* (1931). He also patriotically tried to pump some life into the British film industry by appearing in *Man of Mayfair* (1931) for Paramount's British subsidiary, and the highly successful *Goodnight, Vienna* (British & Dominions Film Corporation, 1932), Anna Neagle's first starring film.

Jack was diversifying his interests by this time, producing and directing as well as acting. He directed and starred in the British film *Yes, Mr. Brown* (1933), and directed the film version of *That's a Good Girl*, with the pert and talented Elsie Randolph (Jack had produced the 1928 stage version, as well). By the mid-1930s, Jack was thought of as something of a middle-aged has-been in the US (where few of his new films were exhibited), but was a popular, hard-working film and stage star in England. He appeared in eleven films in the latter half of the 1930s, all made in England, but few reaching the US. Among others, Jack starred in the umpteenth version of *Brewster's Millions* (1935), starred with Fay Wray in *When Knights Were Bold* (1936), starred in the simultaneous stage and screen versions of *This'll Make You Whistle* (1937), was a suave detective in *Smash and Grab* (also '37), and costarred with Maurice Chevalier in René Clair's *Break the News* (1938).

War broke out while Jack was touring in *Top Hat and Tails*. He remained in London throughout the war years, narrowly escaping death when his flat (atop his West End theater) was hit during the German bombings. He appeared in (and produced) the escapist stage hit *It's Time to Dance* in 1943, as well as a revival of *The Last of Mrs. Cheyney* and *Canaries Sometimes Sing*. After the war, Jack returned to Broadway as one of the many replacement Elwood Dowds in *Harvey* and in the flop comedy *Don't Listen, Ladies* (1948-49). When Ivor Novello died during the run of *King's Rhapsody* in 1950, Jack returned to London to replace his former sponsor. He was still in top form and terrific looking as he approached 60, his charm and comic timing still intact.

Jack always kept his private life private, so everyone was surprised in 1949 when he wed a lovely young woman named Susan ("Suzzie") Bassett—Jack's first, brief marriage was never spoken of and was off-limits even to his friends. This second pairing was a happy one and lasted for life (after Jack's death, Suzzie married JFK's Secretary of the Treasury, C. Douglas Dillon, and became a well-known society swan). In the early 1950s, Jack rented a flat to actor Rex

With Fred Astaire in Vincente Minnelli's *The Band Wagon*, 1953.

Harrison, who idolized him, as Suzzie remembers. "Indeed, when [Rex] was starting, he based his mannerisms on Jack's. They were very much alike in body language and sense of timing onstage. They were not alike in character or temperament," she adds, "thank God, because Rex could be extremely difficult and my chap had a lovely nature."

Hollywood beckoned again in 1953, and Jack was handed one of the great comeback roles of all time. He played the egomaniacal, over-the-top producer in Vincente Minnelli's *The Band Wagon* (MGM), costarring Fred Astaire, Nanette Fabray and Oscar Levant. It was certainly his best film role, and Jack managed to make the self-obsessed, obnoxious character both funny and somehow charming. His "Triplets" number with Astaire and Fabray was a comic triumph, and in "I Guess I'll Have to Change My Plan," Jack proved to be one of Astaire's great partners, their elegant top-hat-and-tails style blending perfectly.

The Band Wagon was, sadly, Jack's last American film, though he also made a spurt of TV appearances in the US, on *Max Liebman Presents* (1954), *The Milton Berle Show* (1954) and Ed Sullivan's *Toast of the Town* (1955). Back on his own side of the Atlantic, he starred in the stage and screen versions of the farce *As Long as They're Happy* (1954); his last two films, the British *Josephine and Men* (1955) and Preston Sturges' French-made swan song *Les Carnets du Major Thompson* (aka *The Diary of Major Thompson*, also 1955) went largely unseen in the US.

By this time, Jack was beginning to suffer the onset of spinal cancer, the worst of afflictions for a dancer. He continued working as long as he could, appearing on the premiere of Scottish Television in Glasgow in 1957. He entered a hospital shortly thereafter, in October 1957, and died on the 20th of that month (some sources list the 21st). He was fondly remembered as one of the last of the great gentlemen of the pre-War period. Though still only in his 60s, he seemed from another age in the day of Marlon Brando and Elvis. Friends recalled his many kindnesses and charities; his loyalty to Scotland (he maintained a home on the island of Arran), and his devilish sense of humor. His widow had Jack's ashes scattered from a Cunard liner off Southampton, a suitably refined ending for his career.

Billie Burke

Calling Billie Burke a "character actress" is like calling the Grand Canyon "quite a slice." Though she's best known for dithering supporting roles in such films as *The Wizard of Oz*, *Topper* and *Dinner at Eight*, Billie was a stage star, silent movie star, and a brilliant dramatic actress as well. Her comic talent was only the tip of the iceberg.

Her trilling voice sounds a bit British, but Billie Burke was an American girl, born in Washington, D.C., on August 7, 1885. Her parents—a successful circus clown named Billy Burke and a Treasury Department worker named Blanche Hodkinson—christened her Mary William Ethelbert Appleton Burke. By the time little Billie (the nickname was almost immediate) was a child, she had picked up the beginnings of that British accent: the family moved to London in 1893, and that's where she was schooled. Vacations were spent following her father's music-hall act all over the world, and soon Billie's mother decided to put her on the stage, as well. "I was as apathetic as a cabbage," recalled Billie, ". . . merely a willing little girl . . . doing what her mother told her."

A beautiful redhead with china-blue eyes and a flawless complexion, she made her stage debut as a singer in 1899, when she was 14. With the help of her stage-struck mother, Billie began getting larger and larger roles in West End comedies and musicals: *Blue Moon* (1905), *The Belle of Mayfair* (1906), *Mrs. Ponderbury's Past* (1907). American producer Charles Frohman whisked Billie back to her native land to star in *My Wife* (1907) opposite John Drew, and she became the toast of Broadway. By this time, Billie had learned to love her profession, along with the fame, money and adoration that went with it. She was, however, no dumb redhead. Billie was known for her sharp wit and numbered among her personal friends Mark Twain, Somerset Maugham, James Barrie, Booth Tarkington and Enrico Caruso.

Billie Burke spent the next few years bouncing amiably from one success to another on the New York stage, all of them produced by Frohman: *Love Watches* (1908-09), *The Mind-the-Paint Girl* (1912-13), *The Amazons* (1913), and others. "I was a contented little thing," she wrote in her memoirs. "I had my work, which was easy, pretty clothes, security and applause." She kept her health and looks by walking five miles a day, washing her hair in champagne, and grudgingly eating a vegetarian diet ("rabbit food," she called it).

Then, on New Year's Eve 1913, came the meeting which was to forever change three lives. Billie attended a party at New York's Astor Hotel. Among the guests were 45-year-old Broadway producer Florenz Ziegfeld, Jr., and his recently divorced common-law wife, actress Anna Held. Held attended with her friends Lillian Russell and "Diamond Jim" Brady; Ziegfeld was accompanied by his mistress, Lillian Lorraine. Friends hoped that Ziegfeld and Held might reconcile: instead, he fell madly in love with Billie Burke at first sight.

Billie felt much the same, at least in hindsight: ". . . the moment he stepped into the room my heart almost stopped beating," she recalled of that first meeting. "I loved him so intensely that I felt as if I would collapse in a dead faint." Billie Burke and Flo Ziegfeld married on April 10, 1914, while she was appearing in Frohman's *Jerry*. Frohman was furious with her (she forever regretted not making up with him, and never saw him again—he died on the *Lusitania* in 1915). Legend states that during the marriage ceremony, the understandably confused minister kept calling the bride "Florence" and the groom "William"—a good story even if unlikely.

In 1916 Billie Burke embarked on what was to be a very impressive silent-film career, all but forgotten in light of her later successes. Her debut was in *Peggy*, a big-budget Scottish love story for Thomas Ince (she was paid a stunning $10,000 a week). To film it, she moved to the West Coast, which certainly did not help her new

Toast of Broadway Billie Burke, ca. 1920.

marriage. With *Peggy's* success, Billie made her only serial, a hugely popular genre for actresses in the mid-late-1910s. George Kleine signed her to star in the 20-chapter adventure *Gloria's Romance* (1916), shot partly in Florida.

Billie and her husband must have gotten together at least once during this time, as their only child, Patricia, was born on October 23, 1916. (Patricia died in 2008, at the age of 91.)

In 1917, Billie signed a long-term contract with Paramount's Artcraft division, insisting that she be allowed to film on the East Coast so she could also appear onstage (and keep her eye on her wandering husband). She made 14 films for the studio between 1917 and 1921, also managing to star in five Broadway shows. Her silent films show no trace of the flighty society matron she would eventually portray; these were roles designed for a many-faceted actress. She played a farm wife in *The Land of Promise* (1917), a brave girl fighting the Germans in *In Pursuit of Polly* (1918), a "modern wife" in *Sadie Love* (1919), an aviatrix in *Away Goes Prudence* (1920), and a chorus girl in *The Education of Elizabeth* (1921).

Her Paramount films—five of them costarring Thomas Meighan— were great successes, and she became a premiere star. Pop culture reflected her status: the lyrics to the novelty song "Take Your Girlie to the Movies" suggest, "Though she's just a simple little ribbon clerk/Close your eyes and think you're kissing Billie Burke." The one-piece pajamas she wore in *Peggy* became popular under the name "billieburkes."

Florenz Ziegfeld was not an easy man to be married to, as Anna Held had discovered. "Flo was a person of triple or quadruple personality," Billie wrote decades later. He was a hopelessly addicted gambler and was frequently broke. He was (as are all good producers) obsessed with his shows—and, sadly, with his showgirls. His affair with Lillian Lorraine put a strain on both of his marriages, and his attachments to his stars Olive Thomas and Marilyn Miller drove Billie to tears and tantrums. "I was destined to be jealous of the entire *Follies* chorus as well as the *Follies* star list for the rest of my married life," she said, "a rather staggering assignment." Still, "there were moments of serenity and fulfillment, and moments of great fun," which made being Mrs. Ziegfeld worthwhile.

Billie's stage career consisted of hit after hit during this time. Among them were Booth Tarkington's *The Intimate Strangers* (1921-22, with Alfred Lunt), the musical comedy *Annie Dear* (1924-25), Noël Coward's *The Marquise* (1927), and *The Truth Game* (1930, written by and costarring Ivor Novello). One of her plays, *Caesar's Wife* (1919-20), resulted in a feud with Dorothy Parker, then reviewing for *Vanity Fair*. Parker wrote that Billie Burke

Billie in the delightful *Dinner at Eight*, 1933.

"plays her lighter scenes as if she were giving an impersonation of Eva Tanguay." This was quite mild for Parker (who, it will be recalled, once wrote that Katharine Hepburn "runs the gamut of emotions from A to B"). But Ziegfeld was furious and—to no one's credit— got Parker fired from *Vanity Fair* (her friend and coworker Robert Benchley walked out too, in protest).

A chic Billie in *Girl Trouble*, 1942.

Billie's only real flop was *Family Affairs*, which closed in one week, just after the 1929 stock-market crash. That crash also destroyed whatever wealth Flo Ziegfeld had managed not to gamble away. It destroyed, too, the public's taste for lavish theatrical spectacles like the ones he produced. Billie turned all her savings over to him, as well as her jewelry. She also went back West in the spring of 1932 to bring in some money with a two-picture contract at RKO.

It was while she filmed her first, *A Bill of Divorcement*, that Flo Ziegfeld died of heart failure, on July 22, 1932. Neither Billie nor their daughter was able to reach him at the hospital in time. Billie returned to work for both emotional and financial reasons.

Anyone who doubts Billie Burke's dramatic talents should see her as John Barrymore's distraught wife in *A Bill of Divorcement* and as Colin Clive's equally distraught wife in *Christopher Strong* (films mostly remembered today as Katharine Hepburn's first two movies). Her quiet, deeply felt performances are miles away from the comedies which soon made her famous all over again. Her Millicent Jordan in *Dinner at Eight* (1933) combined her comedic and dramatic skills, and she all but stole the film from costars Jean Harlow, Marie Dressler and John and Lionel Barrymore. Millicent Jordan's big "You think *you've* got trouble!" aria still brings applause at revival houses.

From then on she was cast mostly as dithering aunts, wives and mothers: Frances Dee's heartless, snobbish mom in *Finishing School* (1934); sweet but dumb matrons in the Clark Gable vehicles *Forsaking All Others* (1934) and *After Office Hours* (1935); Lady Bareacres in the Technicolor *Becky Sharp* (1935); Rosalind Russell's neighbor in *Craig's Wife* (1936). She costarred with Joan Crawford (*Forsaking All Others* and *The Bride Wore Red*, the latter in 1937), Judy Garland (*Everybody Sing*, 1938), Janet Gaynor (as a card-sharp in *The Young in Heart*, 1938) and Loretta Young (*Eternally Yours*, 1939). In *Only Yesterday* (1933), she sat down at a piano and sang— in her high-pitched trill—"Tiptoe Thru' the Tulips," inadvertently supplying Tiny Tim with his theme song and characteristic stage voice three decades later. Her role as the delightfully annoying and annoyed Mrs. Topper opposite Roland Young took Billie through three films: *Topper* (1937), *Topper Takes a Trip* (1939) and *Topper Returns* (1941).

Billie Burke tired of the "bird-witted ladies" (her own words) she played in most of her films. "I am neatly typed today, of course," she wrote in the 1940s, "possibly irrevocably typed, although I sincerely hope not, for I should like better parts . . . But if people will laugh at my work and keep a sound roof over my head, who am I to complain?"

Of course, Billie Burke's most famous role was as Glinda in *The Wizard of Oz* (1939). It was her own favorite role, she admitted. "I never played such a being onstage, but this role is as close as I have come in the motion pictures to the kind of parts I did in the theater." Her lovely, glittering and kindly Glinda has charmed generations of children, just as Margaret Hamilton has terrified them as the Wicked Witch of the West. Many find it hard to believe that Billie Burke was 53 years old when the film was made in 1938.

Billie continued to take every role that was offered to her, jumping from studio to studio in a day when freelancing was not the usual route to take. She moved into a nice little house in Los Angeles, near her daughter (the lavish Ziegfeld homes had to go when Flo died). Billie never quite gave up on the theater. In addition to local theatrical productions, she appeared on Broadway in *The Rock* (1943) and *Mrs. January and Mr. X* (1944). But films paid her rent.

She'd made 31 films in the 1930s and appeared in another 23 in the 1940s (as well as a series of Hal Roach short comedies in 1948). Billie was always delightful; the films not consistently so. Among her better latter-day films were *The Man Who Came to Dinner* (as the unwilling hostess, 1941), *In This Our Life* (a rare and wonderful dramatic performance, 1942), *Hi Diddle Diddle!* (a low-budget but hilarious film with Pola Negri and Adolphe Menjou), and *The Barkleys of Broadway* (the last Astaire/Rogers film, 1949). Most of her later films were not up to much and sank without a trace: *Hullabaloo* (1940), *What's Cookin'* (1942), *So's Your Uncle* (1943), *Breakfast in Hollywood* (1946). But Billie remained a beloved figure in Hollywood, still working steadily and never considered a has-been or uncastable.

With Cameron Shipp, Billie wrote two charming books: her autobiography (*With a Feather On My Nose*, 1948) and an advice book for women (*With Powder On My Nose*, 1959). She appeared in three radio series in the 1940s and braved television as early as 1950, eventually appearing on such series as *Playhouse 90, 77 Sunset Strip*, and *The Ed Wynn Show*. Always up to date, she said in 1949 of TV, " . . . obviously, it is the coming thing . . . so far I have been faithful to all the arts associated with acting, and I intend to remain faithful in this inclusive fashion."

Billie turned 65 in 1950, but hardly seemed to be slowing down. That year alone, she appeared in *And Baby Makes Three, Father of the Bride* (as the mother of the groom), *Boy from Indiana*, and *Three Husbands*. But her career went into low gear over the next decade. There were *Father's Little Dividend* (1951), *Small Town Girl* (with Ann Miller, 1953), *The Young Philadelphians* (with Paul Newman, 1959), and *Sergeant Rutledge* (1960). Her last film was Cantinflas' *Pepe* (1960), in which she played a cameo role.

By that time, Billie Burke was suffering from dementia, brushed off then as senility (and, indeed, brushed off by acquaintances who thought she was simply behaving as vaguely as her onscreen characters). Her condition deteriorated but, happily, Billie had a wealthy and devoted daughter to see that she was well looked-after. Patricia, her husband and their three children lived next door and made sure that Billie's last years were as comfortable and happy as her failing mind and body allowed.

Billie Burke had been out of the public eye for a decade when she died on May 14, 1970, just shy of her 85th birthday. Today, she's still known worldwide for her work in *The Wizard of Oz*, and that will certainly be her greatest legacy. For all her 79 films and some 30 stage roles, it is for her favorite part that Billie Burke is most famous—not many stars are that lucky.

Ina Claire

There are no "ladies" anymore, or at least darned few. The brittle, amusing, "women of a certain age" who used to trade quips and glitter through ballrooms and teas. On film at least, the likes of Alice Brady, Billie Burke, Constance Bennett, made the life of a Park Avenue grand dame seem the height of sophisticated elegance. One of the greatest was the blonde, urbane Ina Claire, who seemed a Dorothy Parker story or *New Yorker* cartoon come to life.

She was not born into an afternoon tea party. Ina Fagan first saw the light of day in Washington, D.C., on October 15, 1892 (sometimes noted as 1893). She attended Holy Cross Academy until her father died, when she and her mother had to move into a boarding house. Her talent for imitating friends and teachers soon brought Ina into vaudeville and success came fairly quickly. By 1909 she was playing at New York's American Music Hall, doing dead-on parodies of Anna Held, Harry Lauder, Eva Tanguay and other contemporary stars. By that time she had changed her name to the more elegant-sounding Ina Claire, which she later regretted. "I should have played up my real name of Fagan and done more varied parts," she sighed when it was too late to change her image.

Ina's first Broadway shows included *Our Miss Gibbs* (in the chorus, 1910), *Jumping Jupiter* (with fellow beginner Helen Broderick, 1911) and *The Quaker Girl* (her breakthrough part, 1911-12). "I may do things that are much finer," Ina said of that latter show, "but I know I'll never recapture the first thrill of that 16-year-old who suddenly discovered that the stories of dressing rooms heaped with flowers and pleasant attention from all sorts of interesting people she hadn't

Ina Claire on Broadway in *Biography*, 1932-34.

dreamed of meeting were things that actually came true." In 1913 Ina took over Julia Sanderson's starring role in the European tour of *The Girl from Utah*, and was back on Broadway in *Lady Luxury* in 1914.

In 1915 she was cast in a small role in Florenz Ziegfeld's *Follies*, then promoted to a top spot when Annette Kellerman dropped out. Wearing a gown by Lucile, Ina (accompanied by Bernard Granville, Bonita's dad), introduced the hit song "Hello, Frisco," written to celebrate the transcontinental cable. (Granville also had the dubious honor of singing "My Radium Girl" to the glowing *Follies* chorus, while strolling through Radiumland.)

Ina appeared again in the 1916 *Follies*, a banner year which also featured Fanny Brice, W.C. Fields, Will Rogers, Marion Davies, Bert Williams, and Ann Pennington. Ina did imitations of Jane Cowl, Geraldine Farrar, and—surprisingly—Ziegfeld's wife, Billie Burke. Earning $1,000 a week, Ina also appeared atop the New Amsterdam Theater Roof in the *Midnight Frolics*.

She made her first dive into films in 1915, when Jesse Lasky scooped her up to appear in two Paramount-released features, *The Wild Goose Chase* (directed by Cecil B. DeMille) and *The Puppet Crown*. But—like many stage stars—she disliked silent films. Ina, especially, was used to projecting her character with voice as much as facial expression, and found filmmaking frustrating. Her only other ventures into silent films were an all-star *Red Cross Pageant* in 1917, and a 1920 Metro version of her 1917-18 stage hit, *Polly with a Past*.

It was back to Broadway for Ina and real stardom, with that original stage version of *Polly with a Past*, a sophisticated, naughty comedy of manners. "Rather rough stuff," she later called her role in that and her next Broadway hit, *The Gold Diggers* (1919-20). She got married for the first time during the run of that show, to newspaper critic James Whittaker (they divorced in 1925).

The 1920s were more than kind to Ina Claire. She starred on Broadway in *Bluebeard's Eighth Wife* (1921-22), *The Awful Truth* (1922-23), *Grounds for Divorce* (1924-25), *The Last of Mrs. Cheyney* (1925-26), and *Our Betters* (1928). Note how when these plays were later filmed only one of them (the 1929 version of *The Awful Truth*) starred Ina Claire: her roles were played on film by her sleekly elegant followers Claudette Colbert, Constance Bennett, Irene Dunne, Norma Shearer, and Joan Crawford.

That early talkie version of *The Awful Truth* was the impetus for Ina's return to films, for Pathé. Costarring the equally brittle and elegant Henry Daniell, it was a critical and box-office failure, but still caused Ina to reconsider a film career. She also made the cover of *Time* magazine that year, a considerable achievement in an era when performers were rarely so honored.

Nineteen-twenty-nine also marked Ina's celebrity marriage to John Gilbert, on the rebound from his passionate, difficult affair with Greta Garbo. The handsome, charming, mercurial Gilbert could not have been a less likely partner for the disciplined, intellectual, cynical Ina Claire. "I'd only known him six weeks," she said later. "We met at a party someplace . . . And he said something derogatory about himself. Not exactly derogatory, but he sees himself as kind of a sex symbol. But it made me laugh, and I thought I wouldn't have expected that from him."

From the start, it was obvious the marriage was not fated to last. The happy couple was interviewed by reporters while starting off on their European honeymoon in the summer of 1929. "What does it feel like to be married to a famous star?" Ina was asked. She sweetly replied, "I don't know—why don't you ask my husband?"

Ina later called this marriage "my biggest mistake. I just don't *know* people who acted like that, and I didn't want to." On the other hand, Ina was hardly the ideal wife for John Gilbert: "No one could ever accuse Ina Claire of being warm and cuddly," said Gilbert's daughter, "and that is, unfortunately, what Jack needed, poor darling." Making things worse for the marriage was the downturn of Gilbert's career in the early 1930s. Whatever the cause (and many have been put forward), he tumbled from the nation's hottest male star to a has-been in a few short years. Ina's successes certainly did not help his mood or his self-esteem any.

By the time Ina left for the East Coast in late 1930 to film *The Royal Family of Broadway* for Paramount in Long Island, the marriage was essentially over. She and Gilbert thought the five-month separation might help them, but nothing had changed when Ina returned to California except that her career had surpassed his. The two split in 1931, their divorce becoming legal the following year.

The Royal Family of Broadway was a brilliant film, still a delight to see. Based on a Kaufman and Ferber play, it was a wicked parody of the Barrymores; Ina played Julie Cavendish, the Ethel part. She was much more Ina Claire than Ethel Barrymore—sarcastic, emotional, temperamental, and very chic and fashionable. Though she shined alongside her costars, Ina had a hard time competing with Fredric March, who did an amazing over-the-top take on John Barrymore.

Her next film, *Rebound* (1931), was shot in Los Angeles for RKO. Ina and Myrna Loy played two points of a romantic triangle. In a small supporting role was Robert Williams, a New York actor brought out west to recreate his stage role on film. His career was promising, but after another few roles, Williams died of appendicitis in November 1931. *Rebound* has not aged particularly well, despite the presence of Ina and her able costars, Loy, Williams, Hedda Hopper, Louise Closser Hale: it's just another dull teacup drama.

The Greeks Had a Word for Them (later retitled *Three Broadway Girls* at the censors' behest) was another cup of tea entirely. Shot by Goldwyn in 1932, it starred Ina as one of three backstabbing gold-digger "friends" (the others being Joan Blondell and Madge Evans). This was not one of those cuddly gold-digger comedies about wisecracking showgirls with hearts of mush—these were hard-bitten hookers who would gladly double-cross one another for the right amount of loot. Ina played the worst of the lot, Jean, an old hand who nabs a millionaire and has to fight off her pals to hold onto him; Ina managed to look like a *Vogue* cover even while playing one of the year's most hard-boiled tarts (and this was 1932, the year of Jean Harlow's *Red-Headed Woman* and *Red Dust*). The scandalous pre-Code film was a hit, due in part to its bluntness.

And then, her film career was essentially cut off. Ina left Hollywood and returned to Broadway in 1932 for S.N. Behrman's *Biography* (1932-34). Film fans may have missed her, but Ina had no regrets: "I'm no good in pictures," she sighed, elaborating on why she preferred the stage. "In the theater—most of all in comedy—there is a close relationship between the actors and the audience. They get something from each other. Pictures are different. When you watch a picture, you are completely detached, and the way the audience feels doesn't affect the film in the least."

Broadway was just as good to Ina in the 1930s as it had been in the '20s. After *Biography*, she starred in *Ode to Liberty* (1934-35), *End of Summer* (1936), *Barchester Towers* (1937-38) and *Once is Enough* (1938). Now in her late 40s, Ina Claire was one of New York's most acclaimed comic actresses. She was admired but not always beloved by her coworkers, though, and was known as a sharp-tongued perfectionist. She acted as her own manager and was famous for driving directors to distraction (she earned Broadway's everlasting gratitude for decking universally hated director/producer Jed Harris on the set of their abortive play, *The Gaoler's Wench*, in 1929).

The always-elegant Ina Claire, returning from vacation in 1932.

"I began to be called difficult because of being somewhat fussy about the material I worked with when I was still in my teens," she admitted. "If there are to be any mistakes, I'd rather they'd be my own." She was also known for her scathing wit and quick comebacks off-stage and on; nothing that happened during a show could throw her. While playing in *End of Summer*, a property lamp lit itself before she could reach the switch. To the delight of costar Van Heflin and the audience, she chirped, "Ah—magic!"

Ina returned to Hollywood to make two last films, one of which has become her chief legacy. As the cool, bitchy villainess, Grand Duchess Swana, in *Ninotchka* (1939), she all but stole the film from Greta Garbo. Ina Claire always denied any similarity between herself and her roles, but Swana does sound a lot like the actress: "Oh, I'm so bored with this face," Swana sighs into her mirror. "Oh, well, I guess one gets the face one deserves." Ina herself had told a reporter three years earlier, "Can you imagine anyone with a nose that tips as mine does playing a noble, tragic character? Look at it. I might get along fairly well being noble and sad until I suddenly turned my profile."

Coworkers were worried about the teaming of the ex-Mrs. John Gilbert with Garbo, but they needn't have been concerned. With Gilbert three years in his grave, the one-time rivals got along swimmingly. Garbo admired Ina's professionalism and success; and Ina Claire never let anyone intimidate her. According to Garbo biographer Barry Paris, Ina amused the star by tap-dancing on the set. On film, Ina provided a sparkling counterpoint to Garbo's dour, drab Soviet envoy, and helped contribute to the film's huge success.

In *Claudia* (1943), Ina played the wise, dying mother of childlike Connecticut housewife Dorothy McGuire. The film itself (based on a Broadway play) lacked plot and pacing, and McGuire's dithery character was more annoying than charming. But the game cast pulled it through, and Ina proved what a powerful dramatic actress she might have been, despite her profile. Sadly, *Claudia* was Ina Claire's last movie.

She returned triumphantly to the stage and continued working till her retirement at the age of 62. Among her latter-day shows were *The Talley Method* (1941), *The Fatal Weakness* (1946-47) and her last, T.S. Eliot's *The Confidential Clerk* (costarring Claude Rains, 1954).

Ina had married attorney William Wallace in 1939, and the two
moved to San Francisco's Nob Hill area. This third marriage lasted
till Wallace's death in 1976. "Oh, it is terrible living alone," Ina said
the following year. "I talk on the telephone with the girls [her friends;
Ina never had children]. I'm invited out quite a good bit, but I don't
feel like going to parties."

Still chic and elegant in her old age, she complained merely of
some loss in hearing and mobility. Almost to the end, she spoke
wistfully of a possible return to acting. But "it has got to be something
modern. I don't want to come back in an old chestnut," she told
a reporter in the late 1970s. Despite her age and infirmities, she
continued to appear at benefits and award shows. Interviewed by
James Watters for the 1984 book *Return Engagement*, she chatted
gaily about friends, scandals and parties but refused to reminisce
about her career: "The memory does *not* linger on," she said.

Ina Claire died in her San Francisco apartment shortly thereafter,
on February 21, 1985, at the age of 92. Nutritionist Nathan
Pritikin and violinist Efrem Zimbalist's obituaries appeared the
same day, but it was Ina Claire who garnered the most newsprint.
Not that hers was still a name on anyone's tongue—but she was the
last of the great light-comic Broadway stars. Something cool and
elegant had gone out of the world, and most op-ed and obit writers
were gracious enough to acknowledge that.

Claudette Colbert

Not many performers are equally at home in drama and comedy; Claudette Colbert was one of those few. It's hard to decide whether she was more brilliant in screwball comedies like *It Happened One Night, The Palm Beach Story* and *Midnight*, or tragedies like *Imitation of Life* and *So Proudly We Hail!* The most modern of actresses, she was also one of the most talented.

Claudette Colbert was born Lily Chaunchoin in Paris on September 13, 1903 (many sources stated 1905, but Claudette herself, refreshingly, insisted on the earlier date). Her banker father suffered reverses and took his wife, daughter and son Charles to New York in 1912. The future Claudette Colbert attended Washington Irving High School; she soon discovered acting, and briefly appeared with New York's famed Provincetown Players, which also gave early opportunities to Bette Davis, Henry Fonda, Katharine Hepburn, and other future Hollywood hopefuls. But the teenager was still unsure as to whether she wanted to be an actress or a clothing designer; she took classes, worked odd jobs.

For someone unsure of her career path, she did remarkably well, making her Broadway debut at 20, in the short-lived *The Wild Westcotts*. She toured in such long-forgotten plays as *We've Got to Have Money, The Marionette Man, The Cat Came Back* and *High Stakes*, among others. She returned to Broadway in the unsuccessful *Ghost Train* and *The Pearl of Great Price* (both 1926), and had her first real hit in *The Barker*, a 1927 play about midway low-life—it was during this show that Walter Winchell famously dubbed her "Legs." She stayed busy during that play's run, marrying costar Norman Foster and making her film debut, in the silent *For the*

Claudette Colbert in 1935.

Love of Mike (1927), with Ben Lyon. Claudette hated the experience ("I had no idea what I was doing") and vowed never to film again. She went to London with *The Barker* and appeared in several more shows (notably the Theater Guild's *Dynamo*, 1929).

By 1929 talking films were obviously the coming thing, and Claudette rethought her decision to avoid movies, signing a five-year contract with Paramount—she was to stay with that studio for the next 14 years. From 1929 through 1932, she marked time in 15 films (her first was a kidnap drama called *The Hole in the Wall*, with Edward G. Robinson). She quickly graduated to leading roles, but the films were pretty divergent in quality, and the scriptwriters and directors didn't yet know what to make of her peculiar charms. A pert, apple-cheeked ingénue, she was still finding her way. She appeared with Maurice Chevalier in the English and French versions of *The Big Pond* (1930), Gary Cooper (*His Woman*, 1931), husband Norman Foster and Ginger Rogers (*Young Man of Manhattan*, 1930) and the irascible George M. Cohan (*The Phantom President*, 1932).

Claudette was seen to better advantage in another Chevalier film, *The Smiling Lieutenant* (1931), as his self-sacrificing mistress who memorably instructs his wife, Miriam Hopkins, how to "Jazz Up Your Lingerie." Director Ernst Lubitsch was one of the first to really bring out Claudette's smart, snappy, sexy warmth. She made a scandalous hit bathing in asses' milk in DeMille's *The Sign of the Cross* (1932); as Poppaea, Nero's vampy wife, she wasn't handed much of an acting role, but she showed a great deal of her Parisienne anatomy, and the public took notice. That milk bath did as much for Claudette as it had for Anna Held, and in 1933 and '34 she became a genuine, top-rated star, appearing in eight films, several of them Hollywood classics.

There were dramas: she was a smuggler's daughter in *I Cover the Waterfront*, a pancake tycoon in the first version of *Imitation of Life* (much less campy than Lana Turner's remake), and she was DeMille's *Cleopatra*, in a silly and unhistoric but highly enjoyable 1934 production (Claudette was not the first movie Cleopatra, of course—maybe a dozen actresses had preceded her). And there were the comedies, a genre she quickly became adept at. The most famous is *It Happened One Night*, on loan to Columbia, with director Frank Capra and costar Clark Gable. Claudette won her only Oscar for that movie, which has since become an icon of its era. But just as enjoyable was the sadly forgotten *Three-Cornered Moon* (1933), a wonderful screwballer about a dizzy Brooklyn family dealing with

Claudette Colbert with one of MGM's Leos, 1939.

sudden poverty in the Depression. Director Elliott Nugent and costars Mary Boland, Richard Arlen, Lyda Roberti and Wallace Ford turn this short film (a little over an hour) into a gem worth searching out.

By 1935, Claudette Colbert was one of Paramount's biggest stars, and this was a studio that also employed Marlene Dietrich, Mae West and Carole Lombard. Not even Paramount always knew how to cast their stars, and Claudette was sometimes put into historical films, the only genre she totally failed at. Stunningly modern and up-to-date, she looked silly and uncomfortable in the period costumes and plotlines of *Under Two Flags* (Victorian, 1936), *Maid of Salem* (17th century, 1937), *Zaza* (ooh-la-la Belle Époque Paris, 1939), and *Drums Along the Mohawk* (Revolution-era New England, 1939).

Claudette Colbert was not Hollywood's greatest beauty, but her trim little figure, round, kitten-like face, and obviously intelligent good humor made her a bit of a sex symbol, much to her own surprise. By 1934 she'd adopted the hairstyle she kept for life: a short, auburn bob with a fringe of bangs. Although a partygoer and social animal, Claudette was also known as a tough-as-nails professional, overseeing her lighting and camera angles. Her right profile was known as "the dark side of the moon," and scenes had to be staged so as not to show it. She was also self-conscious about her short neck—directing her in a 1956 TV show, Noël Coward reportedly snapped, "If only Claudette Colbert had a neck, I'd wring it!" "When it comes to details, I'm a horror," she admitted cheerfully, though downplaying the profile story. "Why *not* have your good side showing?"

She divorced Norman Foster in early 1935 and later that year wed Dr. Joel Pressman, a happy marriage that lasted till his death in 1968. Still, rumors about Claudette's sexual orientation circulated for decades. Her friendship with Marlene Dietrich got gossip going—largely because of a photo of the pants-clad actresses happily straddling each other on a sliding board at one of Carole Lombard's parties. Claudette kept her private life private, and despite winking nicknames like "Uncle Claude," no one knows what did or didn't go on behind closed doors.

She appeared in another 13 films between 1935 and the end of the decade and—unlike many of her contemporaries—her star did not seem to fade. Along with programmers like *I Met Him in Paris* and *It's a Wonderful World* were some real gems: the Russian-émigré comedy *Tovarich* (with Charles Boyer, 1937), the marvelous Ernst Lubitsch comedy *Bluebeard's Eighth Wife* (with Gary Cooper, 1938), and *Midnight* (with Don Ameche and John Barrymore, 1939), one of the funniest and sexiest comedies of the decade.

The 1940s were bound to be tricky for an actress born in 1903 and, indeed, the end of the decade saw Claudette's slide from the ranks of the top-market stars. But things started out well, with the anti-war drama *Arise, My Love* (one of the actress's own favorites) and the shameless tearjerker *Remember the Day* (with a young, stunningly handsome John Payne). In 1942 she starred in one of the last great screwball comedies, Preston Sturges' *The Palm Beach Story*. She—and costars Joel McCrea, Rudy Vallee, Mary Astor (and Robert Dudley, as the memorable Wienie King)—were hilarious in this tale of a warring couple and the millionaires who love them. She had two patriotic wartime hits in *So Proudly We Hail!* (1943), as the den mother of nurses Veronica Lake and Paulette Goddard, and *Since You Went Away* (1944), as one of the loyal women left on the homefront.

Claudette left Paramount at war's end, and her career was never quite the same—to be fair, the breakdown of the studio system toppled many other stars at the same time. Her next box-office success wasn't till the 1947 rural comedy *The Egg and I*, and it was her last. (*The Egg and I* also had the dubious distinction of introducing Ma and Pa Kettle to the screen.) She made 16 postwar films, her last being the 1961 soap opera *Parrish*. None of them were classics, but they certainly covered all genres: comedies (*Without Reservations*, 1946; *Let's Make It Legal*, 1951); dramas (*The Secret Heart*, 1946; *Three Came Home*, 1950); even Westerns (*Texas Lady*, 1955). In 1954 she made two films in her native France, the anthology *Destinées* and Sacha Guitry's historical *Si Versailles m'etait Conte*.

With her film career fading, Claudette took up the challenge of television, as early as a 1954 version of *The Royal Family*. Throughout the 1950s, she gamely acted on many of the anthologies: *General Electric Theater*, *Robert Montgomery Presents*, *Playhouse 90*, *Letter to*

Still stylish and elegant, in *Parrish*, 1961.

Loretta [Young], *Zane Grey Theater*. She also made a handful of full-length TV-movies, including the one that nearly ended with her being throttled by director Noël Coward (*Blithe Spirit*). Indeed, her last appearance before a camera came with the enjoyably glossy soap opera *The Two Mrs. Grenvilles* (1987), in which she played a haughty society dowager who is awfully mean to poor Ann-Margret.

And she never gave up the stage, her first love. Once she was free of the studios—and was financially independent—Claudette was able to dabble on Broadway when an interesting project was offered. She replaced Margaret Sullavan in *Janus* in the mid-1950s, and starred in *The Marriage-Go-Round* (with Charles Boyer, 1958-60), the short-lived flops *Julia, Jake and Uncle Joe* (1961) and *The Irregular Verb "to Love"* (1963), *The Kingfisher* (with Rex Harrison and George Rose, 1978-79), the pallid comedy *A Talent for Murder* (1981), and her swan song, the arch comedy *Aren't We All?* (with Rex Harrison again, 1985). Even when the shows themselves were panned, critics and audiences were so delighted to see a still-lovely and chic Claudette Colbert onstage that all was forgiven.

She and Dr. Pressman spent much time in Europe and bought a large, rambling home in Barbados. Pressman's death in 1968—and the deaths of her mother and brother soon after—left Claudette shaken but unbowed. Her travels, painting, many friends and occasional acting kept her busy and alert, and she hardly seemed to slow down with time. In 1980 she breezed into a photo session wearing "last year's Nina Ricci" and explained hurriedly, "I'll be 77 on Saturday, and Frank [Sinatra] is tossing a party in London. Then I'm going down—or is it up?—the Nile with the Annenbergs, and I hope to have an audience with the Pope on the way back." She often hosted her friends the Reagans in Barbados during their White House years, and was awarded The Kennedy Center Honors in 1989. In 1990 she wished *Vanity Fair* readers "a fabulous new decade. I'm praying to make it to 2000. After all, I'll only be 97."

She didn't quite make it. She suffered a severe stroke in March 1993 and spent a month in the hospital. Frail and partially paralyzed, she returned to her Barbados home, and every so often one saw sad photos of her, white-haired but chin up, being wheeled about by a nurse. When she died at 92, on July 30, 1996, her front-page *New York Times* obit recalled her "wit, gaiety, cupid's-bow mouth and light touch . . . worldly and sophisticated yet down to earth." Claudette herself was quoted, "I've always believed that acting is instinct to start with; you either have it or you don't . . . I did comedy because all my life I always wanted to laugh myself. There was never anything that gave me as much satisfaction as to be in something amusing."

Joan Crawford

In the battle of the Golden Age movie stars, it's long been a given that Bette Davis and Katharine Hepburn were Great Actresses, and Joan Crawford was simply a Movie Star. But time, cable TV and DVDs have evened the field and we can now see that when Davis and Hepburn were good, they were very, very good (*Now, Voyager, The Lion in Winter*); but when they were bad they were horrid (*Beyond the Forest, Suddenly, Last Summer*). As *Mommie Dearest* fades into the past and more of Joan Crawford's films are available to the public, it's apparent that her quiet, often underplayed and well-thought-out performances have aged better than those of many of her more well-regarded peers. Joan *was* a Movie Star, of course, but she was also a damn good actress.

Joan Crawford's birthdate is something of a mystery: the place was San Antonio, Texas; the date was March 23; but the year can only be estimated at somewhere between 1904 and 1908. She clawed her way up from what she described as a miserable childhood of poverty, hard work and little love. Lucille Fay LeSueur was the daughter of Thomas LeSueur (who vanished early) and his wife Anna; she also had a brother, Hal, who proved no comfort to her. Lucille became "Billie" Cassin when her mother wed theater manager Henry Cassin and moved to Oklahoma; it was one of the few happy periods of the girl's life, and her introduction to show business. But that marriage failed too, and the late 1910s and early '20s were an ordeal of waitressing to put herself through boarding school (she also took classes at Stephens College in Columbia, Missouri, but soon dropped out). The social ostracism both toughened the girl and ingrained her with a lifelong terror of poverty and failure. As she told journalist Roy Newquist, "If I hadn't had such a shitty childhood I wouldn't have worked my tail off to get where I am."

By 1924, she had broken into show business in the Midwest as a chorus—and probably burlesque—girl. Her stage career was brief but no doubt grueling: under her birth name, Lucille LeSueur, she was a "Fanchonette" dancer in the traveling Fanchon and Marco touring shows; a chorine in the Shuberts' *Innocent Eyes* (1924, with fellow dancer Jack Oakie, who became a lifelong pal); and was in the Shuberts' *Passing Show of 1924*, which featured pretty much a no-star cast. It was during the Broadway run of that unremarkable show, though, that she stood out enough for MGM talent scout Harry Rapf to spot her, test her, and sign her to a standard starlet contract.

She arrived at the spanking-new MGM studios in January 1925 and was promptly shown off in the short *1925 Studio Tour*, smiling shyly while being fitted by couturier Erté. She advanced quickly, through luck, talent, ambition, and spending every minute of every day at the studio, nosing around, making friends, and offering herself up for publicity shots. She was an extra or bit player in maybe half-a-dozen films in 1925. But, more impressively, she played two leads that very first year: in the Jackie Coogan film *Old Clothes*, and with Constance Bennett and Sally O'Neil in *Sally, Irene and Mary* (Joan was Irene, the bad girl who comes to a bad end). It was also in late 1925 that Lucille LeSueur became Joan Crawford, through a fan-magazine contest (Joan claimed to have hated the new name, but being a team player, she dealt with it).

She starred in nine films in 1926 and '27, some of them "B" films but also opposite MGM's top leading men: Lon Chaney (the sadomasochistic circus thriller *The Unknown*, directed by the über-creepy Tod Browning); sexy John Gilbert (*Twelve Miles Out*). She also starred with First National's comic Harry Langdon (in *Tramp, Tramp, Tramp*, a title which no doubt resulted in much ribbing for the leading lady).

Joan broke through as a star in 1928, the last year of the silent era. But of her seven 1928 films, only one stands out: the flapper epic *Our Dancing Daughters*, which also shot costar Anita Page to the top ranks at MGM. As the good girl to Anita's bad, Joan played

A fresh-faced young Joan Crawford in 1933.

the outwardly naughty but golden-hearted "Dangerous Diana," stripping down to her step-ins and dancing wildly atop tables (Joan was a prize-winning Charleston dancer). Talkies were on the way, and Joan Crawford was suddenly one of the studio's best bets. That same year, her other silents included *West Point* (with lifelong pal William Haines), *Across to Singapore* (a silly seagoing adventure with Ramon Novarro), and the gangster thriller *Four Walls* (with John Gilbert).

She was well on her way to becoming Hollywood's Crown Princess, having been dating Douglas Fairbanks, Jr., since 1928. They married in the summer of 1929, and Joan tried her best to fit into Hollywood's old-guard society. Her father-in law, Douglas Fairbanks, Sr., befriended her, but mother-in-law Mary Pickford (perhaps recognizing a bit of Gladys Smith in the former Billie Cassin), gave Joan the cold shoulder. Joan toned down her clothes and makeup and boned up on her classics: "I became piss-elegant," she later admitted. "The climax came one morning at the studio when I fluffed a line and said, 'Oh, *feces!*'"

By 1929, Joan and MGM were dipping their toes into talkies: of her five films that year, three were silent with "Movietone" scores and sound effects; one (the dreadful "jungle girl in the city" drama *Untamed*) was a talkie; and one was *The Hollywood Revue of 1929*, in which she very gamely sang and danced "Gotta Feelin' for You," a performance really much better than posterity will have it. Joan was no Marilyn Miller, but she carried the tune and her dancing was perky and hot, if not polished.

Joan Crawford was famous for, among other things, her chameleon-like way of shifting her image with the times. As the 1920s ended, her frizzy-haired flapper characters melted into sunken-cheeked, sleek-haired working girls and debutantes. The early talkie years were dangerous; even Norma Shearer and Greta Garbo were given more than their share of stinkers. Joan plowed bravely through such muck as *Montana Moon* and *Laughing Sinners* (in which she is "saved" by Salvation Army man Clark Gable), but she was rewarded with golden opportunities like *Paid* (as a steely, vengeful con-woman), *Dance, Fools, Dance* (as a girl reporter involved with much more believable gangster Clark Gable), and *Possessed* (with Gable again: he's a politician, she's his noble up-from-trash mistress, and they are both wonderful). It was in the early 1930s that Joan Crawford came into her own as an actress. In her silent days, she is clearly learning: all big, scared eyes and self-conscious smiles. Her earliest talkies still show that hesitance, along with a terror-driven energy. But by 1931 she was fully the equal of Shearer or Garbo, her mannerisms smoothing out.

Some say (this author among them) that 1932 was the greatest year of the movies' Golden Age; it certainly was a banner year for

Joan Crawford. She only had three films released and one bombed, but all three stand as milestones. In the all-star *Grand Hotel,* Joan played the kind-hearted but slutty "little stenographer," who poses nude on the side. While Garbo, John and Lionel Barrymore and Wallace Beery, bless their hammy hearts, tore up the scenery in a hugely enjoyable way, Joan Crawford gave a realistic, modern and very moving performance (her latter scenes with Lionel Barrymore are particularly heartbreaking). The silly soap opera *Letty Lynton* is most notable for its costumes, by Adrian: in particular, a white dress with huge ruffled shoulders became a 1930s fashion icon, selling millions of knockoffs and influencing design for years to come.

Then—on loan-out to United Artists—came *Rain.* Playing Sadie Thompson, the whore bedeviled by a preacher, Joan was following in the footsteps of the role's creator, Jeanne Eagels, and Gloria Swanson, who'd filmed *Rain* in 1928. It's a stunning film (Oliver T. Marsh's fluid cinematography set new standards for the era), and Joan and costar Guy Kibbee gave the performances of a lifetime. Oddly, the stage-trained Walter Huston and Beulah Bondi come off as stiff and strident; but Joan gives a polished *movie* performance. Sadly, the public wasn't buying, and Joan always looked upon the film as a mistake.

Box office was important to her: she answered all her own fan mail till it became overwhelming; she stopped and chatted with fans and (after a scolding from Louis B. Mayer), never left the house without looking like "Joan Crawford." Later in life, she said that "To this day, some little—or big—voice inside me says, 'Joan, go out there looking like a *star.*'" On a 1932 trip to England, she was serenaded by her "shopgirl" fans, and burst into grateful tears. One factor that powered Joan Crawford all of her life—onscreen and off—was a quite understandable fear. As someone who'd come up from nothing, she'd seen her once-famous costars Harry Langdon, Marie Prevost, Jackie Coogan, James Murray, reduced to poverty and ruin.

She bounced back from *Rain,* and 1933 and '34 were peak years for Joan (professionally, not personally—she and Fairbanks divorced in 1933, though they remained friendly for the rest of Joan's life). She was as big and marketable a star as any MGM owned, fully the equal of Garbo, Harlow, and Shearer (the wife of the studio's production supervisor, Irving Thalberg). *Dancing Lady* (1933, her third film with Clark Gable) was a goofy, delightful musical, featuring appearances by newcomers Fred Astaire, Nelson Eddy and Eve Arden. She was re-teamed with Gable in *Chained* and *Forsaking All Others* (both 1934). By this time, the two had commenced an on-again, off-again love affair that would continue for decades. They might well have married, but were never single at the same time.

In 1934 Joan also made *Today We Live*, her first of seven films with Franchot Tone, a 29-year-old actor with a wealthy New England background. Tone appealed to the snob in Joan; the two married in 1935. Once again, she went overboard in trying to "better" herself; unfortunately, her efforts were less suggestive of Grace Kelly than of Margaret Dumont. The fact that Tone's film career was largely confined to playing weak-chinned second leads did not bode well for their marriage: they split in 1939, but, again, remained friends.

From 1935 through 1938, Joan's films slowly, almost imperceptibly, lost their sparkle and appeal. *No More Ladies* and *I Live My Life* (both 1935) were glamorous, hollow society dramas; *The Gorgeous Hussy* (1936) was her first box-office bomb since *Rain*. It was one of her few period films; Joan was clearly miscast and uncomfortable, and the movie was one long yawn. Things perked up a bit with another Gable comedy, *Love On the Run* (1936), and a drama with Spencer Tracy, *Mannequin* (1937), but most of her films seemed thin, tired and long-winded (*The Last of Mrs. Cheyney, The Bride Wore Red, The Shining Hour*).

The decade that started so brilliantly was ending on an ominous note for such actresses as Joan, Garbo, Norma Shearer, Katharine Hepburn, Jeanette MacDonald. Younger, fresher faces were catching the studios' attention: Betty Grable, Lana Turner, Hedy Lamarr, Rita Hayworth. Garbo and Shearer retired from the screen; MacDonald went back to the concert hall; Crawford and Hepburn stuck out their chins and reinvented themselves. In 1939, Joan was handed one of her best and one of her worst films: In the ill-conceived *Ice Follies of 1939*, the only thing saving her from complete humiliation was that costars James Stewart and Lew Ayres looked even sillier than she did. In the dazzling *The Women* (directed by George Cukor), Joan brilliantly portrayed a bitchy gold-digger, sharing

Joan at her Joaniest, mid-1940s.

the screen with Norma Shearer, Rosalind Russell, Paulette Goddard, Mary Boland and Marjorie Main.

But she was treading water at MGM, and her time was running out. The only really worthwhile project she got from MGM thereafter was *A Woman's Face* (1941), in which she played a scarred (physically and emotionally) criminal mastermind. The rest of her films, from

1939 through 1943, were either pompous (*Strange Cargo, Susan and God*) or dull (*When Ladies Meet, Above Suspicion*). Joan left MGM, by mutual consent, in 1943, and found herself for the first time in charge of her own career.

It was at this time that Joan's private life ran off the rails. In 1942 she married actor Phillip Terry; that lasted four years. More troublesome was her adoption of four children: Christina (in 1939), Christopher (1941) and twins Cathy and Cindy (1947). The twins came along when Joan's life was settling down, and they maintained a good relationship with their mother. Christina and Christopher were another story: they were problem children from day one, who brought out the worst in Joan (and vice versa). Much too strict and unable to cope with their tantrums and misbehavior, she was eventually skewered posthumously by Christina in her memoirs, *Mommie Dearest* (published in 1978, after Christina found she'd been cut from Joan's will). That book—and the hilariously camp movie version—tarred Joan as a child abuser and emotional maniac for years. Her ex, Douglas Fairbanks, Jr., said, "The Joan Crawford that I've heard about in *Mommie Dearest* is not the Joan Crawford I knew back when," and friend Myrna Loy stated that she knew Christina as a child, and if she'd been Joan, she would have *killed* her, not just punished her. Joan had a rare moment of prescience in 1964, when a scurrilous biography of Jean Harlow was published: "There must be some way you can write your will," she said, "to leave your life story to someone to protect your reputation from exploitation."

Of course, the good works Joan did were rarely made public. She regularly sent Marie Prevost money when that actress was broke and jobless; she helped set William Haines up in his successful interior decorating business when his acting career faltered; she donated money to Hollywood Presbyterian Hospital, so down-on-their-luck film workers could be treated at her expense.

Back on the career front, Joan was determined to star in Warner Brothers' film version of James M. Cain's novel *Mildred Pierce*. She begged, she auditioned, she finally convinced director Michael Curtiz to cast her. It was the moment when critics and audiences began to really respect her talent, and she won a Best Actress Oscar for her performance. Her follow-up at Warners was possibly even better: the underrated *Humoresque* (with John Garfield, 1946). Joan looked her loveliest in this film, all cheekbones and lipstick and huge, welling eyes. But she also gave one of her best performances, as the self-destructive society woman in love with Garfield. Her final scene is a marvel of restraint and under-acting.

Things continued well with *Possessed* (a psychological drama, not to be confused with her 1931 film of the same title). She got another Oscar nomination (losing to Loretta Young in *The Farmer's Daughter*, a performance that has not aged well). But even Warners had trouble finding good projects for her, and she soon spread her wings, with mixed results: *Daisy Kenyon* (20th Century-Fox, 1947) and *Flamingo Road* (back at Warners, 1949), were entertaining and fast-paced, but more than a little tawdry.

Middle age is a dangerous time for actresses, and the 1950s were harrowing for Joan and her contemporaries. Even her appearance worked against her, with the make-up crews not bringing out her best. Joan's fabulous bone structure seemed to harden as she neared 50; her bow-tie lips bigger and eyebrows thicker; her hair worn in an unflatteringly severe style. This was the decade in which she looked the most like a Joan Crawford drag queen.

Joan starred in 11 films between 1950 and 1957, most of them melodramatic "women's pictures." She did her best with indifferent material in Warner Brothers' *The Damned Don't Cry, Goodbye, My Fancy,* and *This Woman Is Dangerous*; the interesting "older woman/younger man" (Jeff Chandler) drama *Female on the Beach* (at Universal); the bizarre, high-camp Western *Johnny Guitar* at Republic. In 1953 Joan returned to MGM for the glitzy color musical *Torch Song*, which proved unfortunate (her singing was dubbed, the script was abysmal, and Carol Burnett's 1970s parody of it was memorably funny).

Some interesting roles did still come her way. In RKO's *Sudden Fear* (1952), she earned an Oscar nomination for her performance as the murder target of husband Jack Palance and his tootsie Gloria Grahame. Columbia handed her a quartette of films in the 1950s: *Autumn Leaves* and *The Story of Esther Costello* were only passably entertaining, but in *Harriet Craig* (as an obsessive housewife trying to hold onto the only thing she has—her house) and *Queen Bee* (as a deliciously monstrous control freak), she managed to project a cool, snake-like menace while occasionally summoning up some genuine sympathy for her characters.

In the mid-1950s, Joan finally found marital happiness. In 1955 she wed Alfred Steele, the graying, bearish vice president of Pepsi-Cola. Joan had finally met her match: Steele was as successful and hard-driving in his world as Joan was in hers. The marriage was genuinely happy, and Joan spent the late 1950s traveling with her husband on behalf of Pepsi, becoming an ace saleswoman. Then, in 1959, Steele died of a heart attack in their New York apartment. Joan threw herself back into acting, to fill her emotional and financial needs (Steele did not leave her well-off, mostly because of outstanding debts). In *The Best of Everything* (1959), she played the soft-spoken but deadly boss from hell, a performance that must have influenced Meryl Streep's Oscar-winning turn in *The Devil Wears Prada*. The film itself has become a cult item for women in publishing and holds up very well, with an equal measure of camp, glamour and genuine drama.

In 1962 Joan made a fateful decision, one that would effect the rest of her career: she agreed to costar with Bette Davis in the low-budget Grand Guignol horror drama *What Ever Happened to Baby Jane?* It was Joan's last hit, but it turned both Joan and her costar into freak-show attractions. Most of her remaining films were low-budget horrors, though Joan never condescended to the material and always gave 100% in such drek as *Strait-Jacket* (1964), *Berserk!* (1967), and the execrable *Trog* (1970). It was an almost unavoidable trap for actresses of a certain age. During that period, Olivia de Havilland, Barbara Stanwyck, Tallulah Bankhead and Deborah Kerr all got pulled into that tar pit.

As smart and driven as she was, Joan also tackled television, beginning with a 1953 appearance on *The Revlon Mirror Theater.* From the 1950s through the 1970s, Joan guested on numerous shows, including the Golden Age anthologies *General Electric Theater* and *Zane Grey Theatre*, as well as the series *Route 66, The Man from U.N.C.L.E., The Lucy Show,* and her swan song, a 1972 episode of *The Sixth Sense.* Joan also good-naturedly appeared on a number of game shows, of which she was a great fan: *Password, I've Got a Secret, To Tell the Truth.*

Joan shows off her own jewelry, early 1960s.

But her best moment on TV (and her best latter-day performance) was in the 1969 pilot episode of Rod Serling's *Night Gallery*. Directed by the 23-year-old neophyte Steven Spielberg, Joan starred as a blind, imperious millionaire who buys the eyes of a hapless donor for just eight hours of sight. Her performance—especially in the last, harrowing moments of the playlet—are a testament to Spielberg's directing skills and Joan Crawford's still breathtaking talent. She continued working, but *Night Gallery* was her last hurrah.

By the 1970s, Joan was looking terrific, though she herself didn't think so (for the first time in her life she began avoiding photographers, after seeing an unflattering photo of herself and Rosalind Russell in 1974). Her hair was a soft strawberry-blonde, her makeup in age-appropriate light pastels, and any plastic surgery she might have had done was very minor—no scary pulled-back face. By 1973, when she was talked into appearing live at Town Hall in New York for a sold-out evening of chat and audience questions, Joan was a living legend. She gave up drinking (which had become a problem by the 1950s), moved into a small but elegant apartment in New York, socialized with friends and fans.

By the fall of 1976, Joan probably knew she had cancer. Out of fear, resignation or Christian Science, she refused medical treatment. In the Christmas 1976 photos taken by John Engstead, she looks like a wraith, all big eyes and pained smile. In the spring of 1977 she gave away her dogs, said goodbye to her friends and waited quietly for the end. It came on May 10. Joan Crawford was eulogized, her ashes buried alongside Alfred Steele's. Happily, *Mommie Dearest* is finally fading into history, while Joan's films are readily available on TV and DVD. Viewers are finally able to see what a professional, talented and restrained actress she was, and her legacy looks brighter than it has since her death.

Dorothy Dell

Few film careers were cut quite so short as that of Dorothy Dell; even James Dean and Clarine Seymour had more time in the spotlight to show what they had to offer. Dell was, along with Alice Faye and Ginger Rogers, one of the most promising musical starlets of the early 1930s. There's every chance she would have gone as far. But her death at the age of 19 left her with only three feature films to her credit, and only one of those is in general circulation.

She was born Dorothy Dell Goff in Hattiesburg, Mississippi, on January 30, 1915, the older of two daughters of Elbert and Lillian Goff. It was rumored that her great-grandfather was a first cousin of Jefferson Davis, but this might have been so much studio PR. Dorothy was a little less than a year old when she won the first of many beauty contests, and she kept right on entering and winning through her teens. In 1925 the Goffs moved to New Orleans, where Dorothy became a close friend of another hopeful young actress, Dorothy Lamour.

While at the Sophie B. Wright High School for Girls, both Dorothys pursued their show-business dreams. Dorothy Goff began performing on local radio shows, developing a warm contralto singing voice. The beauty-pageant trophies kept coming—Miss American Legion, The Girl With the Perfect Back, Miss Biloxi, Miss New Orleans. Dubious press releases claim that she was voted Miss America and Miss Universe in 1930, but there were no pageants for either title that year.

She did sign a Fanchon and Marco vaudeville contract in 1930, which had her appearing in Fox theaters all over the West Coast.

Dorothy's mother, sister Helen, and pal Dorothy Lamour accompanied her. The troupe toured through early 1931, when Dorothy—whose name by this time was changed professionally to Dell—accepted an offer to appear in what would be the last edition of the *Ziegfeld Follies* to be overseen by its creator, Florenz Ziegfeld. The show opened at the Ziegfeld Theater on July 1, 1931, and ran through November 21 before heading out on tour. Ruth Etting revived the old standard "Shine On, Harvest Moon," other costars included Helen Morgan, Hal LeRoy and Mitzi Mayfair, Grace Moore, and Harry Richman. Dorothy's contribution was a very funny and lewd song called "Was I Drunk?" which included such lines as,

> *I said "stop, please behave,"*
> *But what's the using of raving?*
> *He said, "give," so I gave—*
> *After all, what was I saving?*

It was an unusually raw number for the high-toned *Follies*. She also appeared as Miss Universe in the sketch "You Made Me Love You," no doubt leading to the later confusion in her résumé. Back in New York after her *Follies* tour, Dorothy made her first movie. In late 1932 she appeared in the Warner Brothers Vitaphone two-reel musical short *Passing the Buck*, along with Nina Mae McKinney.

She returned to vaudeville for nearly a year, signing a Paramount contract in December 1933. Various projects were announced for her (*Come On, Marine; Good Dame; The Search for Beauty*), but Dorothy's first role was as a dockside saloon girl in *Wharf Angel*, which she wrested from contenders Mae Clarke, Helen Mack and Isabel Jewell.

Wharf Angel began shooting on January 4, 1934. Directed by William Cameron Menzies, it was a rough-edged tale of the San Francisco waterfront, with Dorothy as Toy, who is pursued in love by fugitive Preston Foster and sailor Victor McLaglen. During filming, Dorothy and starlet Grace Bradley, old friends from Broadway, renewed their acquaintanceship and acted like the teenagers they were, engaging in practical jokes and giggling between

Dorothy Dell, 1934.

takes. When *Wharf Angel* opened on March 16, Dorothy Dell was proclaimed the discovery of the season. Hard-to-please critic Richard Watts, Jr., wrote that she provided the only "directness and compassion" in the film and that "with proper guidance [she] may develop into one of the most important recent finds of the cinema."

Dorothy was next given the female lead in the Shirley Temple starrer *Little Miss Marker*, which began shooting on February 28 (before *Wharf Angel* had even been released). Based on a Damon Runyon story, *Little Miss Marker* featured Dorothy as a hardboiled nightclub singer whose heart is melted by abandoned child Temple (bookie Adolphe Menjou is likewise affected and winds up in Dorothy's arms, despite their 25-year age difference). The film was released on June 1, the same day that Dorothy appeared on the cover of the in-house Paramount magazine.

Despite battling laryngitis early in the filming of *Little Miss Marker*, Dorothy came out on top again. In this film she bears a strong resemblance to Alice Faye, also born in 1915 and just beginning her film career: both were pretty, slightly plump platinum blondes with deep, strong singing voices and a warm, maternal air. Both, in fact, worked well with young Shirley Temple.

By the time her third picture, *Shoot the Works*, began filming on April 4, 1934, *Wharf Angel* had premiered to great personal reviews, and Dorothy was beginning to get the star treatment from studio and fans alike. Fan magazines quizzed her on various topics, including her love life. "When I do marry," she said, "I want to fall in love so hard that I shall give up my career for it. Otherwise, it's no-go. I do not want to fall in love with an actor," she added, "because they make boring husbands." The only man known to be in Dorothy's life was 28-year-old Carl Wagner, a doctor who had recently performed surgery on her mother.

Wesley Ruggles directed *Shoot the Works*, a musical comedy starring Jack Oakie as a huckster out to make a star out of Dorothy's character (she was given a hit ballad, "With My Eyes Wide Open I'm Dreaming"). The film featured a cast of great character actors: Alison Skipworth, Lew Cody, Ben Bernie, Roscoe Karns, William Frawley and Arline Judge, as well as young Ann Sheridan in a bit part. Advance word was good: film critic Edward Schallert wrote that Dorothy was "a sort of younger Mae West type which is something

Dorothy Dell having a sandwich between takes of _Wharf Angel_, 1934.

in discoveries. There have been several actresses so nominated, but they haven't fulfilled the idea. It looks as if Miss Dell were really it."

Dorothy attended the funerals of Lilyan Tashman, who'd died on March 21, and her _Shoot the Works_ costar Lew Cody, who'd died on May 31. She was later said to have remarked, with a suspiciously ominous prescience, "I wonder who'll be next," referring to the old theatrical superstition of deaths coming in threes.

Dorothy and Dr. Wagner attended a party in Altadena on the night of June 7. Sometime after midnight, Wagner was driving her home (Dorothy had balked at driving since being injured in an accident in 1932). The car skidded off the road at a curve, bounced off a tree, and smashed into a boulder in a ditch. Dorothy, only 19 years old, was killed instantly, and Wagner died several hours later at Pasadena Hospital.

She remained in the news through early summer. Her memorial service was held on June 10, at which her *Follies* costar Ruth Etting sang; her burial was in a tomb paid for by Paramount in Metairie, outside New Orleans, a few days later. Her last film, *Shoot the Works*, premiered on June 29. The next scheduled Dorothy Dell film was to have been *Now and Forever*, with Gary Cooper and Shirley Temple; her role was taken by fellow Paramount starlet Carole Lombard.

The careers of Alice Faye and Ginger Rogers continued strong through the 1940s, but Dorothy Dell was pretty much forgotten, except by her costars and her childhood friend Dorothy Lamour, who never failed to credit her with jump-starting Lamour's own career.

Marlene Dietrich

Thanks to the cinematography of Josef von Sternberg and the studio photography of Eugene Robert Richee, Marlene Dietrich's image has become an icon of 20th-century glamour: the jutting cheekbones and jawline, the impossibly long lashes, the drag-queen eyebrows. But Marlene was more than met the eye. A versatile performer (aces in drama, comedy, musical), a tireless entertainer in World War II, a *mensch* who would bring sick friends home-made soup, a hard-working professional from her debut in the early 1920s to her painful fade-out in the mid-1970s. Marlene Dietrich was impossible to look away from.

She was born Marie Magdelene Dietrich on December 27, 1901, in Schoenberg, Berlin. After her father's death, her mother married Edouard von Losch, an army man, who died at the Russian front in World War I. That war was doubly traumatic for Marie, whose idolized French teacher was deported. Marie changed her name to Marlene and appeared in several stage productions beginning in 1922: everything from musical revues to George Bernard Shaw. It was the Weimar era in Germany, and the stage and screen were bursting with invention, experimentation, and such colorful characters as Margo Lion, Anita Berber and Lotte Lenya. The stolidly middle-class Marlene flowered in this sexual wonderland. Some of her early recordings (including the delightful lesbian duet "Wenn Die Beste Freundin" with Margo Lion) are available on CD, and show a lighter, tinnier voice than we remember.

She made her film debut in 1923, appearing in a total of 17 films before her "overnight success" in *Der Blaue Engel*. She was briefly visible as a monocle-wearing floozy in *Tragödie der Liebe* (1923), had her first significant role in *Eine Du Barry von Heute* (as yet another floozy, 1927), and was playing leads by *Der Juxbaron* and *Café Electric* (both 1927) and *Ich Küsse Ihre Hand, Madame* and *Gefahren der Brautzeit* (both 1929), among others. She later dismissed these as walk-ons, but existing films and stills belie her: we see a tougher, harder Marlene, with dark hair, rounder face, but that worldly look of amusement already in place.

She married production assistant Rudolf Sieber in 1924 and gave birth to her only child the following year. Marlene Dietrich was emblematic of Weimar Germany: on the one hand, she was a wholesome Aryan wife and mother, romping in the park with her daughter and cooking meals for her family and friends. But the film studios and nightclubs knew her as a sexually adventurous chippie, appearing in tawdry revues, painted and bespangled.

So she was no untested ingénue waiting to be discovered by Josef von Sternberg when he cast her as Lola Lola, the heartless vamp of his talkie *Der Blaue Engel* (1930). International fame came just in time; it gave her a ticket out of an increasingly unfriendly Germany. Several of her friends and coworkers died in concentration camps; her *Blaue Engel* costar Emil Jannings worked for the Nazi regime. But Marlene set sail for Hollywood and Paramount Studios.

Marlene Dietrich's fame rests chiefly on the six bizarre melodramas she and von Sternberg made in the early 1930s; films so surreally glamorous they still take one's breath away. Had she made no other films, *Morocco* (1930), *Dishonored* (1931), *Shanghai Express, Blonde Venus* (both 1932), *The Scarlet Empress* (1934) and *The Devil is a Woman* (1935) would have assured her immortality.

Things started out fairly normally with *Morocco*, the story of a camp follower and her Foreign Legion lover, played by a young and heartbreakingly handsome Gary Cooper. Marlene sang three songs, memorably kissing a woman on the mouth while dressed in a man's tie and tails. It was a lurid pulp novel come to life, with Marlene following the troops into the desert at the end, but her languid, almost sulky glamour was something new to audiences. *Dishonored* was, perhaps, the best of the Dietrich/von Sternberg films, though she later denounced it as trash. She played a character based on Mata Hari, a year before Greta Garbo's own version of the story would be filmed. Dietrich's film is lighter, bitterer, and sexier; her

Marlene Dietrich in one of her most delightful comedies, *Desire*, 1936.

death cell and execution scenes were brilliant, and underplayed by the star, who was gaining a more subtle acting technique.

The two 1932 collaborations, *Shanghai Express* and *Blonde Venus*, were more hallucinogenic and mannered, as von Sternberg took advantage of his free hand at Paramount. In the former, Marlene played a notorious tramp ("It took more than one man to change my name to Shanghai Lily") aboard the title train; she sported a wardrobe of feathers, chiffon and spangles (courtesy of costume designer Travis Banton) and was dramatically lighted by cinematographer Lee Garmes. It was all highly serious and a little glum, despite Marlene's speech impediment (she had trouble with her r's, à la Elmer Fudd or Kay Francis), which resulted in her telling costar Clive Brook, "I am weewee of you now." *Blonde Venus* was even more over the top, with Marlene as Cary Grant's kept woman, singing "Hot Voodoo" after emerging from a gorilla costume.

She took a break from von Sternberg to make *Song of Songs* (1933) with director Rouben Mamoulian; this film showed a much more natural and less mannered actress, and Paramount began to rethink the von Sternberg collaboration. Their concerns were raised further by the high cost, low returns and audience bafflement with *The Scarlet Empress* (an almost absurdist retelling of Catherine the Great's life) and the Spanish melodrama *The Devil is a Woman*, easily the weakest of their films together. It was also their last: Marlene went on to make a number of unremarkable films with other directors: *I Loved a Soldier* (1936, with Henry Hathaway); *The Garden of Allah* (with Richard Boleslawski); *Knight Without Armour* (with Jacques Feyder); the surprisingly dismal *Angel* (1937, with Ernest Lubitsch).

There were two bright spots in the 1930s, both showing Marlene's increasing abilities and versatility. In the marvelous screwball comedy *Desire* (1936, directed by Frank Borzage), she played a jewel thief with Gary Cooper as her stooge. This film is one of those heartbreaking "what-ifs"—Marlene's cohort was supposed to have been played by John Gilbert, but ill health forced him to drop out, and the serviceable John Halliday took his place. And in George Marshall's musical comedy western *Destry Rides Again* (1939), Marlene made herself over as a bawdy, funny dame, belting out what was to become a theme song, "See What the Boys in the Back Room Will Have."

By the late 1930s, many of Marlene's contemporaries were running into rough waters. Garbo, Crawford, Hepburn, Shearer, were all pushing early middle age and their stars were waning. Younger actresses were shoving their way forward, and the "old-timers" (most of them still well under 40) were being eased out.

But Marlene had bigger things on her mind by 1939, anyway. When war broke out in Europe, her mother was trapped in Berlin, and her sister Elisabeth's husband worked at Bergen-Belsen concentration camp (Marlene never spoke to Elisabeth again, snipping her out of all the family photos). War brought out the best in Marlene: "I'm a practical person, a logical person," she said in later years. "No time for dreaming." When ordered back to Berlin by the Nazi government, she refused: "Naturally, we were against the Nazis, of course we were. We knew about the concentration

It's New Year's Eve, 1942, at El Morocco, and Marlene is on the phone.

camps, it wasn't difficult to decide."

Marlene had mixed feelings about her homeland. When she'd taken out US naturalization papers in 1937, the German government released a statement that she'd "spent so many years among Hollywood's film Jews that she has now betrayed her Fatherland." She claimed to feel no guilt, but her wartime excursions took on the air of a holy crusade. Many actresses slung hash in the Hollywood Canteen and trouped in camp shows (though no female stars actually enlisted in the armed forces, unlike their male counterparts). But no actress put herself out like Marlene. She later called her wartime work "the only important thing" she'd ever done, dismissing her acting career curtly as "rubbish," "kitsch."

Marlene made eight films during the war. None of them were very good, but much of her salary went to war work (as did $100,000 worth of her jewelry). She made a few hard-boiled dramas (*Seven Sinners, Pittsburgh* and *The Spoilers*, all with John Wayne; *Manpower*, with Edward G. Robinson), the comedies *The Flame of New Orleans* and *The Lady is Willing*; and the enjoyably garish *Kismet*, in which her famously shapely legs were painted gold. But her 1940s films seemed to be only marking time.

Throughout the war years, Marlene gave speeches, helped Jewish friends escape Nazi-occupied countries; some reports even have her inserting codes into her songs for the US Office of Strategic Services. She devoutly attended the Hollywood Canteen and sold War Bonds, but not until 1944 was she able to arrange an all-out European tour. It lasted two years, through North Africa, Italy, France and, eventually, Germany.

During one show, the corniest of Hollywood clichés came true: a bomb knocked out the camp's electricity, and Marlene finished her act while hundreds of soldiers shone their flashlights on her. Marlene made herself popular with the troops by eating with the enlisted men, helping to right Jeeps, milking cows, performing from truck backs, even sharing in their lice and dysentery. She sang for the wounded and dying—both Allied and Axis—in field hospitals, and nearly died herself of pneumonia in 1945. With a price on her head, she toured perilously close to the front lines; she was nearly captured during the Battle of the Bulge, and led a parade of infantry into Rome after D-Day, like an avenging goddess of classical mythology.

Marlene Dietrich—"daughter of the 71st Infantry"—returned to a hero's welcome in America. She was awarded the US Medal of Freedom and France's Legion of Honor. Her statements about her homeland were clearheaded and unforgiving: "They wanted their Führer and they got him, didn't they? Because all of us Germans are like that. We want a leader."

She made another 15 films between 1946 and her final, fleeting cameo in *Just a Gigolo* in 1979. She aged with steely determination rather than grace; not for her the comfy middle-aged curves and laugh lines. She pulled her face back with rubber bands, dieted and exercised herself to a whisper-thin shadow in painfully tailored

Marlene as a soigné nightclub artiste, 1950s.

Dior gowns and suits. But her art only grew deeper and more impressive. She played a black-market Berliner in Billy Wilder's *A Foreign Affair* (1948), an ice-cold villainess in Alfred Hitchcock's *Stage Fright* (1950; her rendition of "La Vie en Rose" alone was worth the price of admission); she returned to the Old West in *Rancho Notorious* (1952) and *Around the World in Eighty Days* (1956); she was a harsh Gypsy fortune-teller in Orson Welles' *Touch of Evil* (1958); she matched wits with Charles Laughton in the courtroom drama *Witness for the Prosecution* (1957).

Her best later performance came with Stanley Kramer's all-star *Judgment at Nuremberg* (1961), playing the elegant, bitter widow of an executed Nazi. "Do you think we knew those things?" she asks American judge Spencer Tracy. "Do you think we wanted to murder women and children? It was Himmler, it was Goebbels. The SS knew what happened. *We did not know.*"—this from Marlene, who stated in no uncertain terms that they did indeed know.

From 1953 until her retirement in the mid-1970s, Marlene concentrated on her career as a chanteuse. When she brought her act to Berlin in 1960, reaction was strong; she brought back too many memories to a country eager to forget. She was picketed, bomb threats were phoned in, eggs and garbage were tossed at the singer. "It was love/hate," she said. "They behaved just like lovers—one goes away, the other's angry." She never performed in Germany again.

Marlene retreated to her Paris apartment in the early 1980s, keeping in touch with the world through letters and phone calls. "None of us émigrés ever found a home," she sighed to Maximilian Schell when he taped her for the 1984 documentary *Marlene.* Then she did a characteristic about-face: "I have no feelings for cities or things like that—rubbish!" In 1990 she commented on the reunification of Berlin: "Anything that brings people together always makes me happy. Happiness is so rare in this troubled world." Privately, she changed her burial plans. She'd long said she would rest in Paris, but now arranged to be interred next to her mother in Berlin. In early 1991 she chipped in to save her old film studio, UFA, which had fallen on hard times. "I'm still nostalgic for Babelsberg," she said. "I'll cross my fingers for you."

Marlene Dietrich died at 90 on May 6, 1992. Even then, her relationship with her homeland remained stormy. Her May 16 funeral brought out both fans and foes. Mayor Diepgen refused to mount any tributes for fear of right-wing retaliation. A campaign to name a street after her near her birthplace was defeated, but Marlene-Dietrich-Platz, a square near Potsdamer Platz in Berlin, was created in 1997. A memorial film festival was cancelled, to the delight of the Christian Democratic Union, while the Green Party called for a moment of silence. Newspapers debated, speeches were made; even in death, Marlene Dietrich and Berlin were inseparable.

Margaret Dumont

One of the supreme pleasures of films of the 1930s and '40s was the abundance of great dowagers. Whether haughty (Edna May Oliver, Hedda Hopper, Mary Forbes) or fluttery (Billie Burke, Cora Witherspoon, Alice Brady), the society matron reigned supreme. But the undisputed queen of them all was the great Margaret Dumont. Pearls draped over her stately monobosom, glaring through a lorgnette and exclaiming, "Well, *really*," she stole every scene. Or, more to the point, she expertly handed over every scene to her screen partner, whether he be Groucho Marx, W.C. Fields or Jack Benny.

She was born Daisy Baker in Brooklyn, on October 20, 1889. Little is known of her youth, although she later claimed to have been the god-daughter of Uncle Remus creator Joel Chandler Harris. Early photos of Margaret are hard to come by, but considering that she was still a great beauty in middle age, she must have been a knockout in her youth. Credits are contradictory, but the aspiring opera singer may have appeared in the Lew Fields musical comedies *The Girl Behind the Counter* (1907) and *The Summer Widowers* (1910), as well as *The Belle of Brittany* (1909).

In 1910 she married John Moller, Jr., who was variously described in the press as a "sugar tycoon" and a "financier and member of New York society." With his death in 1918, she returned to the stage: *The Fan* (1921), *Go Easy, Mabel* (1922), George M. Cohan's *Mary* (1920) and *The Rise of Rosie O'Reilly* (1923), and *The Fourflusher* (1925). Margaret was also credited with at least two silent-movie appearances, as an aristocrat in the 1917 version of *A Tale of Two Cities*, and as a "French Beauty" in the 1923 Lionel

Barrymore vehicle *Enemies of Women* (in which Clara Bow also had a bit part).

In the summer of 1925, fate stepped in, in the form of the Four Marx Brothers. The team had been working their way through vaudeville since the 1910s, and had already appeared on Broadway in *I'll Say She Is* (1924). For their new show, *The Cocoanuts*, Margaret was hired to play Mrs. Potter, a society matron beset by a crooked real estate promoter (Groucho Marx). The play, which opened on December 8, 1925, did well enough to be filmed (in a delightfully amateurish production) by Paramount early in 1929, at their Long Island studios.

By that time, Margaret was already appearing in the Marxes' next show, *Animal Crackers*, as Mrs. Rittenhouse (wooed by Groucho's Capt. Jeffrey T. Spaulding). When Paramount signed the Marxes to a long-term contract, the brothers very wisely took Margaret Dumont along with them, to recreate her role in the 1930 film version of *Animal Crackers*.

Groucho Marx and Margaret Dumont quickly became one of the era's great comedy teams: they clicked like George Burns and Gracie Allen. Invariably, Margaret was the haughty, imperturbable recipient of Groucho's sarcastic wooing: "You and the moon. I hope I can tell you apart. You wear a red necktie so I'll know you." "I hear they're going to tear you down and put up an office building where you're standing." None of this would have been quite so effective without Margaret's alternately blissful or appalled reaction.

Margaret was, sadly, absent from the Marx Brothers films *Monkey Business* (1931) and *Horse Feathers* (1932), both of which featured the sexier Thelma Todd as leading lady. But she was back in full fettle for the brilliant political satire *Duck Soup* (1933), as Mrs. Teasdale, the wealthiest citizen of Freedonia and bankroller for Groucho's President Rufus T. Firefly. It was the last absurdist hurrah for the Marxes at Paramount before they moved to MGM and their comedy style was watered down.

Groucho Marx's relationships with his female relatives and coworkers were never less than tense. He delighted in embarrassing, shocking or insulting the women in his life, and Margaret frequently found herself in the line of fire. He repeatedly told the press that she was bald and toothless, but the least gentlemanly of his

The imposing Margaret Dumont, 1937.

accusations was that she was humorless. In 1978 he repeated this libel: "She never understood any of the jokes . . . She had no idea why *A Day at the Races* was funny." To this day, some film historians and Marx Brothers fans have fallen for this claim and have dismissed Margaret Dumont as an unwitting stooge.

But interviews with her reveal her to have been a perceptive and talented comic actress. "Many a comedian's lines have been lost on the screen because the laughter overlapped," she said in the 1940s. "Script writers build up to a laugh, but they don't allow any pause for it. That's where I come in. I ad lib—it doesn't matter what I say—just to kill a few seconds so you can enjoy the gag. I have to sense when the big laughs will come and fill in, or the audience will drown out the next gag with its own laughter." A much harder job, it must be stressed, onscreen than onstage.

Margaret Dumont objected to the term "stooge," with her usual dignity. "I'm a straight lady," she insisted, "the best straight woman in Hollywood. There's an art to playing straight. You must build up your man, but never top him, never steal the laughs from him." She showed great insight into the Marx Brothers' brand of humor: "The comedy method which [they] employ is carefully worked out and concrete. They never laugh during a story conference. Like most other expert comedians, they involve themselves so seriously in the study of how jokes can be converted to their own style that they don't ever titter while approaching their material."

Margaret certainly couldn't pay her rent on what she earned with the Marx Brothers; she appeared in only another ten films during the 1930s, for studios both large and small. As a freelance supporting player, she had to scramble for roles, and had little choice in what she was offered. She had depressingly small appearances in *Gridiron Flash* (RKO, 1934), *Fifteen Wives* (Invincible, 1934), *Anything Goes* (Paramount, 1936), *The Song and Dance Man* (20th Century-Fox, 1936), *The Life of the Party* (RKO, 1937), *Wise Girl* (RKO, 1938), and *Dramatic School* (MGM, 1938). In *Reckless* (MGM, 1935), she didn't even have a line: she merely hissed at Jean Harlow from a theater audience.

But larger and more satisfying roles did come her way in several B films, such as the Charlie Ruggles comedy *The Girl Habit* (Paramount, 1931) and the melodramatic *Youth on Parole* (Republic, 1937). One of her best showcases was the sprightly 1937 comedy *High Flyers* (RKO), starring Wheeler and Woolsey and Lupe Velez. Margaret played a crystal-gazing society matron plagued by jewel thieves, runaway carnival workers, and a kleptomaniacal dog named Squeezy.

Margaret Dumont and her arch nemesis, Groucho Marx, in At the Circus, 1939.

She appeared in several of the Marx Brothers films made at MGM, as well. She was Mrs. Claypool to Groucho's Otis P. Driftwood in *A Night at the Opera*, in which she memorably opened the door to an overcrowded ship stateroom. In *A Day at the Races*, she played Mrs. Upjohn to Groucho's Hugo Z. Quackenbush, and had to participate in a highly physical slapstick routine, much to her distress. The quality of the Marx Brothers' films began to fall off thereafter: *At the Circus* (1939; Margaret was Mrs. Dukesbury to Groucho's J. Cheever Loophole) and, finally, *The Big Store* (1941). She was not in the Marx Brothers films *Room Service* (1938) and *Go West* (1940). "I'm afraid I was being taken for granted," Margaret said of those pictures. "Missing [them] was the best thing that could have happened to me."

Margaret Dumont did not only appear in Marx Brothers films; she also accompanied them on cross-country tours. Unusual for film comedies, their MGM scripts were fine-tuned in front of live audiences before going in front of the cameras. Margaret not only had to put up with the brothers' nightly adlibs and practical jokes (Groucho once called her "tits" instead of "toots" onstage), but with heartless teasing on sleeper cars and at hotels (she was repeatedly turned in to house detectives as a call girl). As Groucho Marx biographer Stefan Kanfer noted, "Perhaps because Margaret Dumont represented the onstage symbol of female authority, he made her life hell."

She appeared in 16 films during the 1940s, ranging from supporting roles to little more than walk-ons. Recognizing her talents, directors and comics alike often sought her out. W.C. Fields requested her as his foil in *Never Give a Sucker an Even Break* (1941) and the episodic *Tales of Manhattan* (1942). The Fields/Dumont segment was deleted from the latter film but has been restored in the DVD release. She supported Laurel and Hardy in *The Dancing Masters* (1943) and Jack Benny in his self-derided star vehicle *The Horn Blows at Midnight* (1945). She turned up in any number of high-profile films: Danny Kaye's *Up in Arms* (1944), and Esther Williams' *Bathing Beauty* (1944), as well as in lesser fare for poverty-row studios such as Monogram and Republic.

Director George Seaton sought Margaret out for a bit part in Betty Grable's *Diamond Horseshoe* (20th Century-Fox, 1945). In a 1978 interview, he recalled having tea with Margaret at her Knickerbocker Hotel suite and telling her, "I just hate to offer you this, Maggie, but if you would do it, it would be a great favor to me, because nobody could do it the way you do." Margaret accepted; Seaton gave her the full star treatment, complete with dressing room and wardrobe approval. The kind-hearted Betty Grable played along, telling her, "Miss Dumont, I've admired your work so much over the years. Please, if there's anything you can do to help me with my performance, I would only be too happy to have you tell me." This red-carpet treatment was well-deserved, as Margaret was indeed perfect in her tiny role: as the hostess of a party in a dream sequence, she memorably introduces Grable to "Sir How-Dare-You" and "Lady Your-Slip-Is-Showing."

But by now Margaret was stamped in the public's mind as The Marx Sister. She had mixed feelings about her association with the brothers. "The boys ruined my career," she once complained. "Nobody took me seriously as a dramatic actress. People always thought they saw Groucho peering from behind my skirt." When asked about future Marx teamings, she said it "was fun while it lasted. I wouldn't take a million dollars for the experience, but I wouldn't give a cent to do it again. Making pictures with them is truly living dangerously." When offers for her services slowed down, Groucho himself came to her aid, asking a screenwriter about an upcoming project: "Is there a part for her? I don't want to phone her unless there's a good chance she might get it—and boy does she need it!"

She did indeed need the work as the 1950s dawned: she played only small roles in six films between 1952 and 1962 (*Three for Bedroom C*; *Stop, You're Killing Me*; an unbilled bit in *Auntie Mame*; the William Castle horror-comedy *Zotz!*; as anti-rocker Georgianna Fitzdingle in *Shake, Rattle and Rock*; and the Shirley MacLaine starrer *What a Way to Go!*). Television provided some income: Margaret was a recurring character on the 1952-54 sitcom *My Friend Irma* and turned up on *The Donna Reed Show*, in a memorable episode also featuring Estelle Winwood.

In late February 1965, Groucho Marx asked her to appear on *The Hollywood Palace*, an episode of which he was hosting. They reprised the "Hooray for Captain Spaulding" number from *Animal Crackers*— a great success, but it turned out to be Margaret Dumont's swan song. She died at home of a heart attack on March 6, 1965. Marx later recalled his last glimpse of her: "After the show she stood by the stage door with a bouquet of roses, which she probably sent herself. She was waiting to be picked up. A few minutes later some guy came along in a crummy car and took her away. She was always a lady, a wonderful person. Died without any money."

The age of the society dowager was coming to an end at the time of Margaret Dumont's death. There was a last great flowering in the mid-1960s with such television actresses as Harriet MacGibbon (Mrs. Drysdale on *The Beverly Hillbillies*), Natalie Schafer (Mrs. Howell on *Gilligan's Island*), and Agnes Moorehead and Marion Lorne of *Bewitched*. Groucho Marx continued to alternately call Margaret Dumont "a great lady" and to denigrate her in interviews. But he seemed, at the end, to realize how important she'd been to his career. When accepting his 1974 Lifetime Achievement Oscar, the ailing Groucho told the audience, "I only wish Harpo and Chico could have been here—and Margaret Dumont."

Rosetta and Vivian Duncan

Sister acts have been a part of motion pictures since the beginning. A dazzling array of Gishes, Talmadges, Dollies, Lanes, and Bennetts have entertained audiences, along with the more confusingly named de Havillands, Fontaines, Danas, Masons, Deneuves and Dorléacs. One of the most delightful sister teams is all but forgotten today, only one of their films even remotely accessible to modern audiences. They narrowly missed film immortality when MGM decided against starring them in the all-talking musical smash-hit *The Broadway Melody* (1929). Instead, they live on in the twilight world of faded vaudeville stars and one-shot film wonders. It's a shame, for the Duncans were pure gold.

The birthdates of the Duncan sisters can only be guessed at. Some sources state that Rosetta was born in 1900 and Vivian in 1902. Film historian Billy Doyle stated that Rosetta was born on November 23, 1896, and Vivian on June 17, 1902, in Los Angeles (IMDb claims 1894 and 1897, respectively). Whatever their ages, something is known of their childhoods. Their father was real-estate man Samuel Henry Duncan. Their mother, Charlotte Rosetta Duncan, died in 1903, after giving birth to five children: besides Rosetta and Vivian, there was an older sister, Evelyn, and two brothers, Harold and Alex. The motherless children were packed off to school, where Rosetta made the acquaintance of singer Ellen Beach Yaw, sister of their school's founder.

A manic cut-up and talented singer from childhood, Rosetta impressed Yaw, who began giving her private lessons. Researcher Richard Kukan says of Yaw, "She could sing up into the only-dogs-

Rosetta (left) and Vivian Duncan, returning from an Australian tour in the 1920s.

can-hear range, and trill in thirds, and do other weird things. She's usually referred to as a 'concert singer,' although 'musical freak' is closer to the mark." This explains a lot about both Rosetta and Vivian's future act. Soon sisters Evelyn and Vivian joined in the lessons, singing impressive three-part harmony. It is here that Evelyn leaves our story: she abandoned the sister act to become a serious actress, in stock and such Broadway shows as *Lilies of the Field* and *Fair and Warmer*. She also appeared in a number of silent films for Morosco before retiring. Evelyn eventually married, and died at the age of 79 (more or less) in 1972.

Meanwhile, Rosetta and Vivian determined to make the big time with their singing and clowning. In the early 1910s they played local vaudeville theaters and were signed by Martin Beck to the west-coast Orpheum Circuit, getting as far east as Chicago by 1916. Once there, they wired Beck that they'd like to play New York. "There's a train leaving every day," he jokingly replied. Under the mistaken impression that they'd been fired, the determined sisters packed up and grabbed the next train east.

Their mistake turned out to be a stroke of good luck, as the Duncans were hired to play in a Shubert show at the Winter Garden, *Doing Our Bit* (1917-18, also with Ed Wynn and Rita Hayworth's father and aunt, Eduardo and Elsa Cansino). Their success in that show got them a spot touring with the east-coast Keith vaudeville circuit, and then in the Charles Dillingham show (with music by Jerome Kern) *She's a Good Fellow* (1919). It was their first big hit: the sisters, said one critic, offer "some of the most irresistible 'nut' comedy that musical comedy can offer." They toured further in vaudeville, scoring another success in Fred Stone's show *Tip Top* (1920-21, playing characters named "Bad" and "Worse"). "We've had our success, and everything we have we've gotten by our own efforts," said Rosetta. "Nobody ever gave the Duncan sisters anything."

By now their schtick was established: Vivian was "the pretty one," Rosetta "the funny one." Tall and lovely in a blonde, China-doll way, Vivian trilled in a breathy soprano and played the dumb ingénue. Rosetta (who was by no means unattractive) was the comic imp. Often playing a Baby Snooks-like character, she was brash, wisecracking and sang in a bold contralto. Not all reviewers were charmed by their antics: "Hokum is all right in a musical piece until it is plastered on too generously," wrote one critic. "We have always been an admirer of the Duncan sisters. We admire them yet—in fact, we consider them the best sister harmonizing team on the American stage, but as you may have guessed by this time, we don't like too much of Rosetta's alleged comedy." One of their gags was to throw doughnuts or onions into the audience. "We ought to see about watermelons," Rosetta once cracked. "They ought to make a real hit!"

They were extremely close and devoted to each other; creepily close by today's standards, but this was not unusual in touring vaudeville families. The girls—who called each other Hymie (Rosetta) and Jake (Vivian)—were rarely apart. "I couldn't live without my sister," said Rosetta in 1929. "We have never been apart except for two weeks. I've always taken care of her, and, in a different way, she's taken care of me. I've looked out for her the way a mother would." Again, according to Rosetta, "We call each other up the minute we wake up in the morning, and we're together all the time." *Motion Picture Classic*'s reporter Elisabeth Goldbeck wrote that "Vivian never worries. She's easy-going. She never takes anything seriously. Rosetta worries. Someone has to be serious, and it's always devolved upon her." On the other hand, Vivian had a better mind for facts and figures, and kept the act's songs, dates and bookings straight.

In 1922 the Duncans hit upon the idea which made their fortune: a musical-comedy version of the still-popular play *Uncle Tom's Cabin*, retitled *Topsy and Eva*. The girls claimed to have written the script and songs themselves, though a few ghosts may have been involved. The show ran for six months in San Francisco, a year in Chicago, and was a smash hit on Broadway in 1924-25. Then followed Boston, a return to Chicago, and other cities. Only a car accident, which seriously injured Vivian in 1926, interrupted their frenzied success. The show could hardly be revived today, except as a controversial period piece. One cannot discuss the Duncan sisters without treading into the uncomfortable realm of blackface, a major force in show business from the mid-19th century through the 1930s. Vivian, of course, played the lovable, sweet-hearted Eva St. Clare and Rosetta her pal, the comic "jus' wicked" slave girl, Topsy.

They became the toast of two continents (at least), the good friends and dancing partners of such royalty as Alfonso of Spain, Emmanuel of Portugal, George of Greece, the Duke of York and the Prince of Wales. "We used to think nothing of an 8,000-mile tour through Europe and South Africa," Rosetta later reminisced. Beginning in the early 1920s, they also made about a dozen recordings of their hits, including "The Bullfrog Patrol," "I'm Following You," "Side By Side," and "When it's Sweet Onion Time in Bermuda (I'll Breathe My Love to You)."

The Duncans filmed *Topsy and Eva* in 1927 (a print exists at the Library of Congress). Famed director Lois Weber was hired, but soon threw her hands up in dismay and was replaced by Del Lord. Lord was also stymied, and no less than D.W. Griffith was brought in to sort things out. They also appeared in the 1927 silent W.C. Fields comedy *Two Flaming Youths* as themselves, along with vaudeville and radio stars Weber and Fields, Clark and McCullough, and Moran and Mack.

The sisters' closeness was somewhat tested when Vivian fell in love with Stockholm-born actor Nils Asther, who had appeared as George Shelby in *Topsy and Eva* (he was later seen in such films as *Our Dancing Daughters, The Bitter Tea of General Yen, Bombshell,* and *Sweater Girl*). Their romance was difficult to maintain, as Asther's work kept him in Hollywood while the Duncans toured the US and Europe. Vivian was miserable without him, and when they were together, Rosetta's hovering presence didn't help. "We three are always together," Rosetta admitted. "And if they went to Honolulu or anywhere to be married, I'd be right by my sister's side. Nils understands that."

Whether or not Nils understood was a moot point: he and Vivian married in 1930 and she gave birth to a daughter, Evelyn Rosetta, the following year. The marriage did not last. When she filed for divorce in 1932, Vivian told Judge Bush that the language problem predominated: "You can see how it would be yourself, Judge, to have your husband and your mother-in-law talking about you in Swedish when you don't know what they were saying." Vivian won custody of Evelyn, a large settlement, and moved in with her sister and the countless nieces, nephews and cousins they cared for. Nils Asther never married again (he is one of the many stars whose sexual orientation has provided much vague gossip). He continued working in films and TV till the early 1960s, and died in 1981. Rosetta never married. "I've been engaged three times," she said, "but nothing ever came of it because I couldn't leave 'Jake.' My love for her was stronger than anything else."

Along with nearly every other vaudeville star, the Duncans ventured into the new medium of talking films, and they seemed to have hit the jackpot: MGM wanted them to appear in a loosely disguised version of their own life story in the studio's first all-talking

A glamorous publicity shot for *It's a Great Life*, 1929 (Vivian is on the left, Rosetta to the right).

musical, *The Broadway Melody*. It told the story of a struggling sister act (one pretty and one funny) who hit Broadway and resist all efforts by lovers and producers to split them apart. But someone at the front office (probably producer Irving Thalberg) felt that the Duncans—now in their thirties—were not "box office" enough, and they were replaced by MGM contract players Bessie Love (as Rosetta) and Anita Page (as Vivian). It's hard to fault the decision in retrospect, as *Broadway Melody* was a huge hit and Love and Page were delightful. But it was awfully tough luck for the Duncans.

As a consolation prize (and perhaps to work out a previously signed contract), MGM gave the sisters starring roles in what has become one of the great undiscovered treasures of the era, a movie that begs to be put out on DVD. *It's a Great Life* (released in December 1929, six months after *Broadway Melody*) is a fascinating glimpse at the Duncan sisters in action, and actually is a much better piece of moviemaking than *Broadway Melody*—it was directed by the great Sam Wood, who also helmed *A Night at the Opera*, *Goodbye, Mr. Chips, Kitty Foyle,* and *King's Row.* The girls played the Hogan sisters, Casey (Rosetta) and Babe (Vivian), department-store clerks who rise to vaudeville fame. The act nearly breaks up when Babe marries their pianist (played by Lawrence Gray, the character is amusingly named James Dean), while Casey is pined after by her ex-boss, played by Jed Prouty.

The heart of the film is their act, which was wisely filmed in front of a live audience: the uncanned laughter and the Duncans' interaction with the audience are both natural and electrifying. You can see how and why they became stars. The girls' first number was their theme song, "I'm Following You," done in simple harmony with no schtick. Later, their comic skills are shown in "It Must be an Old Spanish Custom" and a parody of "Tell Me, Pretty Maiden" from *Florodora*. In a color finale, they do the less-effective, audience-free production numbers "Hoosier Hop" and "Sailing on a Sunbeam." As captivating as their singing was, the Duncans' acting was not at all bad, either. Vivian effectively played the dimwitted, indecisive worm who finally turns, and Rosetta's driven, possessive trouper must have struck quite a chord with Nils Asther. After all these years, *It's a Great Life* is a lovely present from the Duncan sisters.

As kind as the 1920s had been to the Duncans, the 1930s were harsh. They lost millions in the stock-market crash, and Vivian's alimony and child-support payments declined along with Nils Asther's career. They filed for bankruptcy in 1932, claiming assets of $22,000 and debts of $400,000. "We're troupers, not bookkeepers," was Rosetta's understatement. Vivian laid their troubles to "gold mines with no gold, worthless stock, the fickleness of Wall Street and signatures on too many dotted lines." Plans for a musical film called *Hungarian Rhapsody* never went through. In 1935 they appeared in their last film, a short comedy called *Surprise!* Made in New York, the two-reeler had the sisters at a boarding school (shades of their stage hit *Tip-Top*) and attending a party in Mexican garb (which, goodness knows how, led to a Topsy and Eva routine).

Fortunately, the Duncans were troupers, and nothing got them down: financial or romantic troubles, the slow death of vaudeville, the onset of middle age. They continued touring the world, appearing in nightclubs, on radio and, eventually, on TV. With the success of the 1945 film *The Dolly Sisters*, some noise was made about filming their life, but nothing came of it. "Lots of people confuse us with the Dolly sisters," groused Rosetta, "but they were dancers." She added that "a friend of ours who caught [our] show overheard two old ladies say, 'Those aren't the original Duncan sisters, they're the daughters of Nils Asther!'" The teenaged Evelyn Asther did join the act, which included what must have been an increasingly bizarre version of their old Topsy and Eva routine. During World War II, they appeared at the Stage Door Canteen, throwing candy into the audience "because of an onion shortage."

"Time hasn't dulled the showmanship of the Duncan sisters," said *Variety* in 1952, and as late as 1957 they were headlining at the Palace (by now they had added rock-n-roll and Calypso to their act). *The New York World-Telegram* described the sisters as "rich and ageless and showing no sign that their spirit has in any way diminished," and both Vivian and Rosetta laughed and joked and reminisced through the interview. Vivian, by now a grandmother, noted that she was "excited because women are now allowed in the Lambs' Club," and Rosetta expressed a wish to drive upstate for some fishing.

But the Palace was their last great stand. In 1959 they were appearing at a nightclub in Lyons, Illinois, when Rosetta apparently fell asleep at the wheel of her car and drove into a bridge stanchion. Suffering multiple broken bones and internal injuries, she never regained consciousness and died on December 4, Vivian at her bedside (she was somewhere between 59 and 65, according to which source one believes). Several months later, Vivian began working as a single for the first time, unable to stay away from show business.

Vivian had married real-estate man Frank Herman in 1947, and the two moved to a two-acre estate in California. As late as 1968, Vivian was still on the road, doing her act in Australia. She made one last appearance, in Vol. III of Richard Lamparski's *Whatever Became of . . .?* books, in 1970. Still blonde and beautiful, she insisted, "I'll never retire. As long as I spend all my time at the piano, I might as well make some money at the same time." By the time she died, on September 19, 1986 (aged somewhere around 90), the Duncan sisters were all but forgotten, figments of another age. Only recently has *It's a Great Life* turned up (all too rarely) on TV, to remind audiences what a real delight they were.

Jimmy Durante

He was comically unattractive. His voice sounded like a motorboat. His acting was enthusiastic, rather than accomplished. But James Francis Durante managed to become a much-loved star in virtually every entertainment medium of the 20th century: stage, screen, radio and television. He is also one of the few showbiz legends about whom not one bad word has ever been spoken.

He was born on Manhattan's Lower East Side, the baby of four children of barber Bartolomeo Durante and his wife, Rosa. Both Durante parents were recent immigrants from Salerno, Italy, and they made a comfortable, if not wealthy, life for themselves and their children in the New World.

It was a tough neighborhood Jimmy Durante was born into, on February 10, 1893, but a loving family. Jimmy was funny-looking from an early age and took a great deal of ribbing in school about his oversized nose. "I'd go home and cry," he recalled. "I made up my mind never to hurt anybody else, no matter what. I never made jokes about anybody's big ears, cross eyes, or their stuttering." His family also helped: they gave him enough love and a good enough self-image so that his ego managed to survive ruthless childhood taunts.

They also gave him piano lessons, though that might never have happened had the Durantes known where their son would start his professional career. Jimmy dropped out of school in the eighth grade and took a number of odd jobs before landing his first show-business position, as ragtime pianist in a series of very disreputable joints. From 1910 till 1914, Jimmy learned his trade at Diamond Tony's on Coney Island, the Chatham Club in Chinatown, Maxine's in Brooklyn, and a dozen or so others. They ranged from bars to cabarets to out-and-out whorehouses. "Ragtime Jimmy" not only became a talented piano player, but he learned the ins and outs of handling crowds—he also became lifelong friends with a singing waiter named Eddie Cantor.

By 1914, Jimmy worked his way up to the Alamo Club in Harlem, where he was made bandleader and talent booker. He worked there till 1921, while also moonlighting at other clubs and making a series of recordings with The Original New Orleans Jazz Band. The Alamo also served as his introduction to two very important people in his life: song-and-dance man Eddie Jackson, and singer Maude Jeanne Olson. Jimmy married Jeanne in 1921.

He made the leap and opened his own club in late 1923, possibly at Jeanne's urging. The Club Durant (no "e") on 58th Street near Broadway only lasted two years, but it made Jimmy a star. One of the most popular speakeasies, it featured a good band, comics, dancing girls, and always a scattering of celebrities in the crowd. It also brought together Jimmy and Eddie Jackson with another song-and-dance man, Lou Clayton. The team of Clayton, Jackson and Durante (also known as The Three Sawdust Bums) became the sensation of the mid-1920s. "I doubt if a greater combination ever lived," said Broadway chronicler Damon Runyon.

When the Club Durant was padlocked by the Feds in 1925, the threesome took off for greener pastures, performing their loud, corny songs and comedy at the Dover, the Parody, and, finally, the Palace Theater. "We was *colossial!*" Jimmy recalled. In the late 1920s, the team toured in vaudeville, to the distress of the home-loving Jeanne Durante.

By this time, much of Jimmy's stage persona had been formed: his fracturing of the English language ("It's a catastrostrophe!"), his asides to the audience ("Surrounded by assassins!," "Everybody wants t' get into the act!," and his signature "Hot-cha-cha!"), and such good-natured tunes as "I Know Darn Well I Can Do Without Broadway (But Can Broadway Do Without Me?)," "I Ups to Him," "Jimmy, That Well-Dressed Man," and, later, his theme song, "Inka-Dinka-Doo."

Clayton, Jackson and Durante made their Broadway debut in Florenz Ziegfeld's *Show Girl* (1929), which made a star out of hoofer

Ladies man: Jimmy Durante in the early 1930s.

Ruby Keeler. The team had several good specialty spots in the show, and Jimmy was also given a number of solo routines. Jimmy's personality, said critic Brooks Atkinson, "batters its way through all barriers." The trio also made their first film that year, *Roadhouse Nights*, shot in Paramount's Long Island studio. Playing Helen Morgan's accompanist, Jimmy again outshone everyone else and brought the proceedings to a screeching halt every time he appeared.

"Jimmy Durante" as a character was seen full-blown in his first film, and his onscreen persona never really varied much. He was brash, friendly, befuddled, and childishly enthusiastic. At 36, he looked almost 20 years older, and even here he came off as more avuncular than anything else. Jimmy was never romantic leading-man material, and his popularity only grew as he aged into the grandfatherly stage.

Clayton, Jackson and Durante sailed into their next Broadway show, *The New Yorkers* (1930-31), playing bootleggers. Their most popular comedy routine, a frenetic tribute to "Wood!," was the hit of this show. It was then that the team was broken up by MGM, which offered Jimmy a five-year contract. Jimmy and Jeanne decamped for Los Angeles, and what was to be a disastrous early foray into films. He appeared in 17 movies over the next four years, all but five of them for MGM. Out of those thirty or so hours, perhaps 30 or so enjoyable minutes could be lifted.

MGM simply did not know what to do with Jimmy's admittedly unique talents. He supported William Haines in one of his unsuccessful talkies, *The New Adventures of Get-Rich-Quick Wallingford* (1931), played brief comic relief in such films as *Cuban Love Song* (1931), *The Wet Parade* (a 1932 Prohibition drama), the submarine adventure *Hell Below* (1933), the Fox musical *George White's Scandals* (1934), and the father-love tearjerker *Carnival* (Columbia, 1935).

Teaming him with struggling silent-film comic Buster Keaton may have seemed like a good idea on paper, but on celluloid it was a "catastrostrophe." In *The Passionate Plumber, Speak Easily* (both 1932), and *What! No Beer?* (1933), the two proved to be oil and water. Jimmy came off as bullying and obnoxious, and poor Keaton looked as miserable and downtrodden as he felt. Both men admired the other's talent, but realized that they were not fated to be the next Laurel and Hardy.

There were a few high spots in Jimmy's early film career. In *The Phantom President* (Paramount, 1932) he stole the show from unlikely lovers George M. Cohan and Claudette Colbert; in *Blondie of the Follies* (MGM, 1932) he and Marion Davies did an hilarious parody of Barrymore and Garbo in *Grand Hotel*; and in *Palooka* (United Artists, 1934) he introduced his hit "Inka-Dinka-Doo." Lovely Mexican comedienne Lupe Velez made a much better partner than had Keaton; the two appeared together in *Cuban Love Song* and three 1934 films, *Palooka, Strictly Dynamite* and *Hollywood Party*.

That last film was probably the high point of Jimmy's 1930s film career. It went through a long, expensive shoot, first planned as an all-star revue. By 1934, though, it had been trimmed and hacked into an odd mish-mash involving jungle star Schnarzan (Jimmy), his Jane (Lupe Velez) and arch-rival Liondora (played by handsome "Greek" comic George Givot, who actually hailed from Nebraska). There are many moments of pure gold: Jimmy's Tarzan parody, Lupe Velez's egg fight with Laurel and Hardy, and some really delightful musical numbers. Even Jeanne Durante got into the act, with a cameo appearance as herself.

Jimmy took some time off to reteam with Clayton and Jackson (as well as with Lupe Velez) in the Broadway show *Strike Me Pink* (1933). The musical got only fair reviews, but "The Three Sawdust Bums" kept it running for 105 performances. A bigger hit—in every way—was Billy Rose's *Jumbo* (1935-36), the last show at New York's famed (and enormous) Hippodrome before its demolition. A circus tale with Jimmy as the press flack, it was filmed in 1962 (with Jimmy recreating his role).

For all his offhand fooling, Jimmy took his work seriously. In the mid-1930s, he lectured at some UCLA acting classes. Student Loretta Lambert later recalled, "He taught us that no matter what role you were assigned to, it was quite necessary to realize that the audience is never fooled—they can always tell when an actor is faking. 'Love them,' Durante would say, 'and they will love you back. It's the way you deliver your lines that counts. That's a lot more important that what's in them.' He'd demonstrate by peeling off joke after joke. Many of them were stale and overworked. But the technique he used made those jokes come alive."

The late 1930s were busy years for Jimmy, although his film career all but dried up. Cut loose from MGM, he appeared in another seven films between 1936 and 1941. The only one which amounted to much was *The Man Who Came to Dinner* (Warner Brothers, 1941), but Jimmy was rather miscast in the Harpo Marx role. He tried mightily in small parts, but failed to save such films as *Start Cheering, Little Miss Broadway* (with Shirley Temple) and *You're In the Army Now*. But he had more than films to keep him busy. There were three Broadway shows: he played an ex-con in Cole Porter's *Red, Hot and Blue!* (1936-37, with Ethel Merman and Bob Hope), a studio flack in *Stars in Your Eyes* (1939, with Merman again), and doing eight numbers in his last Broadway show, the revue *Keep Off the Grass* (1940). There was also radio, and hardly a week passed in the 1930s and '40s without Jimmy Durante appearing on the Eddie Cantor, Jack Oakie, Rudy Vallee, and Fred Allen shows, *Fibber McGee and Molly, Duffy's Tavern* and others.

The early 1940s were a bad time for Jimmy personally: his father, sister and wife all died between 1941 and 1943. When Jeanne Durante died in 1943, he was heartbroken. Jeanne comes across as a very unsympathetic figure in the memoirs of Jimmy's friends: alcoholic, whiny, manipulative. There must have been something to her to keep Jimmy so loyal, but her charms were lost on others. She lived on as "Mrs. Calabash," to whom Jimmy said goodnight at the end of his TV shows (though producer Phil Cohen claimed the name was based on a Calabash pipe and used because it sounded funny).

Oddly enough, when Jeanne Durante died, Jimmy's career took off again. In 1943 he began appearing on the radio with up-and-coming comic Garry Moore on CBS's *Camel Comedy Caravan*, which by 1945 was retitled *The Jimmy Durante-Garry Moore Show*. Moore left in 1947, but Jimmy's show continued, still hugely popular, through 1949. Tapes of this show are still fall-down-laughing funny, and showcase Jimmy's timing and delivery. Guests included ex-partners Clayton and Jackson, with good-natured appearances by Al Jolson, Ethel Barrymore, Carmen Miranda, Frank Sinatra, Lucille Ball, and frequent turns by opera diva Helen Traubel.

Jimmy, still pounding away at the piano, 1953.

By the mid-1940s, Jimmy's film career had also resurrected itself. Balding and almost grandfatherly, Jimmy returned to MGM in 1944, where he made six films over the next four years. Like other middle-aged clowns, Charlotte Greenwood and Everett Edward Horton, Jimmy proved to be a great comic foil for such youngsters as Van Johnson and June Allyson (*Two Girls and a Sailor*, 1944), Frank Sinatra (*It Happened in Brooklyn*, 1947) and Esther Williams (*This Time for Keeps*, 1947, and *On an Island With You*, 1948). He only made three film appearances in the 1950s: in the low-budget, sentimental *The Great Rupert* (1950), as Donald O'Connor's father figure in *The Milkman* (1950), and a cameo in the Jimmy Walker biopic *Beau James* (1957).

Jimmy was busy with other things in those years, possibly his most successful: he became a TV star. He debuted cohosting NBC's *Four Star Revue* in 1950, and hosted *The All Star Revue* (1951-52) and *The Colgate Comedy Hour* (NBC, 1953-54). In 1954 he was given his own show, which ran through 1956. Occasionally seen in reruns, they are just as delightful as his radio show had been. Lou Clayton had died in 1950, but Eddie Jackson was a frequent TV guest. Carmen Miranda made a hilarious appearance in 1955, dying only a few hours later. Other guests included Tallulah Bankhead, Eddie Cantor, Robert Mitchum, Charles Laughton and Peter Lawford. Jimmy tried to get Greta Garbo to appear but— though she sent him what amounted to a fan letter—she declined.

After his show went off the air, Jimmy continued guesting on TV and starring in specials through 1972 (his swan song being *The Sonny and Cher Comedy Hour*). He supplied the narration for the Christmas cartoon *Frosty the Snowman* (1969), which still runs every year. Like some of his aging contemporaries, he occasionally veered into the maudlin, recording such tear-jerkers as "September Song" and "Young at Heart." As Jimmy aged, the awards poured in, from the National Conference of Christians and Jews, the TV Academy, the Catholic Youth Organization, the City of Los Angeles, the March of Dimes, the Los Angeles Press Club. He found personal happiness with Marjorie Little, whom he'd met when she was a hat-check girl in the 1940s. After a 16-year courtship, they married in 1960, and adopted a daughter, Cecilia, the following year.

Along with his TV work, recordings and nightclubs, Jimmy appeared in another four films in the 1960s, the most fondly remembered of which is his last, the madcap all-star comedy *It's a Mad Mad Mad Mad World* (1963). Jimmy only appeared at the beginning, as the man who sets the action in motion by telling of a buried fortune before—literally—kicking the bucket.

Jimmy had appeared to be old for so long that it was alarming when he suffered a debilitating stroke in 1972. His health declined from then on. Wheelchair-bound and visibly frail, he made occasional appearances at awards shows, but they were heartbreaking. He whispered a game "Inka-Dinka-Doo" into a microphone at his 83rd birthday bash in 1976, but it was his last public appearance. He was able to stay at home almost till his death on January 29, 1980, just shy of his 87th birthday.

His obituaries were front-page news all over the world: even little children could manage a fair impersonation of him. His recordings are still used in TV commercials, a kind of immortality which has eluded all but a few. "Lesser comedians squeezed laughs with vulgarity," said the *New York Times*, "but he trusted to his inexhaustible good will and overpowering energy." When asked in the 1950s what he'd like to be remembered for, Jimmy said with prescience, "For makin' people laugh, and makin' them feel good."

Cliff Edwards

His moments of fame were few, but lasting in the memory: the chirpy, upbeat voice of Jiminy Cricket in *Pinocchio*, handing out advice and crooning "When You Wish Upon a Star," or decked out in a slicker and strumming a uke, lightly crooning "Singin' in the Rain" in *The Hollywood Revue of 1929*. But Cliff "Ukulele Ike" Edwards also turned in affecting character performances in 74 films and sold millions of records as a pop singer in the 1920s and '30s. His life was a series of bankruptcies, divorces, and struggles with substance abuse, but right till the end he kept his chin up and his uke strumming.

Clifton Edwards was born in Mark Twain's hometown, Hannibal, Missouri, one of four children of Edward (a railroad worker) and Nellie Farnus Edwards. He was always coy about the year. "The doctor apparently never recorded my entrance," he said in the 1950s, "so you can say I'm anywhere between 50 and 90." But the date seems to have been June 14, 1895. When ill health took his father off the job, young Cliff left school and took on a variety of odd jobs: in a shoe factory, a foundry, a movie house, a carnival. "I bought my first ukulele in a pawn shop in Chicago and learned to play it by ear after I swung a spot in a traveling musical show," he later recalled. Had he possessed a few dollars more, Edwards would have bought a set of drums instead.

By 1918, he was touring in vaudeville as "Ukulele Ike." His crisp Midwestern tenor, moon face (with Barney Google eyes), and his gentle falsetto and scat-singing set him apart from other crooners such as Frank Crumit, Nick Lucas and "Whispering" Jack Smith. That year, he had his first hit with the nonsense ditty "Ja-Da," and

Cliff Edwards doing what he did best, ca. 1930.

was soon headlining both as a single and variously teamed with Joe Frisco, Lou Clayton, and Pierce Keegan. He appeared in the 1918 *Follies,* as well as Ziegfeld's racier rooftop *Frolics.* A brief (1919-21) marriage to Gertrude Benson resulted in the birth of his only child, Cliff, Jr.

Cliff's real success began in 1923 when he signed to record for Pathé. Through the decade, he became one of the top-selling recording artists in the country, putting his stamp on hundreds of songs, from ballads ("It Had To Be You," "June Night," "Reaching for Someone") and upbeat ditties ("Red Hot Mama," "Meadowlark," "That's My Weakness Now"). Just as Boop-a-Doop girl Helen Kane became the female voice of the Roaring Twenties, "Ukulele Ike" became its male emblem. He introduced "Fascinatin' Rhythm" in the 1924-25 Gershwin show *Lady Be Good* (with Fred and Adele Astaire), costarred with Marilyn Miller in Ziegfeld's *Sunny* (1925-26) and performed "Shakin' the Blues Away" in the 1927 *Follies*. Life couldn't be any better for Cliff, and in the late 1920s the advent of talking films only increased his marketability.

MGM signed him up for two musical short subjects in 1928, then to a long-term contract, beginning with a small part in the Marion Davies film *Marianne* (1929). Cliff stayed with MGM through 1932, playing character parts in 22 features and a handful of shorts (including a voice-over in one of the studio's bizarre "Dogvilles"). His biggest splash came as one of the hosts of the all-star *Hollywood Revue of 1929*, in which he introduced "Singin' in the Rain." Cliff appeared with Joan Crawford in three dramas, *Montana Moon* (1930), *Laughing Sinners*, and *Dance, Fools, Dance* (both 1931); in the latter, he quite effectively played a hard-boiled, ill-fated reporter. Cliff turned up in a number of high-profile MGM movies: *So This Is College* (1929), *Good News* (as an aging collegian, 1930), *The Sin of Madelon Claudet* (1931), *Hell Divers* (1932), as well as such low-budget fare as the Buster Keaton programmers *Parlor, Bedroom, and Bath* and *Sidewalks of New York* (both 1931).

But Cliff's private life was not keeping pace with his career. A good portion of his salary was going to pay alimony and child support. Still more was lost to gambling, bad investments, and, rumor has it, to alcohol and cocaine. He married again (to actress Nancy Dover) in 1932; the following year his teenage son lost his legs in a train wreck, and still more child support was added to Cliff's monthly dues. In March of 1933 he filed for bankruptcy: He owed some $68,000 to various creditors, and his only assets were the clothes on his back. He divorced his second

Newlyweds Cliff Edwards and Nancy Dover, 1932.

and last wife in 1936, resulting in still more alimony payments.

But the work kept coming in, even after Cliff's MGM contract lapsed. As a freelancer, he made another ten films for them through the 1930s, including such A-list assignments as Jean Harlow's swan song, *Saratoga* (1937), *The Girl of the Golden West* (1938), and even a tiny role in *Gone With the Wind* (1939). He also found work at Fox (*George White's Scandals*, 1934 and '35), Universal (*The Man That I Marry*, 1936) and Columbia (*Little Adventuress*, 1938). By this time, the short, plumpish actor's past as a best-selling songster was all but forgotten; he was better known as one of the movies' busiest character actors. He made one last Broadway appearance in George White's 1935 *Scandals* and began singing over the radio: he had his own shows on NBC (1932) and CBS (1932 and '34), and frequently guested on other shows as well. Still, financial woes kept Cliff on the vaudeville circuit, worldwide. In the late 1930s he also made a series of "blue" records for Novelty, which were delights of double-entendre: "I'm a Bear in a Lady's Boudoir," "I'm Gonna Give It To Mary with Love," and "I Like Mountain Women" may have been shocking and tawdry in 1936, but they're a positive hoot today.

The Western came to Cliff's aid in the early 1940s, and he played grizzled sidekicks and wisecracking cowpokes in such Saturday matinée fare as *Riders of the Badlands* and *Prairie Stranger* (both 1941), *Red River Robin Hood*, and *Sundown Jim* (both 1942), *Fighting Frontier* and *Sagebrush Law* (both 1943).

It may not have paid much, but Disney's *Pinocchio* (1940) bestowed immortality on Cliff Edwards. He tested for and lost the title role but was called back to test for sidekick Jiminy Cricket. "Walt said, 'Cliff, you've got to talk like a cricket,'" he later recalled. "I reached for Walt's hand and said, 'It was nice knowing you. Hope we can get together sometime soon on something else.' He pulled me back. 'You can do it,' he said. 'Just talk natural.'" Cliff talked and sang naturally, and his voice became an emblem for Disney (later, their weekly TV show opened with his rendition of "When You Wish Upon a Star"). "I've been in the business a long time, and now I achieve my greatest success playing a bug," he mused.

More voice-over work followed, as a crow in Disney's 1941 hit *Dumbo*. Cliff worked steadily (though mostly on low-budget projects) through the war years, including some musical short subjects. He appeared in 360 hospitals and army camps, both in the US and abroad. None of this made him much money. He continued appearing on the radio (he briefly hosted his own shows in 1944 and '46). Mostly he returned to his vaudeville roots and toured the US and spent 30 months performing in Australia. Cliff was one of the first to jump into television, with two short-lived CBS variety series in 1949.

But by the 1950s Cliff was an aging reminder of a lost era, his drinking making him less and less employable. Disney came to his aid with a number of TV voice-overs and *Mickey Mouse Club* gigs. He made only one film in the '50s (*The Littlest Outlaw*, 1955), and his financial situation continued to deteriorate. But Cliff refused to complain or fall prey to nostalgia. "Me, I live today," he said in 1955. "Then there's tomorrow, and that means today again. But there's no yesterday. Yesterday's dead. The hour's always now, not then."

But Cliff Edwards' upbeat attitude was not rewarded with good luck. By 1969 he was long unemployed (his last film being a voice-over for the 1964 film *The Man from Button Willow*). Health and money troubles forced him into a nursing home, as a welfare patient. When he died of heart failure on July 21, 1971, his body went unclaimed, and he was buried in a charity grave. Still, even at his lowest, Ukulele Ike had voiced no regrets: "Do you go back to the early chapters of a book you've read? Not unless there's something you've missed. And I can't think of anything. Mistakes, sure. But they've happened, they're done. No, you go out and buy another book. The next one might be the best, you know."

Peg Entwistle

For every star in Hollywood, there are a dozen bit players and character actors who barely hang on by the skin of their teeth. And there are hundreds—thousands—of young hopefuls who never make a name for themselves, who wind up pumping gas or waiting tables. It's one thing that never changes about show business. Indeed, with the Screen Actors Guild and other unions becoming more and more closed societies, unavailable to newcomers, it is even harder to get a foothold in the movie or TV business. One young actress in the early 1930s had it all: beauty, talent, family connections, a Broadway career behind her. Yet she is only remembered for her supposed career failure and her brilliantly symbolic suicide. If Joan Crawford stands for all the small-town girls who dragged themselves up to success from nothing, then Peg Entwistle is an emblem for all those hopefuls who found movie stardom beyond their reach.

Peg's early years had been clouded in mystery until sterling researcher James Zeruk, Jr., began digging out the facts of her life and death, with help from Peg's niece, Lauretta Slike. Peg was born Millicent Lilian Entwistle, on February 5, 1908, in Port Talbot, Wales (though she was raised in London). Her parents were both on the stage: her father, Robert Entwistle, and his second wife, Lauretta (along with various uncles and cousins), arrived in New York with Peg sometime in the mid-1910s (Peg's half-brothers, Milton and Robert, Jr., were born in the US). Robert Entwistle acted fairly steadily through the 1910s, appearing on Broadway with such stars as Estelle Winwood and Blanche Bates; by 1920 he had retired from show business and ran a successful business making

Broadway actress Peg Entwistle in the late 1920s.

fancy gift boxes. Robert Entwistle died after being struck by a car in New York in 1922, leaving 14-year-old Peg and her brothers in the care of her uncle, Harold, an actor and theater manager. By this time, she had already decided to follow her father and uncle into acting.

And her early successes came with astonishing speed—she got a place with the Henry Jewett Players in Boston by 1925, and reportedly made her Broadway debut as a bit player in *Hamlet* that same year. She toured with Blanche Yurka in *The Wild Duck*, as Hedwig—Bette Davis, decades later, recalled this show as a turning point in her life: "When 'Hedwig' died, I died. When the lights came up in the theater, I knew what I had to do. Before that performance, I wanted to be an actress. When it ended, I *had* to be an actress."

Peg worked her way up through such shows as *The Man from Toronto* (her first real role on Broadway, in 1926); *The Home Towners* (a George M. Cohan comedy, 1926); a 1929 revival of *Sherlock Holmes* starring William Gillette; she costarred with Dorothy Gish in the prestigious Theater Guild revival of Shaw's *Getting Married* in 1931; she played Amy in a revival of *Little Women* in 1931. Like everyone else, Peg had her share of short-lived flops. In *The Uninvited Guest* (1927), *The New York Times* wrote that "Peg Entwistle gave a performance considerably better than the play warranted." *She Means Business* opened and closed like a camera shutter in 1931; *Just to Remind You* lasted two weeks that same year. Peg's biggest success on Broadway was in the 1927 comedy *Tommy*, in which she played the female lead (William Janney, later a film juvenile, played the title role).

In 1929, while touring with the Theater Guild in California, Peg spoke of her acting: "To play any kind of an emotional scene I must work up to a certain pitch," she said. "If I reach this in my first word, the rest of the words and lines take care of themselves. But if I fail I have to build up the balance of the speeches, and in doing this the whole characterization falls flat. I feel that I am cheating myself. I don't know whether other actresses get this same reaction or not, but it does worry me."

In the spring of 1927, Peg married actor Robert Keith, and recently discovered letters show the marriage to have been a genuine love match. Writing to an aunt in late 1927, she said, "We get along splendidly. He's a sweet thing and I love him terribly. We've been married eight months and we haven't had an honest-to-God fight yet." Keith—ten years Peg's senior—acted on Broadway between 1921 and 1951, and appeared in dozens of movies and TV shows— he's best remembered today as the sheriff in *The Wild One* and as the vengeful, dying patriarch in the 1964 *Twilight Zone* episode

Peg in Hollywood, 1932.

"The Masks." Keith was already twice-divorced when he and Peg wed, and he had a six-year-old son, who grew up to be the noted character actor and *Family Affair* star Brian Keith. By the time the couple split in 1929, though, Peg asserted that "her husband snatched large handfuls of hair when he was contrary-minded."

The Depression had its effects on Broadway along with all other industries, and Peg's career was slowing down. In the spring of 1932, she appeared with Laurette Taylor in one of two James Barrie one-act plays: she was in *Alice Sit-by-the-Fire*, which got great reviews—till Taylor's health (she was a brilliant but unreliable player) caused her to drop out and the show closed abruptly.

By this time, Uncle Harold Entwistle was in Los Angeles, enjoying a career as a character actor and bit player—he appeared in dozens of films before his death in 1944, including *She Done Him Wrong*, *Mutiny on the Bounty*, *Romeo and Juliet*, *Easy Living*, *Wuthering Heights* and *Kitty Foyle*. In May 1932, Peg took a train west and moved into Harold's bungalow on Beachwood Drive. As James Zeruk, Jr., has recently discovered, she did not do so because she was in despair over her stage career and was hoping to break into the movies—she had actually been offered a role in a West Coast stage production of the comedy *The Mad Hopes*, which got a great reception at Los Angeles' Belasco Theater in May and June 1932. Along with Peg and Billie Burke, the cast included Humphrey Bogart—by this time, with her marriage over, she and Bogart were an item. Peg may or may not have planned to follow *The Mad Hopes* back to Broadway, where it opened for a very brief run in December 1932 (none of the L.A. cast went east with it—Jane Wyatt played Peg's role on Broadway).

Peg had other irons on the fire by the time *The Mad Hopes* closed in Los Angeles. Most writings on Peg Entwistle have her crawling to Hollywood when her stage career fizzled, only able to find one tiny role in a B film and killing herself in despair. As Zeruk and Peg's niece now reveal, that is not the story at all. By mid-1932, it's true, most of the studios had their Broadway émigrés sewn up. In the very early years of the talkies (1928-31), the ranks of studio players were filled out by a flood of fresh-faced New York stage players: Claudette Colbert, James Cagney, Joan Blondell, Bette Davis, Ginger Rogers, Edward G. Robinson, Katharine Hepburn, Miriam Hopkins, Paul Muni, Barbara Stanwyck, Spencer Tracy and others had their contracts all signed and locked up by the time Peg arrived in Los Angeles.

Still, Peg got a call from RKO studios, tested for—and won—a role in *Thirteen Women*, a wonderfully lurid potboiler based on an even more lurid novel by Tiffany Thayer. Shot in July 1932, it starred Myrna Loy—still in the early, Asian temptress phase of her career—as a half-caste who had been so teased and spurned by her former sorority sisters that she decides to kill them or drive them mad, one by one (frankly, they really have it coming, too). There were not indeed thirteen women; the victims in the film were winnowed down to Irene Dunne, Jill Esmond (married at the time to Laurence Olivier), Florence Eldridge (Mrs. Fredric March), Kay Johnson (mother of character actor James Cromwell), Mary Duncan, and Peg. Billed ninth in the opening credits, Peg played Hazel Cousins, who appears early in the film: she and Kay Johnson watch in horror as one of their sorority sisters, a circus acrobat (must have been some sorority!), lets her partner plummet to her death. Shortly thereafter, Peg meets her own doom: she stabs her husband to death, screams prettily in close-up, and her yearbook photo is crossed off by a smug Myrna Loy. Then off to the next victim.

The film did not do well in pre-release screenings, and various sources have it held up till either October or November 1932. It pretty much sank without a trace; *Thirteen Women* was re-cut after the Production Code came into effect and re-released briefly in 1935, at only an hour's length. Now seen occasionally on TV, *Thirteen Women* survives as an enjoyably silly thriller, and shows Peg to be lovely (in a quiet, Ann Harding way), with a perfect talkie voice and—within the strictures of the script—great potential as a film actress.

But it came to an end on the night of September 16, 1932. Peg left her uncle's home, telling him she was going to the drugstore and to see friends. She put a heartbreaking note into her bag: "*I am afraid I am a coward. I am sorry for everything. If I had done this a long time ago, it would have saved a lot of pain. P.E.*" She headed for the HOLLYWOODLAND sign looming overhead on Mount Lee. The 50-foot sign had been erected in 1923, beyond Griffith Park, to promote a real-estate development (it has read HOLLYWOOD since the last four letters were torn down in 1949). Built of wood and sheet metal, the letters were already a local landmark and emblem of the movie community by 1932, though they were beginning to fall into disrepair. A carpenter's ladder leaning against the H gave Peg her access (it must be noted that if one is going to climb a giant letter, H is really the way to go—you can rest halfway up).

Peg put her coat, bag and shoes at the base of the H and climbed—no one knows how long she perched there, looking out over the town, before she jumped. Peg was not found for two days: a female hiker discovered the shoes, coat and bag, with the note inside, and spotted Peg's body down the hillside; she made an anonymous call to a police station. Peg's body was found and eventually identified, becoming the sensation of the newspapers for a week or two.

More than career failure must have plagued Peg. After years onstage, one minor glitch would not have pushed her to desperation—indeed, new information reveals that her career was not in as bad shape as had previously been thought. Her marriage had failed, but Peg's romance with Humphrey Bogart indicates that she was bouncing back from that, as well. There is no evidence of drug or alcohol problems in her life. No one knows what else may have been eating at her: depression, an ongoing physical ailment; the possibilities are endless, though her note hints at some long-time, deep-seated sorrow.

It was the cause of her death—such a brilliant exit, jumping from the very symbol of the movie business—that shot her to fame and has made her a cult figure today. She was the only documented suicide from the HOLLYWOOD sign (which was completely renovated in the late 1970s, and is now cordoned off from hikers). Peg's ashes rest today next to her father's in Ohio; with a biography of her now in the works, one hopes that the many questions of her life will be answered, and her life and career will finally be as well known as her death.

Greta Garbo

Greta Garbo had been such a walking ghost, a legendary figure, for the fifty years of her retirement, that her actual death in 1990 seemed almost redundant. The biographies, memoirs and "I knew/walked with/saw her in a grocery store" books began pouring out of the publishing houses immediately. Her films were already available on TV and video; now many are out on DVD (even one reel of the long-missing *The Divine Woman* turned up in the late 1990s). And yet the question remains: who *was* Garbo? What did she have, besides her stunning looks and undercurrent of eroticism (and neuroticism)? Was she one of the movies' greatest actresses, or largely a trick of the light and the cameraman's art?

Greta Lovisa Gustaffson was born on September 18, 1905. Her childhood was a mixture of deprivation and Huckleberry Finn-like romps. Living in a poor neighborhood of Stockholm, the Gustaffsons barely scraped by, and when father Karl Alfred (to whom Greta bore a strong likeness) died in 1920, life took a turn for the worse. Greta loved her mother, a jolly potato-shaped woman named Anna Lovisa, and was fond of her brother, Sven, and her sister, Alva. Greta also loved the Swedish countryside and grew tall and healthy, taking long walks and swims.

In school and at work, Greta was quiet and self-conscious, but could also be a normal, mischievous teenager. She found work at a barbershop, then as a hat salesgirl and catalog model at a large department store. By this time, Greta was stage-struck as well, spending her extra money going to films and the theater. After appearing in several advertising films, she quit her department-store job to study at the Royal Dramatic Theater in Stockholm (later students there included Ingrid Bergman, Max von Sydow, and Bibi Andersson). Her earliest professional film appearance was as a bumptious bathing beauty in the two-reel short *Luffar-Petter* (*Peter the Tramp*, 1922). Seen today, the 17-year-old appears to be a healthy, happy country girl. Some sources also list her as a bit player or extra in *En Lyckoriddare* (*A Happy Knight*, 1921) and *Kärlekens Ögon* (*A Scarlet Angel*, 1922).

Mauritz Stiller was one of Sweden's most famous directors when he discovered Greta in 1923 and renamed her Garbo. The handsome, magnetic 40-year-old Stiller had directed such epic and popular films as *Thomas Graals Bästa Barn* (*Thomas Graal's Best Child*, 1918), *Herr Arnes Pengar* (*Sir Arne's Treasure*, 1919), and, most recently, *Gunnar Hedes Saga* (*The Story of Gunnar Hede*, 1923). His new project, *Gösta Berlings Saga* (*The Story of Gosta Berling*), was based on a popular novel about a reckless defrocked priest in the early 19th century—it starred Swedish heartthrob Lars Hanson, and introduced the newly-named Greta Garbo in a supporting role as one of the ill-starred women in his life. The film was very long and convoluted (and was only seen in the US in a highly edited version)—Garbo made an impact, but was certainly not an overnight star.

After an abortive attempt to make a film in Istanbul, Stiller and Garbo took off for Berlin and its active film scene. But it was another brilliant director—G.W. Pabst—who directed the young Garbo next, in the marvelous, dark *Die Freudlose Gasse* (*The Joyless Street*, 1925). Dealing with the contemporary financial and moral crisis in Berlin, it starred the great Danish film queen Asta Nielsen, but gave Garbo a challenging role as an impoverished girl who must sell herself to support her family.

On a talent-hunting tour of Europe, MGM's vice president in charge of production, Louis B. Mayer, snapped up both Mauritz Stiller and Greta Garbo, and shipped them off to the US (opinion differs on who he wanted more, Stiller or Garbo—Mayer was cagey and not one to tip his hand). Garbo arrived in Los Angeles in the summer of 1925, and was tossed into the same starlet hopper with the other newcomers: she was plucked, slimmed, coiffed and gowned to look like the current popular idols (they chose a Gloria

Greta Garbo in the early 1930s.

Swanson/Evelyn Brent look for Garbo). She slowly learned English, posed for silly publicity shots (her MGM contemporary Joan Crawford thrived on this; Garbo *hated* it).

Her first MGM films, *The Torrent* and *The Temptress* (both 1926), were unhappy experiences for her and did little to establish her as something new and different. In *The Torrent*, she played a lovelorn Spanish opera singer; in *The Temptress* she was a heartless Parisian vamp who falls for architect Antonio Moreno. She got good reviews, and the films did well enough, but Garbo herself was miserable: she hated the US, was lonely and felt her roles were silly. Mauritz Stiller was fired from *The Torrent* (it was directed by Monta Bell), and was sent back to Sweden after working on a handful of films at Paramount; he died in 1928. Just as upsetting, her sister Alva, also on the brink of an acting career, died of tuberculosis in 1926, at the age of 23.

In the fall of 1926, Garbo filmed *Flesh and the Devil*, and met two men who were to transform her as an actress and a sex symbol. Director Clarence Brown was to helm seven Garbo films between 1926 and 1937, and was as responsible as anyone else for her onscreen persona. And her leading man, John Gilbert, got the public interested in her as the icon of tragic romance she was to become. Gilbert, about 30 (sources vary), was film's hottest sex god, what with Valentino in his grave. Dark, mercurial, with a tempting bad-boy quality, he had the habit of falling madly in love with his leading ladies (his four wives were all actresses). John Gilbert and his costar—a naïve, unworldly 21-year-old, remember—were soon involved in a red-hot affair, which translated very well onscreen.

A frustrated director and screenwriter as well, Gilbert coached Garbo into the acting style that suited her talents best. Relying on her expressive face, she slowed down and let her eyes do her talking. Revealing a real talent for drama—or at least the ability to express great, hurt emotions through her eyes and downturned mouth—for the first time "Greta Garbo" became "*Garbo*" and was spoken of in hushed tones as the new Bernhardt of the screen. This all took a few years, of course, but the *New York Times* reviewers were singing hosannas through the end of the silent era: "Singularly fine acting . . . Sometimes she reminds one of a blond Mona Lisa and on other occasions she is gentle and lovely" (*Love*); " . . . fascinating . . . if anything more impressive than she has been in other films" (*The Kiss*). All ten of her MGM silents were successes, though Garbo did much better in the cities than the hinterlands, where tragic heroines tended to get laughed out of town.

Of her silents, some were genuine masterpieces, while others were dull programmers—par for the course. It's impossible to critique the missing *Divine Woman* (1928), though reviewers were not kind. *The Mysterious Lady* (1928) was an unremarkable spy story, with the rather pallid Conrad Nagel as leading man. *Wild Orchids* (1929) was . . . *odd*. A romantic triangle set in Java, with Garbo as the frustrated wife of an older man (Lewis Stone, her most frequent costar), it fell into self-parody at moments. In *The Single Standard* (1929), she was a rather pompous and self-important young lady on a quest for "freedom, equality, and honesty in love" (p.s. she finds it, with Nils Asther). Her last silent, *The Kiss* (also 1929), was another overwrought love triangle (a love square, actually, with young Lew Ayres, Conrad Nagel and Anders Randolf battling for her affections). Only Garbo's participation raised these films above programmer status.

But a handful of Garbo's silents were thoroughly enjoyable, and brought out the best not only in her but in MGM's vast crew of directors, cinematographers, set and costume designers and costars. The previously mentioned *Flesh and the Devil* was a melodrama, but the top of its genre. Garbo was reteamed with John Gilbert in a modern-dress *Anna Karenina*, retitled *Love* (so the billboards could herald, "GARBO AND GILBERT IN LOVE!"). This version—miles better than her talkie remake—showed her acting skills at their quietest and most effective; her chemistry with Gilbert still burned through the screen. He also *lightened* her effect somehow, keeping her from falling into the grandeur that sometimes plagued her acting. Garbo and Gilbert were together again in *A Woman of Affairs*, based on the scandalous novel *The Green Hat*— Garbo was a doomed, tragic young society butterfly, and this film was one of the great delights of the late silent era.

By the end of the 1920s, Garbo's love affair with Gilbert had burned out, though the two remained friends. Of course, it's impossible to discuss Greta Garbo without bringing up her love life and sexuality, which were gossiped about at the time, and since— an equal number of proponents cast their votes for her being straight, gay, bisexual, asexual. She was never able to maintain a happy romance with either a man or a woman. She hated her glamorous image and in private life often wore no makeup and men's clothing. Ever since she was a child, Garbo referred to herself as "one of the Gustaffson boys," a bachelor, an old man. When asked what roles she wanted to play, she chose male roles: Hamlet, Pierrot. None of this so much says "gay" as it hints that she may have been transgendered—born a half-century later, she might have been able to live happily as a man. All of this is sheer wild speculation, of course—Garbo never discussed her private feelings with anyone.

Garbo was MGM's last major star to dip her toe into talkies—the studio was nervous, understandably, about her deep voice and heavy Swedish accent. After casting about for a suitable vehicle and intensive voice and language coaching, *Anna Christie* opened in early 1930, with the memorable ad line "GARBO TALKS!" The film, based on Eugene O'Neill's 1921 play, is long, talky and morose; but Garbo came through with flying colors: "Greta Garbo is even more interesting through being heard than she was in her mute portrayals," said the *New York Times*. "Unlike most of the film actresses in their débuts in talking films, Miss Garbo suits her actions to the words. She thinks about what she is saying and accompanies the lines with suitable gestures and expressions."

By this time, the Garbo Legend had already emerged. She refused interviews, fled from photographers, closed her sets; her purported catch phrases, "I vant to be alone" and "I t'ank I go home now," were already objects of jest. Some felt she was genuinely shy; others that she was high-hatting Hollywood and her fans. She was respected, parodied, idolized (by "Garbomaniacs"), pursued. Her acting career now seemed almost secondary to her role as a glamorous, elusive phantom.

Few of her earliest talkies were much good, but Garbo rose above the middling scripts (the genius of cinematographer William Daniels helped—she looks breathtaking in all of these films). In *Romance* she was an Italian opera singer; in *Inspiration* a naughty artist's model; she and Clark Gable were wasted in *Susan Lenox: Her Fall and Rise*. Finally, in 1932, she was given a role she could sink her teeth into: *Mata Hari*. While not as sexy or gritty as Marlene Dietrich's 1931 version (*Dishonored*), Garbo's *Mata Hari* is well

Greta Garbo, happy to be vacationing in Sweden, summer 1935.

worth seeing (the bizarre costumes by Adrian are worth the price of admission alone).

Her next film, *Grand Hotel* (1932), is certainly one of the greats of its era, still hugely enjoyable. It's also a mélange of acting styles— the relatively low-key and modern performance by Joan Crawford; the boisterous hamminess of John and Lionel Barrymore and Wallace Beery (why is he the only one in the movie attempting a German accent?) and Garbo's "neurasthenic posturing," as one critic put it. But, still, her performance—as weird as it is—works. Her Grusinskaya is *supposed* to be a self-dramatizing, over-the-top ballerina, and one wouldn't expect her to behave any other way.

After the interesting Pirandello "mystery play" *As You Desire Me* (1932), Garbo again threatened to "go home now" and was issued a new contract by MGM: she now got a flat salary per film, and made only one film per year, each one necessarily a hugely budgeted production. Each Garbo film was now an Event, despite the star refusing to do publicity or spend more than one day per film in the photo studio. As big as she was, Garbo's biggest audiences were in US cities and overseas—as the situation in Europe worsened through the 1930s, her films brought less money into the studio (unlike today, of course, when flops can more than make back their investment through DVDs). Her most personal film was *Queen Christina* (1933), a biopic about the 17th-century Swedish monarch who abdicated in 1654 for reasons that are still debated. In Garbo's version, it was for the love of Spanish ambassador John Gilbert (cast at her genuinely kind insistence, as he was down on his luck and needed the work). This pre-Code film had enough gay references in it to keep audiences whispering: Garbo going off on her own dressed (unconvincingly) as a man, kissing her lady-in-waiting on the lips, calling herself a "bachelor," refusing to marry and have heirs. Garbo's friend Salka Viertel worked on the script, and rumor had it that Garbo herself had much input.

The Painted Veil (1934) was, arguably, her worst talkie. A teacup drama based on a Somerset Maugham novel, it took Garbo (with costar Herbert Marshall) through a Chinese cholera epidemic and a series of unfortunate hats. But after that came her marvelous doomed duo, *Anna Karenina* (1935) and *Camille* (directed by George Cukor, 1936). Garbo had no one to work against: Fredric March's Count Vronski was stiff and sexless, and Robert Taylor's Armand Duval was a boy ingénue. But she hauled out her heavy artillery and proved herself indeed the new Sarah Bernhardt, the high-tragedy queen of the early 20th century. She toned down her posturing (having good scripts made it unnecessary) and turned in excellent, low-key performances with just the right, light touch of head-tossed-back despair.

And then it was back to the bottom of the roller coaster with *Conquest* (1937), a dull, overlong costume drama about Napoleon (Charles Boyer) and his mistress Maria Walewska. It's all full of noble self-sacrifice and invasions and it lost a great deal of money for

Toward the end of her career, 1939.

MGM. Something had to be done: in 1938 came the now-notorious "Box-Office Poison" list, published in *The Independent Film Journal*. The piece complained that films starring Garbo, Mae West, Joan Crawford, Katharine Hepburn, Marlene Dietrich and Fred Astaire, among others, simply were not drawing audiences—it was stressed that the inferior vehicles, not the performers themselves, were to blame.

Thus, *Ninotchka*: MGM shifted gears entirely and put Garbo into her first comedy since her early pre-Stiller days. It was a foolproof vehicle, with a script by Charles Brackett and Billy Wilder, Ernst Lubitsch directing, costarring the velvety Melyvn Douglas and the brilliant wit Ina Claire (the fact that John Gilbert married Claire right after breaking up with Garbo caused no friction on-set: Gilbert was dead and the ladies found each other charming). Garbo was perfectly cast as a dour Russian functionary adrift in Paris; she poked fun at her own image ("GARBO LAUGHS!" was the advertising tagline). It earned Garbo her fourth Oscar nomination and was a huge hit with fans and critics alike: "It must be monotonous, this superb rightness of Garbo's playing," wrote the *New York Times'* critic. "We almost wish she would handle a scene badly once in a while just to provide us with an opportunity to show we are not a member of a fan club. But she remains infallible and Garbo."

The *Times* ate those words when Garbo's next—and final—film came out late in 1941. *Two-Faced Woman* is not nearly as bad a film as legend will have it; it's a silly, fluffy little comedy about a woman who pretends to be her own sexy twin sister to teach her husband a lesson. Claudette Colbert or Carole Lombard could have made it into an enjoyable, forgettable soufflé without turning a hair. But Garbo was lost at sea, even with brilliant comedy director George Cukor and Melvyn Douglas holding her up. Still lovely at 36 and still a top star, she walked away from her career and never acted again.

If Garbo had died in the 1940s, she'd be remembered as one of Hollywood's greatest stars. It was her afterlife as the Flying Dutchman of actresses that made her a legend. Settling into a Manhattan apartment and traveling the world, she spent the last fifty years of her life as the world's most famous recluse (money was not an issue: she collected Impressionist artwork and still had the first dollar she ever made). Of course, the faster she ran, the faster the fans and reporters chased her; a Garbo sighting became a badge of honor for even the most jaded socialite. Still chic into the 1960s, she thereafter adopted a hag look: shapeless hats and coats, long, disheveled white hair, huge sunglasses hiding her ravaged face (all great beauties age, but those who do not use sunscreen *really* age).

Opinion was divided on whether or not she was shy like a fox, cagily preserving her legend by playing up her enigmatic schtick. Certainly, had she appeared on *The Tonight Show* or sat down with *People* magazine, the bubble would have burst. Her friends never talked to anyone about her, or they were dropped, but various acquaintances described her as either witty, sociable and warmhearted; or self-centered, humorless and a dull conversationalist. When she died of kidney failure, on April 15, 1990, it was somewhat surprising to learn that she left a close family of affectionate nieces and nephews behind, and that her never-seen apartment was sunny and cheerful. It was all so *normal.*

The question remains: how great an actress was she? It's hard to see past that face, with its perfect bone structure and deep eyes. Certainly she was a gifted actress, within a very limited range. Her main flaw was that she could not (or was never given the opportunity to) create distinct characters. Her Mata Hari, Anna Karenina, Camille, and Ninotchka were all the same woman, interchangeable. This is not to minimize the talent that Greta Garbo did have, or the impact she left on the century. One hundred years from now, people will still be watching Garbo films, and they will never wonder "what did people *see* in her?"

Betty Grable

Very few stars have so succinctly summed up their appeal as did Betty Grable. "As a dancer I couldn't outdance Ginger Rogers or Eleanor Powell," she admitted later in life. "As a singer I'm no rival to Doris Day. As an actress I don't take myself seriously. I had a little bit of looks yet without being in the big beauty league. Maybe I had sincerity. And warmth. Those qualities are essential." That sincerity and warmth—and more talent than Betty gave herself credit for—made her the most endearing actress of her era. Lacking the high-voltage glamour of Rita Hayworth, Veronica Lake or Hedy Lamarr, Betty Grable was the personification of the bubbly but knowing World War II gal next door.

Ruth Elizabeth "Betty" Grable was born into a comfortably middle-class family in St. Louis, Missouri, on December 18, 1916. Her mother, Lillian, pushed both of her daughters into show business, but Betty's older sister, Margaret, would have none of it. By the time she was old enough to walk, little Betty was taking dance, acrobatics, saxophone, and ukulele lessons. In 1929, with talking pictures a temptation she could not resist, Lillian left her husband and older daughter in Missouri and set out for Los Angeles with Betty.

She was only 12 when she got her first movie job, in the chorus of Fox's *Happy Days* (filmed in 1929 and released in 1930). Casting directors were not too careful about checking the ages of their chorines, especially when they were as hard-working, photogenic and talented as the mature-looking, curvy Betty. From 1930-32, she appeared in 19 movies, as a chorus girl, background extra, and bit

The million-dollar smile of Betty Grable, 1941.

player (sometimes billed as Frances Dean). Eddie Cantor took a liking to her and she wound up featured with him in *Whoopee!* (leading the opening chorus), *Palmy Days* (a very funny bit in the opening scene as well as chorus work) and *The Kid From Spain*. She also turned up in Mary Pickford's *Kiki*, the gold-digger comedy *The Greeks Had a Word for Them*, and even Noël Coward's 1933 *Cavalcade*, as a background extra.

In 1934 she was signed by RKO, at the age of 17 (she was, remember, born in December). She spent the next few years filling bit parts and walk-ons that could have been done just as well by perky blonde starlets Toby Wing or Joan Marsh. A few of her mid-1930s films were memorable, and she did proud by herself: she did a hilarious song and dance with Edward Everett Horton in the Astaire/Rogers musical *The Gay Divorcee* (1934), sang back-up for Rogers in *Follow the Fleet* (1936), was a cute co-ed in *Pigskin Parade* (1936).

By this time her peculiar charms were becoming evident: not beautiful but cute, with a slightly receding chin, small but sparkly eyes, a mile-wide smile, and a puppy-like adorableness that jumped off the screen. Her crystal-clear Midwestern singing voice and impressive dancing skills made her easy to cast, and she worked like a racehorse. By her mid-teens, she was a thorough professional: always on time, letter- and step-perfect, cheerful, easy to get along with. But, somehow, her career stalled. She was dropped by RKO and picked up by Paramount, but the films and the roles got no better: in *College Swing, Campus Confessions, Million Dollar Legs*, she was spinning her wheels. After the disappointing Joe Penner comedy *The Day the Bookies Wept* (1939), Betty Grable gave up on Hollywood and moved east to Broadway.

In December 1939, just before her 23rd birthday, Betty opened in *DuBarry Was a Lady*, a Cole Porter musical starring Bert Lahr and Ethel Merman. She was a smash in a supporting role, and suddenly, Hollywood took notice. Before the show closed in December 1940, Betty Grable was back in Hollywood, signed by 20th Century-Fox as an "overnight star," after ten years in the movies.

Betty's personal life had not stood still while she worked nonstop. In 1937 she wed 23-year-old ex-child star Jackie Coogan, who had fallen on hard times. His father had died in a car accident, his engagement to Toby Wing broke up, his career was on the skids, and his mother and stepfather had robbed him blind. Betty stood by him during the historic lawsuit which resulted in the Child Actors Bill, known as the Coogan Act, setting aside a trust fund for child performers to protect their earnings. The Coogan/Grable marriage, however, lasted only two years, after which Betty enjoyed relationships with George Raft, Artie Shaw, Desi Arnaz (pre-Lucy, of course) and others. The love of her life was still a few years in her future.

In October 1940, Betty Grable's real reign began with the release of *Down Argentine Way*, a glossy color musical comedy in which she was romanced by hugely unconvincing "Argentinean" Don Ameche and coped brilliantly with scene-stealers Carmen Miranda and Charlotte Greenwood. It was the beginning of a five-year stretch of cotton-candy musicals, nearly all of them bright, chirpy, silly and the perfect remedy for the horrific war-filled newsreels that preceded them. World War II and Betty Grable's popularity ran concurrently, and it was certainly no coincidence.

It was her wholesome, all-American chipper sincerity that made her stand out; during her high-camp musical numbers she seemed to be in on the joke and thoroughly enjoying singing and dancing to such goofy numbers as "Down Argentine Way," "Down On Ami Ami Oni Oni Isle," "O'Brien Has Gone Hawaiian," and "Run, Little Raindrop, Run." But she was also able to carry off classic ballads such as "Cuddle Up A Little Closer" and "I Can't Begin to Tell You."

By all accounts, Betty Grable was one of the nicest, best-liked people in Hollywood, though she was no pushover: years as a chorus girl had given her a ribald sense of humor and a way with a stinging wisecrack. Outtakes show that when she (or a costar) flubbed a take, she laughed, apologized and shrugged her shoulders, rather than bursting into a volley of curses like so many of her contemporaries. Fan magazines and gossip columnists tried to foment feuds between Betty and costars Carole Landis, Alice Faye, Carmen Miranda, June Haver, Marilyn Monroe—all of whom became lifelong pals with her instead.

From 1940 through 1945, Betty starred in 11 musicals; not all of them were terrific, but there really was not a stinker in the lot. Her presence alone could make such otherwise lackluster films as *Song of the Islands, Footlight Serenade,* and *Sweet Rosie O'Grady* worthwhile. And there were some real gems, too, their rock-candy cheerfulness still shining through after all these years: in *Tin Pan Alley* (1940), she and Alice Faye played WWI-era vaudeville songstresses, romanced by John Payne and Jack Oakie; Betty and Carole Landis were wholesome gold-diggers in *Moon Over Miami* (1941); she

A rarely seen pose from Betty Grable's most famous pin-up photo session, 1943.

teamed with John Payne again in the delightful *Springtime in the Rockies* (1942); *Pin-Up Girl* (1944) played up to the iconic bathing-suit shot (smiling back over her shoulder) taken in 1943 by Frank Powolny; she and equally blonde June Haver were wildly miscast but enjoyable as the dark, Hungarian *Dolly Sisters* (1945). The supporting casts in these films only add to the sparkle: Charlotte Greenwood, Carmen Miranda, Edward Everett Horton, Jack Oakie, Phil Silvers, Cesar Romero.

There were also two forays into drama, the war romance *A Yank in the RAF* (1941, with Tyrone Power) and the noir *I Wake Up Screaming* (1941, which resulted in the amusing newspaper ads, "*I Wake Up Screaming* with Betty Grable!"). But as a dramatic actress, Betty was no more than competent; she knew it, and had no desire to continue along those lines.

It was while making *Springtime in the Rockies* that Betty's romance started with orchestra leader and ace trumpet player Harry James (also born in 1916). Betty Grable and Harry James married on July 5, 1943, and for the next two decades were one of show business' most high-profile couples (a contemporary song parody went, "I want a girl just like the girl that married Harry James"). They had two daughters, Victoria and Jessica (who have, thank goodness, never written books about their parents). The marriage was a genuine love match right up to—and beyond—their divorce in 1965, but drinking, gambling and infidelity finally proved too much (James died on what would have been their 40th anniversary).

Betty Grable's career took an imperceptible but, in hindsight, inevitable downturn with the end of World War II. She remained with Fox for the next ten years, making more than a dozen films before her contract ended in 1955. But all of the wartime pin-up girls found themselves to be old hat, while still in the bloom of youth and beauty: Betty, Rita Hayworth, Hedy Lamarr, Dorothy Lamour, all had to reinvent themselves.

Betty made four fairly nifty films with Dan Dailey, a male version of herself: blond, talented, cheerful (*Mother Wore Tights, When My Baby Smiles At Me, My Blue Heaven, Call Me Mister*). The rest of her musicals were a blur of agreeable but unremarkable time-wasters such as *The Shocking Miss Pilgrim, Wabash Avenue, Meet Me After*

Betty Grable and Harry James on TV in 1954.

the Show, and her last, *How to Be Very, Very Popular*. Her biggest hit was the nonmusical *How to Marry a Millionaire*, costarring Lauren Bacall and newcomer Marilyn Monroe. It's perhaps apocryphal but typical of Betty that she was said to have told Monroe, "Honey, I've had it. Go get yours. It's your turn now."

But Betty Grable, happily, did not disappear; she went on working right up till her death. She'd been making TV appearances since her 1954 debut on *Chrysler Shower of Stars*, and was seen on dozens of shows over the next two decades: *The Ed Sullivan Show, The Lucy-Desi Comedy Hour, The Carol Burnett Show*, and as a presenter at the 1972 Oscars. She also signed on as spokeswoman for the vitamin supplement Geritol, and was seen in print and TV ads in the late 1960s and early '70s. Looking trim and fit, her face pulled back by lift-tapes, her legs as good as they'd been when insured by Fox for a quarter of a million dollars, Betty also kept active onstage. She was one of the seemingly thousands of Dolly Gallagher Levis on Broadway (in 1967), she toured in *Belle Starr* and *Born Yesterday*, and was one of Las Vegas's most popular acts.

But it ended too soon: Betty was diagnosed with lung cancer in May 1973; despite surgery and chemotherapy, the disease metastasized. The summer of 1973 was a particularly sad one for film fans. That June and July saw the deaths of Fay Holden, Ernest Truex, Joe E. Brown, Veronica Lake, Lon Chaney, Jr., Robert Ryan, Jack Hawkins and Bruce Lee. Betty Grable entered St. Johns Hospital in Santa Monica on June 28, and she died there on July 3.

Betty Grable's life was not, goodness knows, a bed of roses: a stage mother, two problematic marriages, a relatively early death. But the horrors and scandals visited upon her contemporaries, Rita Hayworth, Hedy Lamarr, Veronica Lake and Carole Landis, did not tarnish Betty's life, and today her films bring unalloyed delight in one of the brightest and cheeriest actresses ever to set foot before the movie camera.

Charlotte Greenwood

Many a bad movie has been made more bearable—and many a good movie terrific—with the aid of talented character actors. One reason films of the 1930s and '40s are so enjoyable is the horde of stock players populating them: Edward Everett Horton, Billie Burke, Hattie McDaniel, "Cuddles" Sakall, and their other less glamorous and lower-salaried coworkers. One of the best—boasting a 50-year career—was Charlotte Greenwood.

She was not a great beauty. Tall (estimates run from 5' 10" to 6' 3"), gangly, with a long face and a broad grin, she was never cut out to be an ingénue. Born on June 23, 1890, Frances Charlotte Greenwood was the daughter of a Philadelphia barber and his wife. The family was what used to be called "impoverished gentility," and Charlotte claimed to be descended from a Revolutionary war soldier named Andrew Jacquette. Her parents separated, and Charlotte moved with her mother to Boston, Virginia, and eventually New York, where Mrs. Greenwood managed the actor-friendly Times Square Hotel. Charlotte left school in junior high and joined the chorus of *The White Cat* (1905)—her first Broadway show, at the New Amsterdam Theater. The early 1910s saw Charlotte and her partner Eunice Burnham trouping in vaudeville as "Two Girls and a Piano" (their delightful ad in *Variety* boasts, "Oh, We're So Perfect and Flawless!"). Charlotte's first real acclaim came with *The Passing Show of 1912*. Already her persona was set: a gawky, happy-go-lucky gal gifted with a pleasing contralto and an acrobatic dancing style.

She'd already perfected her trademark dance steps: a painful-looking split and a nonchalant high kick which literally reached her head. "One day I happened to put my foot up and twist it round a little," she told a reporter in 1916. "Something in the way I did it made the audience laugh . . . as I found it amused people I began to do more and more weird stunts." Even by the mid-1910s, she recognized that "I'm so identified with this kind of part that I'm afraid I'd have a lot of trouble if I tried to take up anything else. If I were playing in an Ibsen tragedy, the audience would probably expect me to put one foot on the mantelpiece."

It was the "Letty" series that cemented Charlotte's fame. In *So Long, Letty* (1916-17), she created the character that was to carry her for years: *Linger Longer, Letty* (1919-20), *Letty Pepper* (1922), all the way to *Leaning on Letty* (1935). She also appeared in the 1913 *Ziegfeld Follies, The Tick-Tock Man from Oz* (1913), Irving Berlin's *New Music Box Revue* (1922), toured in England and Australia, and headlined at the Palace on Broadway.

After a brief engagement to vaudeville partner Sydney Grant, Charlotte eloped with Cyril Ring (younger brother of vaudeville star Blanche Ring) in 1915. The marriage ended in scandal five years later when Charlotte and two detectives burst into a Philadelphia hotel room to find Ring and "a woman in scanty attire"—Ann Fleming, a chorine from Charlotte's current production—having what newspapers referred to as "improper relations." Charlotte married composer Martin Broones in 1924; that second marriage lasted for life.

It took the movies some time to catch on to Charlotte's appeal. She appeared in a handful of silents: *Jane* (with her first husband, 1915), the short comedy *Stepping Some* (1918) and *Baby Mine* (with the comedy team George K. Arthur and Karl Dane, 1927). "Someday I want to make a really first-class film," she said during her silent days. "The trouble is that one can't appear in a musical comedy and act for the pictures at the same time. It is too exhausting . . . Someday I intend to take a good rest and then try again." Studios seemed at a loss as to how to handle her—then talkies arrived.

Letty once again came to her aid, and her talking feature debut was in 1929's *So Long, Letty*. Seen today, the film is stiff and awkward, but Charlotte's performance shines through with a good-natured glee. She made eight films over the next three years, including two short comedies (*Love Your Neighbor* and *Girls Will be Boys*). The best of her features was the Eddie Cantor comedy *Palmy Days* (1931),

An elegantly fur-trimmed Charlotte Greenwood returning from a European trip in 1934.

which featured Charlotte as the lovestruck gymnastics coach at a chorus-girl-staffed bakery ("Glorifying the American Donut"). Besides working brilliantly with the nervous-nelly Cantor, Charlotte sang the terrific opening number, "Bend Down, Sister" (a teenaged Betty Grable can be easily spotted in the chorus).

Sadly, the rest of her early talkies fell short of *Palmy Days*. *Parlor, Bedroom and Bath* was typical of Buster Keaton's early, sad forays into talking comedy. She played a maid in *The Man in Possession* (1931, later remade as *Personal Property*, with Jean Harlow and Robert Taylor).

In the wild comedy *Flying High*, Charlotte's acting style did not mesh well with the equally over-the-top Bert Lahr's; the film is too loud by half. *Stepping Out* (1931, with Reginald Denny and Cliff Edwards) and *Cheaters at Play* (1932, one of Thomas Meighan's last films) may very well be good films, but they only exist today in archives. After the British-made *Orders is Orders* (as the secretary of a movie director, 1933), Charlotte gave up on talkies, and talkies gave up on her.

In 1932 Charlotte happily returned to the stage with *Wild Violets* in London; she also made a rare dramatic hit in *The Late Christopher Bean* (1933). She appeared in the Jerome Kern/Oscar Hammerstein operetta *Three Sisters* and *The Gay Deceivers* in London, and toured with *Leaning on Letty* until World War II put a stop to her wanderings.

It's for a series of 1940s musicals that Charlotte Greenwood is best-remembered today. She returned to Hollywood in 1940's *Young People*, a terrifically enjoyable musical featuring Charlotte and Jack Oakie as the retired vaudeville parents of 12-year-old Shirley Temple. It's funny, dramatic, heartwarming, has some great musical numbers—a last hurrah for Temple's childhood, and a welcome back to Hollywood for Charlotte.

She made 15 movies through the 1940s, all but a handful of them with 20th Century-Fox (*Up in Mabel's Room* and *The Great Dan Patch* were for United Artists; the sweet-natured *Driftwood* was for Republic). Among her Fox wartime musicals were a handful of classic, tune-filled movies that have come down to us as jewels of their era—still enjoyable, still funny, yummy slices of Americana. Charlotte played aunts, dowagers and older pals, looking askance at her up-and-coming costars Alice Faye, Betty Grable, Carmen

Charlotte in one of her later films, *Peggy*, 1950.

Miranda, John Payne and Don Ameche; she romanced equally talented scene-stealers Edward Everett Horton, Jack Haley, Charles Ruggles, and S.Z. "Cuddles" Sakall. She also—in nearly every film, even if it had to be dragged in from left field—got to do her acrobatic high-kick. Buying any of these—or all of them—is a great investment: *Down Argentine Way* (1940), *Moon Over Miami* (1941), *Springtime in the Rockies* (1942), *The Gang's All Here* (1943), *Oh, You Beautiful Doll* (1949).

Surrounded by Hollywood beauties, Charlotte remained admirably unselfconscious about her looks and height. "I always tell my tall girlfriends to look up and just act as if the rest of the world had some growing up to do to catch up to us," she told a reporter in 1940. Years later, she noted, "The kind of wrapping you come in has nothing to do with it. As quickly as you realize that, contentment and peace come—from the heart. Happiness is within you." Charlotte had a lot in common with fellow loud-mouth comics Jimmy Durante, Bert Lahr and Jack Oakie. None were sex symbols; their singing, dancing and acting skills were bumptious rather than brilliant. But all projected an overwhelming likability, a palpable need to please and entertain.

After the war, Charlotte—now in her mid-fifties—slowed down her career, but only slightly. She played *I Remember Mama* onstage; her last Broadway show was Cole Porter's *Out of This World* (1950). The role of Aunt Eller in *Oklahoma!* had been written with her in mind, but Charlotte had been too busy in Hollywood to play it (Betty Garde had that honor). In 1955, Charlotte did, happily, recreate the role in the film version: unrecognizable as the granite-hewn farmwoman, Charlotte gave the last of her great turns, and even got to do classic "Charlotte Greenwood" numbers with "Kansas City" and "The Farmer and the Cowman."

She made another four films in the 1950s, none of them very special (and *The Opposite Sex*, an ill-conceived 1956 remake of *The Women*, was a real horror). Her swan song was a 1961 pilot for a TV series (*The Best of the Post*) that never sold. Although she thereupon retired, Charlotte remained active socially. Interviewers were surprised to find a chic, elegant woman: placid, well-spoken and no longer given to high kicks. Her husband died in 1971 and Charlotte followed him a few years later; she was 87 when she died in Los Angeles on January 18, 1978. Word of her death broke a few weeks later, and a surprising number of papers around the country carried articles. Charlotte Greenwood's Broadway successes were some 60 years in the past, and her biggest films 30 years old, so most obituaries were brief—but many of them carried a small, blurred photo of the actress in action, one leg flung delicately in midair.

Daisy and Violet Hilton

Daisy and Violet Hilton only made two films: one of the best of the 1930s, and one of the worst of the 1950s. But no one who saw these women can ever forget them. The only conjoined twins to star on the big screen, Daisy and Violet somehow overcame their novelty status and shone as talented singers and charming, if often unhappy, women.

Their life story is as horrifying as anything Dickens or Poe could have concocted. Their early years are somewhat hazy: they were born in 1908 (possibly on February 8), either in San Antonio, Texas, or Brighton, England, depending on which source you believe. The babies were joined at the base of the spine, and their parents were anxious to be rid of them. They sold the girls when still toddlers to a woman named Mary Hilton, who began exhibiting them in freak shows. Like many twins, conjoined and otherwise, the girls had very different personalities: Daisy described herself as "impulsive and talkative and quick-motioned," while Violet said, "I'm not a talker and I seldom do anything on impulse." They had to work hard to get along, but, the girls told a reporter for *The American Weekly* in 1944, "It is as though some Power greater and stronger than ourselves, has given us this inner harmony to compensate for our being forced to live constantly as an entity."

Mary Hilton, her daughter Edith, and various husbands and lovers, trained Daisy and Violet in singing and music (they played piano, violin, clarinet, and developed excellent singing voices). They were taught to dance the Black Bottom by young vaudevillian Bob Hope when they played on the same bill together in the 1920s. But mostly their lives were loveless and brutal. Touring the world with their

Daisy and Violet Hilton in the early 1930s.

increasingly successful act, Daisy and Violet were tormented, beaten and emotionally abused by their keepers. They were kept secluded, as "people would not pay to look at us if they could see us for nothing."

"Doctors punched, pinched and probed at us till we were almost crazy," one of the girls later remembered. They were not anxious to be separated, however, as each was all the other had. They lived by their own rules: "Among them is not to seek advice from each other, not to advise, ever, and not to speak aloud our thoughts."

By the mid-1920s Mary Hilton had died, and their career was taken over by her husband, a go-getter named Meyer Meyers. Soon, the girls were working their way up in vaudeville; they toured on the west coast Orpheum circuit, appeared with Eddie Cantor and Charlotte Greenwood, and met with great success. More than a novelty, Daisy and Violet perfected a finely-honed act that would have worked even if they had been separate. Playing instruments and singing (in close harmony, not unlike the Boswell Sisters), they proved a hit with audiences and critics alike (even *Variety* raved about them). The Hiltons toured Europe, India, Egypt, and Central America. In 1930 they won a court battle to free them from the thieving Mr. Meyers, but they were left penniless.

They both had romances—the other twin separating herself (or so she said) from what was going on over her shoulder. Violet became engaged to bandleader Maurice Lambert, but their marriage application was turned down in 21 states "on grounds of morality and decency."

In 1932 the girls appeared in their first film, Tod Browning's *Freaks*. In small supporting roles, they essentially played themselves. *Freaks*, one of the most shocking films ever made, concerned a star-crossed love affair between a gold-digging bareback rider (Olga Baclanova) and a gullible midget (Harry Earles). A "normal" love story, between Leila Hyams and Wallace Ford, was thrown in as well. A score of circus performers was rounded up by Browning to fill out the cast. In addition to the Hiltons, there were Harry Earles and his sister Daisy (both were heavily-accented German midgets), the legless Johnny Eck, the armless Frances O'Connor, the entirely limb-free "Prince Randian," and a number of "pin-heads," portrayed by people born with microcephaly or nanocephaly.

Daisy and Violet were thrown in for their name value, and for color and comic relief. They did not take part in the horrifying finale—nor, sadly, did they get a chance to sing. Looking lovely in chiffon frocks, Violet cracked wise while Daisy got engaged in the film to annoying stuttering comic Roscoe Ates, leading to much suggestive dialogue (and cringe-making stuttering). Their acting was distinctly amateurish, but the Hiltons were utterly charming.

Violet (left) and Daisy Hilton, working in a Miami snack bar, 1955.

Daisy and Violet spent the rest of the 1930s scratching out a living in the dying days of vaudeville. They did surprisingly well, headlining around the country as late as 1937. But their private lives continued to be frustrating. In 1936 Violet married dancer James Moore, after campaigning for permission from the courts. Sadly, the marriage turned out to be a publicity stunt, and Moore soon vanished. In 1941 Daisy married actor Buddy Sawyer. That, too, failed almost immediately: "I guess I am not the type of fellow that should marry a Siamese twin," Sawyer told the press.

In 1951 Daisy and Violet appeared in their second and final movie, the low-budget exploitation film *Chained for Life*, released through Classic Pictures (belying its name, the company was never to release a classic picture). By this time, Daisy had dyed her hair blonde and put on a few pounds, while Violet looked rather gaunt, so the sisters were quite easy to tell apart. Costarring Warner Brothers' veteran character actor Allen Jenkins as their manager, the film was a crude retelling of Violet's publicity-stunt marriage, with a murder plot thrown in for good measure. Vivian Hamilton (Violet) shoots her sister Dorothy's two-timing fiancé, leading to a bizarre and, actually, rather thought-provoking courtroom scene. Would the innocent sister die in the gas chamber or spend life in jail, or would the guilty sister be set free? Like Ed Wood's *Glen or Glenda?*, *Chained for Life* is a sympathetic but very badly-made film on a fascinating topic. At one point, Daisy has a touching (if unconvincingly filmed) dream sequence, imagining herself rising from their bed, separate from her sister—walking through a garden, admiring her figure, dancing with her fiancé. And the sisters finally got to sing on film, four terrible numbers admirably performed.

From there on, the Hiltons' careers declined. They followed showings of *Freaks*, which had an afterlife in midnight and tent shows as *Forbidden Love, Nature's Mistakes, The Monster Show* (it didn't become a cult classic till the 1960s). Their money (and their manager) ran out on them in Charlotte, North Carolina, around 1960. An admirer found them an apartment, and Daisy and Violet got jobs as the most efficient check-out clerks at a local supermarket (one rang you up while the other bagged your groceries). They settled down in Charlotte, more or less forgotten; their names did not appear in the press again till their death of the flu on April 21, 1966.

In 1990 an off-Broadway musical about the sisters, called *20 Fingers, 20 Toes*, opened starring Ann Brown and Maura Hanlon. It was "all thumbs" according to the *New York Times* and quickly closed, but in 1997, a more successful adaptation of the girls' lives, *Side Show* (starring Alice Ripley and Emily Skinner), opened at the Richard Rodgers Theater on Broadway and was nominated for four Tony Awards. It played less than a year, but did bring the Hiltons back into the limelight, and resulted in frequent, sympathetic press coverage of their lives.

Judy Holliday

B londe movie stars in the 1950s seem to have been pretty
much divided between breathy bombshells (Marilyn Monroe,
Jayne Mansfield) and slim, elegant swans (Grace Kelly, Eva Marie
Saint). Producers didn't really know what to do with Judy Holliday,
a brilliant, versatile actress who simply didn't fit into any easy category.
Though she left behind a handful of delightful films, one can't help
feeling a sense of waste that her gifts were not better handled by
Hollywood (or, for that matter, by Broadway). Perhaps, like Lucille
Ball, Judy Holliday would have blossomed with a really good sitcom;
but, unlike Lucy, she never got one.

She was born Judith Tuvim, on June 21, 1921, to Abraham and
Helen (Gollomb) Tuvim. Growing up in a left-wing, intellectual Jewish
community in New York had a lifelong effect on Judy, who never
let her enthusiasm for literature, music or politics wane. She was a
brilliant student, winning a city-wide essay contest at twelve: "I ate up
all the books I could get my hands on," she said, "and when I couldn't
get books, I read candy wrappers and labels on cereal and toothpaste
boxes." Her first brush with the theater (barring childhood ballet
classes) came in high school, when she acted in a play to promote a
school magazine, for which she also wrote and edited.

Judy applied to Yale's drama school, but instead took a receptionist
position with the Mercury Theater, where her father had connections.
Brushing elbows with Orson Welles, John Houseman and Agnes
Moorehead fired Judy's ambition; by late 1938 she was making her
own career plans. Her friend Adolph Green was putting together a
music and comedy-sketch group, which also included Betty
Comden, John Frank (who would leave the group in 1943) and

Alvin Hammer. The Revuers accepted Judy into their fold and opened at the Village Vanguard nightclub in late 1938. It was to be Judy's perfect entrée into show business.

The Revuers caught on, with their clever, up-to-the-minute routines, and Judy quickly found her footing. Her deadpan comedy, strong if untrained singing voice, slide-whistle giggle and tall, showgirl appearance made her a major drawing card. The group played the Rainbow Room at Rockefeller Center and Radio City Music Hall, and in 1940 had their own NBC radio show for 16 weeks. But the jobs brought in little real money and were too far apart for comfort. When offered small parts in the play *My Dear Public*, The Revuers jumped at it. The show never made it to Broadway, folding during out-of-town tryouts in 1942.

By early 1944, The Revuers had gone as far as they could on the East Coast, and they pooled their resources for a move to Hollywood. A few club dates got them an offer from 20th Century-Fox to appear in the musical *Greenwich Village* (1944). When the film opened, The Revuers found their work had landed on the cutting-room floor (they can be spotted in the background of an apartment party sequence). Dismayed, Comden and Green broke up the group and went on to their own brilliant careers writing such shows and movies as *Singin' in the Rain*, *The Band Wagon*, *On the Town*, *Wonderful Town*, *Subways Are for Sleeping* and *On the Twentieth Century*. Judith Tuvim stayed at Fox, to be slimmed, bleached and renamed Judy Holliday.

She didn't give Betty Grable any sleepless nights. After bit parts in *Something for the Boys* and *Winged Victory* (both 1944), her Fox contract was allowed to quietly lapse. It was during this time that her fabled (and perhaps apocryphal) encounter with Fox's Darryl F. Zanuck took place. Curled, made-up and squeezed into a slinky Starlet Dress, she sashayed into his office, to be pawed and chased by the studio head. When one of her falsies popped out, Judy supposedly stammered, "That's all right, Mr. Zanuck, it belongs to you," and fled. It probably never happened, but made a good party story nonetheless.

Judy arrived back in New York in 1945, where she got a supporting role in *Kiss Them for Me*, as the lovable trollop drawn to three sailors on leave (the show was made into an unwatchably bad film in

1958, with Jayne Mansfield in Judy's role). *Kiss Them for Me* won Judy her first solo acclaim, as well as a Clarence Derwent Award for Best Supporting Actress. It also won her a chance at her star-making role: Billie Dawn in *Born Yesterday*. She got the role when Jean Arthur dropped out at the last moment, and when the play opened on Broadway in early 1946 she became an instant star. Playing the instinctively smart but totally uneducated mistress of a political thug (Paul Douglas), Judy brought new life to the cliché of the dumb blonde. Tough but not cheap, sweet but not saccharine, her Billie was both broadly funny and a recognizable human being. What Judy didn't realize at the time was that Billie Dawn would forever type her: "I guess I owe everything to Billie," she later said. "But some mornings I wake up cursing her."

Judy remained with *Born Yesterday* through May 1949, marrying classical clarinetist David Oppenheim in 1948 (her only child, Jonathan, was born in 1952). By this time, Hollywood was once again interested in Judy, and Columbia's Harry Cohn was convinced against his better judgment to sign her for a supporting role in the Tracy and Hepburn legal comedy *Adam's Rib*. Playing the defendant (a jealous wife who shoots husband Tom Ewell), Judy stole the film, won a New York Critics' Circle Award and a seven-year contract with Columbia.

Judy Holliday certainly looked like star material in 1950, when her contract went into effect: tall and blonde, with big brown eyes and photogenic dimples, she was easily as pretty as the thousands of starlets who flooded Los Angeles each year. Her figure was a bit zaftig, but could be kept under control and was not a big problem in the days of long-line girdles and handfuls of diet pills. What Cohn didn't reckon on was Judy's ambition to be a good, serious actress in worthy projects; her self-doubts; the depressions and temper brought on by her sometimes chaotic private life. Raised in a literary world, she didn't think much of her accomplishments. "Acting is a very limited form of expression, and those who take it seriously are very limited people," Judy once said.

No sooner had Columbia signed their new acquisition than disaster struck: *Red Channels*, a list of entertainment figures allegedly involved in Communism, was published in June 1950, and contained Judy Holliday's name. As Judy was filming *Born Yesterday* (with

One of Judy's best films: *It Should Happen to You*, **1954.**

Broderick Crawford and William Holden), her career teetered in the balance as the FBI investigated her political past. Judy was cleared (and she later denied any involvement in Communism), but the threat lingered through 1952, when she testified in Washington and was again given a clean bill of health.

Born Yesterday was released late in 1950 and was just as popular on film as it had been onstage. Judy even won a surprise Best Actress Oscar (many felt that Gloria Swanson's Norma Desmond and Bette Davis' Margo Channing had cancelled each other out that year). Her success calmed Cohn's doubts (and his fears of her Red-tainted associations), and her career continued its upward spiral. She made six appearances on Tallulah Bankhead's NBC radio program, *The Big Show*, in 1951, and returned to Broadway in the limited-run play *Dream Girl* that spring. She and her husband also bought an 18th-century farmhouse in upstate New York.

She returned to Columbia to film her second contract movie, *The Marrying Kind* (with the gravelly-voiced Aldo Ray; it was released early in 1952). A kitchen-sink comedy/drama about the trials of a young married couple, the film did a good job of temporarily distancing Judy from Billie Dawn and showing her serious acting ability; but it was not the follow-up hit Columbia had hoped for. The acting, the script, the New York location scenes, were all top-rate, but the film was so damn *depressing*. Much better was her next film, begun after Judy had given birth (and dropped from 190 pounds to 127, on a near-starvation diet).

It Should Happen to You (1953) was, arguably, Judy Holliday's most enjoyable film, her most nearly perfect showcase. It introduced her to costar Jack Lemmon (in his film debut), a perfect foil for her. Seemingly half her size, his worried, modern neuroticism balanced perfectly off her deadpan flights of fancy. The film (directed by George Cukor and written by Garson Kanin) was a satire on modern fame: Judy played Everywoman Gladys Glover, who yearns for the spotlight and achieves it when, through various plot twists, she gets her name and image splashed on billboards around New York. Suddenly famous for being famous, Gladys "comes to her senses" and leaves the glamorous life for a down-to-earth marriage to Lemmon.

Judy worked steadily through 1954, appearing on the TV shows *The Huntress* (an NBC drama with Tony Randall) and *Sunday in Town* (also NBC, a 90-minute color special). She reteamed with Jack Lemmon in a divorce comedy with the unfortunate title *Phffft*. Released late in 1954, *Phffft* starred the duo as a successful writing team on the outs, mulling over a reconciliation, while various temptations (including Kim Novak, as a venal dumb blonde) got in their way. Alternately dark and frothy, the film goes on a bit too long and is not a patch on *It Should Happen to You*, but it still features that wonderful cast and displayed Judy's ever-growing talent.

It was newcomer Kim Novak, not Judy, whom Columbia decided to build as their answer to Fox's Marilyn Monroe. Judy Holliday was never really seen by studios as a sex symbol. It wasn't that she was funny: so were Monroe, Mansfield, and a number of other hot properties. Perhaps it was her intensity and intelligence which set Judy apart from the crowd of hopeful sexpots. One always got the feeling that she was smarter than her leading men, that she could easily devastate them with her wit or even break them in half with her bare hands. She might have been a heroine in Depression-era films, like the tough Barbara Stanwyck, Jean Harlow or Glenda Farrell. But the 1950s found Judy a bit off-putting.

She played another smart dumb blonde in *The Solid Gold Cadillac* (1955), which had been a Broadway success for middle-aged character actress Josephine Hull. The role of Laura Partridge was aged-down and glammed-up for Judy, and she turned in another enjoyable variation on Billie Dawn. Like many another successful star, she found herself playing the same character over and over again, but she was so good at it that one can understand the studio's reliance on such a sure bet. But her next Columbia film, *Full of Life* (1956), seemed a departure for her. A drama about a middle-class marriage, pregnancy and religion, it proved to be a rather dreary and self-righteous tract which did nothing for Judy's career. It was her last film for Columbia: after Harry Cohn's death in 1958, the rest of her contract was allowed to slide.

Her marriage fell apart at about the same time; she and Oppenheim separated in early 1956 and officially divorced two years later. Judy became involved with suave, dark-haired actor Sydney Chaplin, a son of Charlie's. He was cast opposite her in what would be her last success on Broadway, the musical *Bells Are Ringing*. The show was written specifically for Judy by her old friends Comden and Green, who (with Jule Styne) tailored the songs to her somewhat limited vocal range. She played a lovelorn answering-service operator involved with a playwright client; the script was not up to much, but it gave Judy full opportunity to

Judy Holliday in 1956.

show off her brashness and vulnerability. The songs ("The Party's Over," "Just in Time," "Drop That Name," the show-stopping finale "I'm Going Back") carried the show and made the cast album a bestseller.

Judy with Gerry Mulligan around the time she filmed *Bells Are Ringing*, 1960.

Bells Are Ringing opened at the Shubert Theater in November 1956, won Judy a Tony Award, and ran through the spring of 1959. Encouraged by the workout her voice was getting, she recorded a solo album, *Trouble is a Man.* In 1958 she met jazz saxophonist, composer and arranger Gerry Mulligan, who became her last love (as well as her collaborator on the 1960 album *Holliday with Mulligan*).

When *Bells Are Ringing* was bought by MGM and filmed in late 1959, Judy was picked up as well (this was not a sure thing: Broadway stars such as Ethel Merman, Julie Andrews and Mary

Martin often lost out when their shows became movies). *Bells Are Ringing*—Judy's last film—turned out to be a delight. Her curls are gone, her hair is done up in a smooth bouffant; the paler makeup of the early 1960s and chic Walter Plunkett costumes showed Judy in a more mature, ladylike light. Smooth, laid-back costar Dean Martin melded perfectly with Judy; she quickened her pace to set off his delivery, and many of their scenes together were as good as anything she'd done with Jack Lemmon.

The film was released in 1960, and Judy spent that summer preparing for her dramatic Broadway debut, playing actress Laurette Taylor in the biographical project *Laurette*. The play never made it past tryouts, folding in Philadelphia in October. One unpublicized reason for the failure was Judy's health: the 39-year-old was diagnosed with breast cancer. A mastectomy was performed (newspapers, shy about breasts, let alone cancer, reported it as a throat problem). Judy stayed out of the spotlight through 1961 and '62, spending time with Mulligan and her son in their apartment (in New York's fabled Dakota on the Upper West Side).

Her last project was another ill-fated show, the musical comedy *Hot Spot*, in which Judy portrayed a Peace Corps worker involved in a well-intentioned scam. Unlike *Laurette*, *Hot Spot* did make it to Broadway, but folded in the summer of 1963 after just 43 performances. Judy returned to her upstate New York farm, her finances in dire shape. Her health deteriorated as well, as the cancer spread. Her mother, Gerry Mulligan and friends looked after her as she sank over the next year. Her death at New York's Mount Sinai Hospital on June 7, 1965, came as a huge shock to the public. She was buried in Westchester Hills Cemetery; her headstone reads "Beloved Mother, Dear Daughter."

Judy Holliday has not inspired any cult-like followings, unlike her 1950s contemporaries Monroe, Dean, Hepburn, and Mansfield; but her reputation has soared with the availability of her films on cable TV and DVD. She is always mentioned as one of the brightest comic talents of the 1950s and of the 20th century—with less than ten starring films to her credit (and maybe four of those are real classics), a good Judy Holliday film festival could be seen in one day—and, indeed, should be seen regularly.

Phillips Holmes

Phillips Holmes is proof that good looks, contacts, and family don't always spell success. Phillips had all of these—plus a bit of talent—yet his stardom was brief. Phillips Raymond Holmes was born on July 22, 1907, in Grand Rapids, Michigan. This was no ordinary Midwestern family: father Taylor Holmes was a popular matinée idol who later acted in the movies and on TV; mother Edna Phillips was a Broadway actress who had costarred with E.H. Sothern; younger siblings Ralph and Madeline also joined the profession. Phillips attended the Newman School in Lakewood, New Jersey, where he was regarded as a good scholar but a bit of a hell-raiser. Various sources report that he attended Cambridge and/or Grenoble Universities—but by 1927 he was certainly enrolled at Princeton. It was there his film career began. Fan magazines state that director Frank Tuttle discovered the college athlete while filming Paramount's *Varsity* on-campus; however, Phillips' family connections indicate that his entry into films was hardly an accident.

His bit part in *Varsity* led to a Paramount contract and another small role in Clara Bow's *The Wild Party* (1929). His first real role came later that year in *Stairs of Sand*, with Wallace Beery and Jean Arthur. He finished out the 1920s with parts in *The Return of Sherlock Holmes, The Studio Murder Mystery,* and *Pointed Heels* (as a young composer in this musical with a fabulous cast: William Powell, Fay Wray, "Skeets" Gallagher and Boop-a-Doop Girl Helen Kane). Phillips made more than a dozen films for Paramount through 1932, along with several on loan-out to Pathé (a *Frankie and Johnny* clone called *Her Man*, 1930), Fox (*The Dancers*, 1930), Warner Brothers (*Man to Man*, 1930), and Columbia (*The Criminal Code,*

The gorgeous blond Phillips Holmes in 1933.

1931). By now he was starring (or costarring): in 1930 alone he appeared opposite Gary Cooper (*Only the Brave*), Nancy Carroll (*The Devil's Holiday*), and stage great Mrs. Patrick Campbell (*The Dancers*).

In 1931, Phillips was given his big chance by director Josef von Sternberg, who was on a break from Marlene Dietrich. He was cast as the social-climbing murderer in *An American Tragedy*, from the Theodore Dreiser novel (based on an actual 1906 case). The film was critically acclaimed but never reached much of an audience, and Phillips' career didn't skyrocket as he'd hoped. The *New York Times* singled Phillips out for panning: "[He] gives a peculiarly flabby conception of his role until he appears on the witness stand . . . Mr. Holmes does splendidly during these stretches." Seen today, Phillips seems more "subdued" than flabby, perhaps at von Sternberg's behest.

It wasn't for lack of talent (the *Times* notwithstanding) or looks: he was, perhaps, born too late. His chiseled face with its soulful expressiveness was made for silent films. Under a D.W. Griffith he might have become another Robert Harron or Richard Barthelmess. But Phillips' voice could be oddly inexpressive and his physique was wispy compared to tough '30s he-men Clark Gable, James Cagney, or Spencer Tracy. And already Phillips was gaining a reputation as a troubled, unhappy young man. Rumors of a drinking problem and depression didn't help him with the studio bosses. "That poor, poor baby," recalled costar Sylvia Sidney decades later. "He had *such* problems."

Phillips made another four films for Paramount; at least one, Ernst Lubitsch's anti-war drama *The Man I Killed* (1932), was quite good. Even the *Times* cheered him in that: "Mr. Holmes is splendid as the saddened Frenchman. He moves as if dazed, and one appreciates that night after night he sees the figure of the dying German." He moved from Paramount to MGM, where he made nine films in 1932 and '33. He had made a kind of screen test already at MGM; he was borrowed from Paramount for *Night Court* (1932). Though a B film, it was a tidy crime melodrama costarring Walter Huston and Anita Page. All three stars gave superb performances (Huston was a crooked judge, railroading dewy blond newlyweds Phillips and Anita).

But a starring role in a B film, even at MGM, was not what Phillips needed—at 25 years old and five years into his career, he was treading water. In 1933, he appeared in nine films—some of them big-budgeted, some with starring roles; it was his

Sporting a very impressive topcoat and ascot, returning from England in 1934.

make-or-break year. He was Irene Dunne's love interest (with a British accent) in *The Secret of Madame Blanche*; supported Kay Francis in the World War I drama *Storm at Daybreak*; and was a wonderfully rotten playboy in *Beauty for Sale*. But some of his roles were getting smaller: supporting roles in the A-films *Penthouse, Stage Mother* and *Dinner at Eight*. This last was Phillips' biggest film (and most-seen today), but one of his least-rewarding parts. He was nearly invisible as Madge Evans' fiancé Ernest, appearing only in the movie's closing moments and only for a brief scene.

In 1934 he left MGM and had the misfortune to appear in Samuel Goldwyn's *Nana*, one of the year's most notorious disasters. It wasn't a total flop, and got some respectful reviews. But Goldwyn had been counting on a huge hit to recoup costs and to make a star out of his new discovery Anna Sten. The air of disappointment hung over the production. Things did not improve much with Paramount's *Private Scandal* (a 1934 crime drama) and Universal's *Great Expectations*—Phillips starred as Pip, but this low-budget version (released in late 1934) fades into the background in comparison with David Lean's 1946 film; also, MGM's *David Copperfield*, a year later, became the standard to beat in the Dickens race.

For the rest of his career he freelanced, in such projects as RKO's *Chatterbox* (an enjoyable 1936 comedy with Anne Shirley), the low-budget spy film *The House of a Thousand Candles* (Republic, 1936), and the unfortunately-titled *General Spanky* (Hal Roach's odd Civil War drama, with Phillips playing straight man for Our Gang kids Spanky, Buckwheat and Alfalfa). He also made several films in England: *Ten-Minute Alibi* and *The Divine Spark* (both 1935), *The Dominant Sex* (1937) and his last film, *Housemaster* (1938).

In 1935 Phillips had taken up with 32-year-old torch singer Libby Holman, which was akin to picnicking on the third rail—calling Libby "unlucky" is like calling Mount Everest "a bump." Her husband, tobacco heir Zachary Reynolds, had been shot in 1932, and Libby was acquitted by the skin of her teeth. Later, her pal Montgomery Clift came to a sad end, and her son died in a 1950 mountain-climbing accident—now Phillips found himself entangled in her sympathetic but apparently cursed circle. Phillips followed Libby around like a puppy as his career slowed down; the two broke up after several public scenes in 1938. This would have been upsetting enough, but she thereupon took up with his younger brother Ralph. They married in 1939, and some felt Phillips never really got over it.

Like the rest of his family, Phillips alternated his screen work with the theater. Though he never appeared on Broadway, he toured in *Golden Boy* (1939) and later in *The Male Animal* and *Journey's End*. One of his last performances was a stage production of *The Philadelphia Story*, in the summer of 1941.

Phillips had already (in honor of his Canadian-born mother) joined the Royal Canadian Air Force when war threatened; when the US entered the fray, he gave up acting and became a fulltime pilot. In the summer of 1942, he postponed his leave to take an additional training course. On August 12, 1942, while being shuttled to a training session, his plane collided with another over Armstrong, Ontario, on its way from Winnipeg to Ottawa. Phillips Holmes, 35 years old, and five other airmen died.

The curse of Libby Holman was not through with the family: Ralph Holmes (still married to but separated from Holman) committed suicide in 1945, at the age of thirty. Holman herself died mysteriously in 1971, possibly a suicide, by carbon monoxide poisoning in her car.

Edward Everett Horton

Very few actors are beloved enough to elicit applause during the opening credits. But to this day, the appearance of Edward Everett Horton brings forth happy little yips from audiences who know that his presence will brighten up even the deadliest of films. For five decades, Edward popped in and out of nearly 150 movies, and is fondly greeted even by audiences born after his retirement.

Edward Everett Horton, Jr., was born on March 18, 1886, in Brooklyn, the son of Scottish immigrants. As his name indicates, he was their oldest child, and he remained close to his family all his life: his mother lived with him till her death at the age of 101, and his brothers George and Winter Davis, and his sister Hannahbelle, spent their later years at his Encino estate.

The Hortons were regular theatergoers, and young Edward was introduced to the stage at an early age, frequently traveling over the East River to see the great performers of the day with his father. Edward relocated to Ohio to attend Oberlin Academy and Oberlin College, then moved back to New York to take business courses at the Polytechnic Institute and at Columbia. But at Columbia he began acting in student productions, and that was all the impetus he needed: he began singing in a Gilbert and Sullivan company on Staten Island, and in 1908 got a job as a gofer and walk-on in the theatrical company of actor/producer Louis Mann. Edward had small parts in the Mann shows *The Cheater* (starring John Bunny), *Elevating a Husband*, and *The Man Who Stood Still*, slowly learning his craft.

Edward also developed a lifelong love affair with stock companies, which he was to carry on even at the height of his movie fame. Through the 1910s, he appeared in various companies across the US: The Orpheum Players and Beaulah Jay's company in Philadelphia; The Baker Stock Company in Oregon; Harry Davis' in Pittsburgh; the Crescent Theater in Brooklyn; Thomas Wilkes' in Los Angeles. He played in dramas and comedies; portrayed old men and young lovers. When he was well into his eighties, Edward maintained, "I'm a stage actor, happiest when I'm on the stage in a good play with a nice audience." It was at Wilkes' Los Angeles company that Edward really came into his own, playing leads in such comedies as *Clarence* and *The Nervous Wreck*—exactly the kind of "nervous nelly" roles that he would later specialize in onscreen.

His success in the Los Angeles area led, naturally enough, to film offers. Edward Everett Horton made his movie debut in 1922, at the age of 36, in the comedies *Too Much Business* (as a man in love with his boss's secretary), *Ladder Jinx* (as a man with a superstitious fiancée) and *A Front Page Story* (as a crime-busting reporter). Another two films followed in 1923; the first (*To the Ladies*) was a pleasant enough comedy, but the second made Edward a real presence. In *Ruggles of Red Gap*—based on a successful Broadway comedy—he played an English valet who must cope with the rough-and-tumble Wild West family of his new employer.

He made a total of 19 silent movies, never rising to the level of stardom, but establishing himself as a reliable favorite with audiences and coworkers alike. His two most frequently seen silents today are *Helen's Babies* (1924), starring Baby Peggy Montgomery and featuring a young Clara Bow as Edward's love interest, and the 1926 MGM blockbuster *La Bohème*, starring Lillian Gish and John Gilbert, with Edward as one of the Bohemians. His other '20s films included the romantic comedy *Marry Me* and the Broadway hit *Beggar on Horseback* (both 1925).

His work—always as a freelancer, never a studio contract player—brought him enough money to buy a large estate in Encino in 1926, where he lived for the rest of his life. Edward was well-liked in the Hollywood community, and acted as manager of the Majestic Theater and the Hollywood Playhouse, providing acting showcases for the up-and-coming and down-and-outers alike.

Edward Everett Horton never much liked acting in silent films, and took to the talkies with alacrity, making two in 1928 and 11 in 1929 (seven of them two-reel shorts produced by Harold Lloyd). "How I longed to talk!" he said at the dawn of the 1930s. "Speech became more dear to me every moment. While playing before the cameras I would think of the most engaging lines, and I just *had* to speak"—thus, his tenure as a stage actor and stock-company producer, while appearing speechless in silents by day.

Edward was one of the busiest character actors of the 1930s, appearing in 66 films over the decade, ranging from big-budget blockbusters to poverty-row Bs. He was lucky enough to be cast in several films which have since become classics of the 1930s and '40s: as a fussbudget reporter in *The Front Page* (1931); third-billed as the Ambassador in *The Merry Widow* (1934); as a corrupt official in the last Dietrich/von Sternberg film, *The Devil is a Woman* (1935); in the charming Errol Flynn comedy *The Perfect Specimen* (1937); as Claudette Colbert's bankrupt father in *Bluebeard's Eighth Wife* (1938); as a concerned asylum caretaker in *Arsenic and Old Lace* (1944); and as an other-worldly messenger in both *Here Comes Mr. Jordan* (1941) and *Down to Earth* (1947). Among his best showcases were his roles as Fred Astaire's pal in the terrific musicals *The Gay Divorcee* (1934), *Top Hat* (1935) and *Shall We Dance* (1937). He was especially good in the first, as the dithery Alice Brady's husband, Egbert, who "fancies dolls"—he also had a great musical number with unbilled chorine Betty Grable.

He was occasionally given the chance to display his impressive talents as a dramatic actor, too: as a tragic and ultimately heroic captive in Manchuria in *Roar of the Dragon* (1932); as a geologist in *Lost Horizon* (1937); as the wisely sympathetic friend in the 1930 and '38 versions of *Holiday*. Though his bread and butter was his supporting parts, he did star in a number of B films, playing his trademark milquetoast: *Ten Dollar Raise, Your Uncle Dudley* and *His Night Out* (all 1935), as a country mouse in *Nobody's Fool* (1936), as a hypochondriac in *Oh Doctor* (1937), as Baby Sandy's *Bachelor Daddy* (1941). Edward was well contented with his place as a character actor, once telling an interviewer that "I never argue about a film. I just want to know how many weeks it will take and how much money they will pay."

Edward Everett Horton in front of the Hotel Athenée, Paris, 1936.

Edward specialized in fussbudget nellies; longtime bachelors and unwed uncles who were understood by the *cognoscenti* to be gay, but who were safely sexless and inoffensive to mainstream audiences. Indeed, his onscreen relationship with British "gentleman's gentleman" Eric Blore in six films (including his three Astaire/Rogers musicals) shows them as an affectionately sparring couple. Such characters—also played by actors Franklin Pangborn, Grady Sutton, Bobby Watson, and Tyler Brooke, among others—were permitted onscreen even after the clamping down of the Production Code in mid-1934. Real-life gay performers were tolerated if they were safely desexed; leading men William Haines and Ramon Novarro made studio bosses nervous, but no one saw Edward Everett Horton as a threat—and he was self-protective enough to keep his sexuality private.

Edward's companion for many years was actor Gavin Gordon, who was 15 years his junior. Documentary evidence of their relationship is hard to come by; film historian William J. Mann says that "Horton's papers appear to have been meticulously gone through, because they are so banal and bland . . . no mention about Gordon at all." Gavin Gordon appeared in more than 60 films between 1929 and 1964, including *The Bitter Tea of General Yen, The Scarlet Empress, The Bride of Frankenstein* (memorably, as a plummy Lord Byron in the prologue), *Notorious, High Society,* and *The Matchmaker*. He and Edward only appeared together in one film, 1961's *Pocketful of Miracles*, starring Bette Davis.

Edward Everett Horton worked busily through the 1940s, in 27 films: dizzy musicals (*Springtime in the Rockies, I Married an Angel, The Gang's All Here, Earl Carroll's Sketchbook*), dramas (*Ziegfeld Girl,* Rene Clair's war film *Forever and a Day*). His own favorite film from this period was *Summer Storm*, a 1944 Chekov adaptation directed by Douglas Sirk. He was also a popular performer on radio, guesting frequently and hosting his own show in 1945.

His movie career finally slowed down in the 1950s, when he appeared in only two films: the dreadful all-star *The Story of Mankind* (as Sir Walter Raleigh, 1957), and an uncredited walk-on in *No Time for Sergeants* (1958). He appeared in five films through the 1960s, the most notable of which were *Pocketful of Miracles*, Stanley Kramer's all-star romp *It's a Mad Mad Mad Mad World* (1963) and the

As the other-worldly messenger in *Here Comes Mr. Jordan*, 1941.

vulgar *Sex and the Single Girl* (1964). Edward's last film was the comedy *Cold Turkey* (1971), in which he played the president of a tobacco company.

The small screen provided much work for Edward as his movie career wound down; he made his TV debut in 1948, on *Hollywood Screen Test*, and he starred in the short-lived series *Holiday Hotel* (1950-51). Over the next few decades, his cameos brightened up such sitcoms as *I Love Lucy, Dennis the Menace, F Troop* (as medicine man Roaring Chicken), *Batman*, and *Nanny and the Professor* (his swan song, in 1971). His best TV gig came with *Rocky and His Friends* (1959-64), for which he narrated the popular "Fractured Fairy Tales." Baby boomers might also remember him narrating the unintentionally bizarre bike-safety film *One Got Fat* (1963), shown in public schools for years. In 1951, Edward returned to Broadway for the first time since *Elevating a Husband* in 1912, starring in a revival of *Springtime for Henry*.

By the end of his life, Edward Everett Horton was revered as one of the Grand Old Men of his profession, and he was still being offered work well into his eighties. "I'm fortunate that I've had a good time right from the beginning when I was earning $12.50 a week in the theater," he said in 1970. "I love my work and I love sitting around here remembering . . . Sometimes I have to tell myself to get up and do something. So I move to another chair." When he died, on September 29, 1970, at the age of 84, his obituaries were lengthy and affectionate: "A master of comic befuddlement," *The New York Times* called him.

Peggy Hopkins Joyce

Some performers are fated to be better known as joke fodder than as actors or actresses. In the 1920s and '30s, that was the lot of Peggy Hopkins Joyce: just mentioning her name resulted in a quick and easy laugh, and many nightclub and radio comics cashed in. Peggy Hopkins Joyce worked for more than a decade as a showgirl and actress, on stage and screen. But she is remembered for her marital escapades (six husbands and goodness how many broken engagements). She was also an inspiration for the literary, stage and film anti-heroine Lorelei Lee, in Anita Loos' *Gentlemen Prefer Blondes.*

She was born into ordinary enough circumstances: Margaret "Peggy" Upton was the daughter of the village barber in Farmville, Virginia, about 100 miles north of Norfolk. She did her best to cover her tracks in later years, but the year seems to have been 1893. Her father, Sam, and her mother, Dora, split up when Peggy was still a child. Neighbors later recalled her as "quite like the other children, with the exception perhaps that she was a little more fond of pretty clothes, that she could dance unusually well, and that she possessed a vague something which made her particularly attractive."

Peggy took her "vague something" off to the nearby resort of Ocean View, where she met and married her first husband, the wealthy Everett Archibald, Jr., of Denver, in 1910. That marriage lasted only six months, and was annulled "because of the bride's age." Peggy was probably 17 at the time, so this excuse may or may not hold water. It took the divorcée only two years to find a second husband. Running away from the private school her parents had sent her to, she married New York attorney Sherburne Philbrick Hopkins in 1913. With this new marriage, she hit Manhattan like a cyclone and took the stage name "Peggy Hopkins" when she began making the rounds of theatrical agencies.

The hopeful showgirl was, in her early twenties, a tall, slim blonde with a slight Southern accent and nearly perfect features (only a slightly receding chin set her apart from cookie-cutter perfection). She befriended vaudeville comic W.C. Fields, who had a long-term relationship with a fellow showgirl, Bessie Poole. (Poole died some years later while defending a man in a speakeasy brawl.) Peggy's stage career blossomed in 1917, when she appeared in that year's *Ziegfeld Follies*. It was a stellar edition, starring Fields, Fanny Brice, Eddie Cantor, Bert Williams and Will Rogers. The other showgirls that year included Dolores, Allyn King, Lilyan Tashman, the Fairbanks twins and Dorothy Dickson. Peggy also appeared in *Earl Carroll's Vanities* and in vaudeville, but her offstage life was moving at an even faster pace than her professional endeavors.

By 1915, Peggy had shed Mr. Hopkins and collected her second in a series of impressive settlements. Multi-millionaire lumberman J. Stanley Joyce became her third husband in 1920, thus completing her final stage name. Between spending time at her homes in Chicago, Paris and Miami, Peggy worked at her acting career. She made her first film appearance in 1922—but only in the newsreels. When a South American embassy employee reportedly killed himself for love of her in Paris, the Ohio Film Board censored the Selznick newsreel coverage of her return to the US. When asked why men were willing to die for her, Peggy smiled, "Now, if a woman tells you the secret of her fascination, you say she is vain. If she doesn't— it means there is something she shouldn't tell."

In 1921, there was a widely publicized divorce from Joyce, at which time it was revealed that he'd given her more than $1 million in jewelry (which he wanted back, and which Peggy hung onto like glue). "He taught me to like expensive things," she said of Mr. Joyce. "I had a marvelous apartment in New York. I had motors, clothes and jewels . . . Now I know why he gave me these gorgeous presents. He wanted to show me off—to put me on parade. He wanted the world to be his dollhouse, and he wanted to make me the doll." Joyce, for his part, charged her with adultery with six

Peggy Hopkins Joyce in *The Skyrocket*, 1926.

co-respondents. Peggy walked away from this marriage a very wealthy—and notorious—woman. This not only got her more acting work, but a job writing an advice to the lovelorn column. She spent much of her time traveling between her roosts in London, Paris and New York, attending the races at Auteuil and the casinos in Monte Carlo. "If she ever knew the frustrations common to most people, she never let on," commented one astonished onlooker.

Husband number four was Count Gustave Morner, a wealthy Swedish nobleman who Peggy wed in Atlantic City in 1924. This was her longest marriage to date, lasting until 1928, but it was hardly a love match. Within a month, Morner had filed for annulment, accusing Peggy of staying out nights. She countersued, calling him a "rotter" and claiming that he'd borrowed $10,000 from her. "I cannot live without men," she told the press. "I am not the flippant man-hunter and home-breaker that I have been pictured," she claimed. "These reports have driven me nearly insane . . . But I have faith and confidence in the American people, and I know that I will get a square deal."

By the mid-1920s, Peggy Hopkins Joyce was more a "personality" than an actress. It took author Anita Loos to make her a star. In 1925, Loos' hilarious novel *Gentleman Prefer Blondes* was published. Written as the diary of a faux-naïve gold-digger, it became an instant classic, later to be successfully translated to stage and screen. Loos made no secret of the fact that Peggy had been one of the main inspirations for the character; though she stopped short of claiming that Peggy and Lorelei were one and the same (Loos did not want to incur a lawsuit, *or* share her royalties). Peggy latched happily onto her renewed fame and wrote (or at least signed her name to) her own book, titled *Men, Marriage and Me* (1930). It was a stylistic duplicate of Loos' book. Although a delightful period piece and a collector's item today, the book did not sell.

In 1933 Peggy's second book, *Transatlantic Wife*, was published. A novel about a wealthy, frustrated wife who falls in with gangsters and gigolos, it, too, did not make much of a literary splash. "I like writing," the authoress said in 1933, adding that "It would be silly of me to make out that I am literary. I read novels. They give me ideas."

Peggy's first feature film, *The Skyrocket*, had been released by the independent Celebrity Pictures on Valentine's Day, 1926. Directed by Marshall Neilan, *The Skyrocket* was the story of a tough orphanage girl who grows up to be a Hollywood star. When her irresponsible, unprofessional ways bring her to grief, she is taken back by her childhood pal Mickey (Owen Moore). Supporting Peggy in this film were Gladys Brockwell as her mother (in a flashback sequence) and Lilyan Tashman as one of her cohorts.

Neilan's friend Colleen Moore later recalled the trials Peggy put him through. "Though Peggy photographed like an angel, she couldn't act," Moore wrote. "Mickey was going out of his mind trying to get a performance out of her." Peggy astonished everyone on the set by showing off an old shoebox containing what she claimed were $5 million dollars worth of diamonds. It was also during this shoot that she had a brief, passionate affair with Charlie Chaplin—a romance broken up by the combination of Peggy's extravagance and Chaplin's cheapness.

She appeared in minor plays such as *A Sleepless Night* and *It Pays to Flirt*, neither of which made it to Broadway. Her last Broadway appearance was as a courtesan in *The Lady of the Orchids*, in 1928. Brooks Atkinson of the *New York Times* called her "competent and convincing," hardly a ringing endorsement.

After that, Peggy haunted the film capitol for scripts, offering to write her own and trying to find sugar daddies willing to back her (she must have envied Marion Davies by this time). But too many people had seen *The Skyrocket*, or just didn't take her seriously enough as an actress. The talkie revolution came and went, but Peggy's stage training didn't make her any more marketable. She was inconvenienced but not broken by the stock market crash and managed to avoid having to auction off her villa near Monte Carlo. "The water beats right up to my walls," she said of this favored home. "You can sit right in my bed and think you're in the middle of the Mediterranean."

Peggy's second and last film (and her only talkie) was the wild comedy *International House*, released by Paramount in June 1933. This film, directed by Eddie Sutherland, remains one of the delights of the pre-Code era and Peggy's real claim to immortality, aside from Anita Loos. The plot—such as it was—involved a bidding war over a new television machine, held in a hotel in Wu Hu, China. "I don't know what those stranded people do in Shanghai," Peggy said prettily before filming began. "The script isn't finished." The cast included Peggy's old pal W.C. Fields (who probably got her the role in the first place), Burns and Allen, Bela Lugosi (surprisingly sexy as Peggy's jealous ex-husband), and rube comic Stuart Erwin (as her unwilling traveling companion). Making cameo appearances were Cab Calloway, Rudy Vallee and Baby Rose Marie.

Peggy as herself in the delightful *International House*, 1933.

Peggy portrayed herself in *International House*: notorious, much-married showgirl Peggy Hopkins Joyce. This could either be interpreted as an indication of her great fame, or as confirmation that she had already become more of a joke than an actress. Either way, she acquitted herself quite well, playing straight woman to Erwin and Fields (with the latter, she had some particularly lewd and funny scenes). She was brisk, glamorous and, as Brooks Atkinson had said, "competent and convincing."

Peggy's life in the 1930s was spent drifting from home to home, her name linked in the newspapers with playboys, movie stars and café society hangers-on. She talked of doing more shows and movies, but nothing came of it. Tragedy brushed Peggy in 1936 after she announced her engagement to Vivian Jackson, a British horseman and professor of astrophysics at London University. It was an unlikely pairing, which was not to be. The couple was sleigh-riding in Switzerland when their horses bolted, and they were thrown at high speed. Peggy suffered a broken leg, and the 30-year-old Jackson was killed.

The publicity grew squalid in the early 1940s, when Peggy began dating singer Bowen Charleton Tufts, who later changed his name to "Sonny" and took up acting. Their relationship was a stormy one and degenerated into public brawling. After a bout in the Stork Club, Tufts bragged, "You ought to see her—she's black and blue from head to foot. Sure I did it. But she packs a mean wallop herself. I don't think I have an unbruised spot on me."

Peggy, then in her early fifties, married British engineer Anthony Easton in 1945. "This is my first marriage in 19 years!" she enthused. "We're going to settle down to a normal marriage, and we certainly want children . . . You can say this is the last marriage." Alas, it was not: the two eventually split up, though records do not give the precise year. "You never know a man until you marry him, and then you wish you didn't," Peggy sighed bitterly. She had pretty much faded from the headlines as newer editions of her old self (such as the Gabor sisters) took up the torch. In 1953—by now looking like a plump, agreeable grandmother—Peggy married for the sixth time, to Andrew Meyer, a retired New York banker. This marriage proved to be the charm, and the couple stayed together, living a quiet, contented life in Woodbury, Connecticut.

Peggy hit the newspapers for the last time in 1957, when she entered a New York hospital, suffering from throat cancer. She died on June 12, 1957, her sixth husband at her bedside. The obituaries were astonishingly large for someone with such a minor film and stage career, someone who had been out of the spotlight for more than two decades. Photos, summaries of her marriages, and snappy quotes enlivened the papers that day. Louis Sobol mourned that "There has never been a more colorful or joyous figure to invade the Broadway scene . . . As far as reporters were concerned, she was always a good Jo."

The *World Telegram* summed it all up by calling the late showgirl "a symbol of the gaiety and irresponsibility of the 1920s, of easy money, expensive clothes, good furs and jewelry, and the best possible relations between the United States and France and England on the non-cultural level."

Helen Kane

It's the story of two actresses: an older, established one, perhaps a bit past her prime but still with a huge fan base, and a younger, flattering protégée, who takes over her elder's career and soon surpasses her, leaving her in the dust. It's a musical cartoon version of *All About Eve*, starring the now-forgotten Helen Kane and her young nemesis, the still-famous Betty Boop.

Helen Kane was born Helen Schroeder, on August 4, 1903, in the Bronx. Things were not easy for Helen or her brother Louis; their Irish mother took in laundry, while their German father drifted from job to job. From an early age, Helen was starstruck. When she was in school at St. Auselin's, she managed to convince her mother to come up with $3 to pay for a queen costume for the school pageant. By the time she was 15, Helen was onstage professionally, touring the Orpheum Circuit with the Marx Brothers in their pre-movie days. Helen spent the early and mid-1920s trouping in vaudeville as a singer, playing New York's Palace Theater for the first time in 1921. "I was on with Clayton, Jackson, and Durante," she later reminisced. "Bill Robinson, Ken Murray, Lulu McConnell, Ruth Etting. When you came in here you had to be tops. There was a great deal of talent."

But there wasn't a great deal of money, and Helen was not yet enjoying a star's lifestyle. "I lived way up in the Bronx," she recalled, "and worked nightclubs far downtown. After the show at night I'd go home alone, with never the slightest fear . . . You could go anywhere without carrying your life in your hand." In the mid-1920s Helen married department store buyer Joseph Kane and took his name professionally.

But she was a divorcée by 1928, when she was appearing at the Paramount Theater in Times Square. There, the old cliché came true; Helen Kane went out a youngster and came back a star. Helen was singing the popular song "That's My Weakness Now," when she interpolated the scat lyrics "boop-boop-a-doop." "I just put it in at one of the rehearsals," she later mused. "A sort of interlude. It's hard to explain—I haven't explained it to myself yet. It's like vo-de-o-do, Crosby with boo-boo-boo and Durante with hot-cha-cha."

The audience went crazy, and four days later, Helen Kane's name went up in lights. Seemingly overnight, the world changed for Helen. "One day I had fifty cents," she laughed, "and the next day I had $50,000." It wasn't quite that dramatic, but Helen's agent Harry Besney got her $5,500 a week in Oscar Hammerstein's show *Good Boy* (where she introduced her hit "I Want to Be Loved By You"). From there it was back to the Palace, but this time as a headliner for $5,000 a week. "Money was falling off trees," she said of her big success in 1928. "I got $5,000 at one of those big society parties just to sing four or five choruses of 'Button Up Your Overcoat.'"

She recorded scores of records (all novelty songs but for one ballad, "I Owe You"). As she took on the status of a full-fledged fad, there were Helen Kane dolls and Helen Kane look-alike contests, appearances on radio and in nightclubs. In late 1928 and early '29 you couldn't throw a brick without hitting Helen Kane. She was certainly something new: tiny (about five feet tall) and slightly plump, she looked like a Kewpie doll come to life. Her round face with its huge brown eyes was topped by dark-brown, curly hair; her voice was a baby squeak with a distinct Bronx accent. Audiences found Helen adorable, though admittedly she grated on the nerves of more than one critic.

In mid-1929, Paramount signed Helen to make a series of movie musicals. Her first of three 1929 films was *Nothing But the Truth*, a comedy starring Richard Dix as a man who has to go 24 hours without telling a lie. Helen's role was small, but she got to sing "Do Something," and made a good impression. From there she went into a cute college musical, *Sweetie*, which starred Nancy Carroll and Stanley Smith. Helen sang several numbers and was teamed with the delightful Jack Oakie—as usual, the comedy couple handily stole the film from the romantic duo. Helen's third

Helen Kane at her Boopiest, 1929.

1929 release was *Pointed Heels*, also in a small supporting role. This backstage romantic triangle featured William Powell and Phillips Holmes vying for the attention of Fay Wray, while Helen and the always-wonderful Richard "Skeets" Gallagher provided the comedy.

In 1930, animators Dave, Max, and Louis Fleischer decided to cash in on Helen's popularity. They assigned staff animator Grim Natwick to come up with a girlfriend for their cartoon character Bimbo the Dog; the result was a caricature of Helen Kane, with droopy dog ears and a squeaky, Boop-a-Doop singing voice. "Betty Boop," as the character was dubbed, became an instant smash hit and the star of her own cartoons. By 1932, she became human, her long ears turning into hoop earrings (typical of Fleischer, though, she continued her inter-species romance with Bimbo). The Betty Boop cartoons of the early 1930s (before censorship set in) were brilliant, exhibiting a sexuality and dark surrealism missing from Disney's cartoons. Helen Kane had some real competition on her hands.

In 1930 Helen made another three films for Paramount, none of them with scripts equaling Fleischer's cartoons. The first was an all-star revue, *Paramount on Parade*. Helen had a cute musical number in which she played a teacher instructing her young students in Boop-a-Dooping. In *Dangerous Nan McGrew*, Helen moved up to her first female lead, as an Annie Oakley-type character in a Canadian medicine show. Her next film, *Heads Up!*, costarred her with Charles "Buddy" Rogers (he was a Coast Guard officer, she was his rich girlfriend). The songs were by Rodgers and Hart, seemingly a good omen for Helen's career. But *Heads Up!* was her last feature film.

By late 1930, Paramount felt that the Boop-a-Doop craze was passing, and let Helen's option lapse. She returned to the stage and radio, which still offered her a good measure of fame and fortune. All the time, though, Betty Boop was gaining in popularity; the Helen Kane dolls and look-alike contests of the late 1920s became Betty Boop dolls and look-alike contests by the early '30s.

1932 was a busy year for Helen: she married actor Max Hoffman, Jr. (son of dancer Gertrude Hoffman), but the marriage lasted only a year. "He didn't do any more stage work after we were

Helen returning from a European trip, 1931.

married and he left me in Chicago in 1933," she told Judge Allegretti at her divorce hearing.

In May 1932, she filed a $250,000 suit against Max Fleischer, his studio, and Paramount Publix Corporation, charging unfair competition and wrongful appropriation of her voice and image in the Betty Boop cartoons. The trial dragged on for two years, the testimony getting more and more surreal as Helen Kane and Betty Boop films were screened by Judge McGoldrick (no jury was called). Betty Boop voice-overs Mae Questel, Margy Hines and Bonnie Poe were brought in to testify; Helen denied copying her own singing style from child performer Baby Esther or from a 1914 French song, "Bou-Bou-Ba-Ba-Bou." The stenographer nearly had a nervous breakdown transcribing Boop-a-Doops and Bou-Bou-Ba-Ba-Bous. Amazingly, McGoldrick ruled against Helen in 1934. The judge "held that she had failed to prove that the defendants had appropriated her 'baby' style of singing," according to one paper. "I consider it very unfair," Helen quite naturally stated, "as all of my friends believe the cartoons a caricature of me." Watching Helen and Betty side by side today, it's impossible to fathom Judge McGoldrick's decision.

That ruling wasn't Helen's only trouble: in 1933 she had been fined $46,500 for a bad business loan. She'd invested in a dress firm through one Murray Posner in 1930; when the firm went bankrupt, Helen was left holding the bag.

Indeed, the only good news for Helen was the show *Shady Lady*, which opened in July 1933. "I am not going to talk any more baby talk and they will not get me to say Boop-Boop-a-Doop," she insisted. "I am going to be a sort of miniature Mae West." After *Shady Lady* closed, Helen went back to the grind of vaudeville, radio and nightclubs. In 1934 she went on a strict salt-free diet and exercise regime and dropped 43 pounds. She was unrecognizable: slim, with longer hair and delicate bone structure which had been lost under her baby fat. At 31, she looked like a Hollywood ingénue.

But in 1935, Helen Kane dropped out of show business. "I was tired, worn out, and I quit," she explained in the 1950s. "I could have gone on. I bought a home in California, went to Europe—a command performance before the King and the Queen of England—to Mexico, and spent a lot of money. Followed the seasons. I bought houses, swimming pools, invested in business." But, she added, "I worked too hard until I finally knocked myself out. It was crazy— I was rich but I wasn't having any fun. Before I was famous I always had a good time."

Helen wed for the third and final time in 1939. Her husband was master of ceremonies and well-known Broadwayite Dan Healy; the bride was 36, the groom 52. They opened a nightclub on 52nd Street, but it lasted only a year. Theirs was a happy marriage, and

Helen decided to settle down "and be Mrs. Healy for awhile." She faded from public view in the 1940s. The Healys moved to a small home on 35th Avenue in Jackson Heights and Dan opened Healy's Grill, on 66th and Columbus in Manhattan.

Fame came calling again in 1950 when MGM filmed *Three Little Words*, the story of songwriters Kalmar and Ruby. Starlet Debbie Reynolds was cast as Helen Kane and given the song "I Want to Be Loved By You." Helen was called in to dub Debbie's voice, and was suddenly back in the limelight, at the age of 47. Television beckoned, interviewers were calling, and she even played the Palace once again in 1956. "With maturity has come a wonderful sense of humor and a great heart. She's fat and funny and the face is as beautiful as ever," wrote one reporter.

In the late 1950s, Helen developed breast cancer and underwent two mastectomies, starting radiation treatments at Memorial Hospital in Queens. When columnist Jim Bishop publicized her courageous fight, she snorted, "*Courage?* I was born scared and running." Dan Healy nearly died of an ulcer, and the cancer spread to Helen's stomach, but she kept on working and planning. "I'd like to do the type of thing Shirley Booth is doing in *Hazel*," she told a reporter in late 1963. "Or do funny commercials. They can put a red nose on me, or give me a broom. I know I can get laughs."

Healy's Grill didn't bring in much money, and Helen admitted that "Dan and I couldn't change a quarter." Plump and cute again as in her Boop-a-Doop days, Helen was still choosy about the appearances she selected. "There is nothing more pitiable than a middle-aged person, especially a woman, acting coy," she once said. In March 1965 she appeared on *The Ed Sullivan Show*; it was her last hurrah. On September 25, 1966, she and Dan watched Debbie Reynolds in *Three Little Words* on TV. "She's kind of cute at that," she laughed. The next day, Helen died, at the age of 63. She was survived by her husband, brother Louis, and Betty Boop, who today continues to confound her unwilling doppelgänger.

Winnie Lightner

Some performers never make it to the top through no fault of their own; they are simply too similar to another current star. Dolores Del Rio always had to wear the tag of "the poor man's Garbo," Ramon Novarro and Gilbert Roland were in the shadow of Rudolph Valentino. And the delightful Winnie Lightner—a brash, vulgar vaudeville star—found herself following in the footsteps of Sophie Tucker. Oddly, though, Winnie had slightly more success in films than did "Soph," though both found it difficult to crash the movies.

Winnie was born Winifred Josephine Reeve, on September 17, 1899. She grew up in Long Island with her brothers Fred and William and her older sister Thea. Their father, Chauncey Reeve, was a patrolman for the Greenport Police Department. The children gravitated toward the stage: by 1909, Thea was onstage (as Thea Lightner) with a partner, Dolly Jordan, and a piano player, Newton Alexander, whom Thea later married. Winnie joined the act in 1915, straight out of high school, replacing Dolly Jordan. "The Lightner Girls and Newton Alexander" played on the Keith vaudeville circuit through the early 1920s, gaining expertise and audience devotion. Winnie took over the act by dint of her natural talents and exuberant personality. The *Toledo Times* called her "a born comedienne" as early as 1916, and in 1918 one newspaper noted that she stole the show from star Bessie McCoy: "While not billed as the headliner, Miss Lightner captured the bulk of the first-nighters' applause." Another review the following year called Winnie "a female Eddie Foy." A brief marriage produced a son, Richard, born in 1922 (there were rumors of other marriages, including one to broker George Holtry).

Winnie Lightner being serenaded by Frank Fay in *The Show of Shows*, 1929.

In addition to her wildly successful vaudeville tours, Winnie spent much of the 1920s appearing in high-profile, star-packed Broadway revues. She was featured in *George White's Scandals* in 1922, '23 and '24—in the last of these, she introduced the now-classic song "Somebody Loves Me." She appeared in the Shubert revue *Gay Paree* in 1925 and '26, and in *Harry Delmar's Revels* in 1927-28, costarring Bert Lahr, Patsy Kelly, and Frank Fay. Like many vaudeville stars, Winnie also filmed some musical shorts in New York in the late 1920s. By 1927, her sister had dropped out of the act and Winnie, billed as "The Song-a-Minute Girl," was playing at the Capitol on Broadway with Van and Schenck. Then the talkies took root, and movie studios began raiding Broadway.

When Winnie was signed by Warner Brothers in 1929, she hardly looked like movie-star material. At 30, she was more like the cheerful, chatty waitress at your local diner. Barrel-shaped, with a pug nose and frizzy auburn hair, she flummoxed even Warners' beauty department. Her first feature film was *Gold Diggers of Broadway*, an all-talking, Technicolor extravaganza. A backstage musical costarring Lilyan Tashman and Ann Pennington, *Gold Diggers* featured Winnie as a nervous and forgetful chorus girl. She belted out "Mechanical Man" and her refreshing brashness was roundly adored by critics and fans. Sadly, only fragments of this film still exist, and Winnie is seen but fleetingly.

Winnie also made a hit in Warners' all-star *The Show of Shows* (1929). One of the more enjoyable of the studio revues, it featured turns by John Barrymore, Myrna Loy, Beatrice Lillie, Ted Lewis, and hordes of famous (and not-so-famous) contract players. But the brightest star was Winnie, who cut through the sometimes ponderous goings-on with two songs. First, she belts out the amusing and coarse "King Congo" ("minus coat and minus pants, you should see His Highness dance"). Then she led the hilarious "Singin' in the Bathtub" production number, a jab at MGM's "Singin' in the Rain."

She Couldn't Say No (1930) was Winnie's first non-musical film, and an indication that the studio did not know what to do with her. Much like the dreary melodramas given to Fanny Brice and Sophie Tucker, this film cast Winnie as a nightclub singer in love with gangster Chester Morris, who in turn loves the prettier Sally Eilers.

Winnie in 1930.

It was a complete waste of Winnie's talents. In the now-lost *Hold Everything* (also 1930), she supported French boxer Georges Carpentier and fellow comic Joe E. Brown—at least this was a comedy, and Winnie got to sing. Her third film of 1930 was a step up: *The Life of the Party* was a bright, funny gold-digging comedy starring Winnie and Irene Delroy as music-store salesgirls who trail a millionaire to Florida. Unfortunately, Winnie only had one song, but that, "Poison Ivy," was a treat in itself. The film cost little to make, and earned a small fortune for the studio, which cast Winnie in three films set for release in 1931.

By that time, the makeover artists were having their way with her. She managed to shave off about 15 pounds; her hair was smoothed and styled, her eyebrows plucked. She was decked out in chic frocks and cute tilted hats for fan-magazine layouts. She was back with Joe E. Brown to start 1931 with *Sit Tight*, playing a health-clinic director training a wrestler. She was a delight in *Gold Dust Gertie*, as a bathing-suit designer vamping crotchety Claude Gillingwater (and harassed by ex-husbands Olsen and Johnson). It was a perfect Warners B-movie: fast, nonsensical, cheaply made and very funny. Less enjoyable was *Side Show*, with Winnie and Charles Butterworth trying to make a traveling carnival pay off.

Manhattan Parade (1932) was a change of pace, the kind of "woman's film" that Kay Francis and Ruth Chatterton were making: Winnie played a successful businesswoman whose husband wants her to stay at home and raise their child (the preternaturally cute Dickie Moore). Winnie did her best, but was somewhat uncomfortable in this new, subdued mode (the film was stolen by Jewish comedy team Smith and Dale as quarreling Broadway producers, Bobby Watson as the world's queeniest costume designer, and the delightful Polly Walters as an unflappable switchboard operator). It might have been a good film for Francis or Chatterton, but Winnie was wasted in it.

Warner Brothers put her back into comedy, thank goodness, as gold-digger Loretta Young's pal in *Play-Girl* (1932); she went from business mogul to bawdy pre-Code shopgirl, with some wonderful eyebrow-raising dialogue. After losing her last pair of panties when the clothesline breaks, Winnie is asked by Loretta, "What are you going to do?" "Stay off of stepladders, for one thing!" she replies.

But after ten films, Warners had squeezed all the pep out of Winnie that they could: her contract was dropped at the end of 1932 (just when she had $7,000 in back taxes to pay off). She had proven her abilities as a supporting player, but was not considered to be star material. Winnie spent the rest of her brief career as a freelancer. First National reteamed her with Loretta Young in *She Had to Say Yes* (1933), in which Loretta had to choose between suitors Regis Toomey and Lyle Talbot, neither of whom (in the film, anyway) was much of a prize package. MGM hired her for a very small role in the delightful *Dancing Lady* (1933)—as Joan Crawford's burlesque pal, she had little to do but sing "Hold Your Man" (from the MGM Jean Harlow film of that name) while Joan and her fellow chorines took it off. *I'll Fix It* (Columbia, 1934) was Winnie's last film; it was a B-film romance between Jack Holt and Mona Barrie, with Winnie given little to do. And with that, her film career was over.

But in another way, Winnie's life was only beginning. Her first divorce long in the past, she married 39-year-old director Roy Del Ruth in 1934 (he adopted her son Richard, and the couple had another son, Thomas, in 1942). Del Ruth had helmed her films *Gold Diggers of Broadway, Hold Everything, The Life of the Party* and *Side Show*, and went on to direct such films as *Born to Dance, DuBarry Was a Lady* and *On Moonlight Bay*. The Del Ruths' son Thomas became a successful cinematographer (*The Breakfast Club, Stand By Me, ER, The West Wing*).

Roy Del Ruth retired in 1960, by which time the couple had settled down in Sherman Oaks, California. Winnie's voluble presence was silenced by her long, happy marriage and motherhood; she vanished from the Hollywood scene and was apparently forgotten until March 5, 1971, when she died of a heart attack at the age of 71. Her obituaries were brief; Winnie's 15 years of vaudeville, brief Broadway stardom and five years onscreen earned her only six column inches in *The New York Times*.

Ben Lyon

Ben Lyon was not easy to fit into any mold, and that is perhaps why he never became as big a star as his near-contemporaries Gable, Cagney or Valentino. He was too boyishly cute to be a believable gangster or working-class tough guy; too tall and athletic to be a juvenile; not a strong enough singer for musicals. He was just a likable, good-looking and reliably talented fellow, which was enough to carry him through a 37-year movie career. He was also lucky enough to enjoy one of show business' happiest marriages, to occasional costar Bebe Daniels.

Ben Lyon, Jr., was born on February 6, 1901, in Atlanta, Georgia. His father, Ben, Sr., was a pianist-turned-businessman, who had eloped with Ben's mother, Alvine. Young Ben was the baby of the family, having an older brother and two older sisters. In 1906 the Lyons moved to Baltimore, where Ben made his theatrical debut in amateur productions. After a normal childhood of schooling and sports, Ben moved with his family to New York in 1916. On finishing high school, he began thinking about an acting career, to his parents' dismay. He got a few unbilled extra roles and bit parts at the New York and Fort Lee film studios, then got his first stage role starring in Booth Tarkington's *Seventeen*. "How I got the part, I never knew," he later said. "I really didn't know how to act."

Ben stayed with *Seventeen* until he turned 20, then played opposite Jeanne Eagels in *The Wonderful Thing*, and appeared in New York and on tour with such shows as *Three Live Ghosts* and *Mary the Third*, and as juvenile lead with Jessie Bonstell's stock company. From time to time, he got minor roles in films, including Warner Brothers' *Open Your Eyes* (1919), Vitagraph's *The Heart of Maryland* (1921) and Fox's *The Custard Cup* (1923).

Ben Lyon in *High Hat*, 1927.

That year, Ben was tabbed by First National for a supporting role in the Jewish comedy *Potash and Perlmutter*, based on a popular novel and play about the garment district. When that film was a success, he was signed to a long-term contract and sent off to California, bidding farewell to his promising stage career. Ben Lyon was to stay with First National through 1927, making 20 films for them and another three on loan-out. These loan-outs, all in 1924, were no small potatoes: he costarred with Pola Negri in *Lily of the Dust* and with Gloria Swanson in *Wages of Virtue* for Paramount, and with William Haines in *Wine of Youth* for Metro.

But First National was his home base, and they spent the mid-1920s building Ben into one of their top leading men (among their other male stars were Milton Sills, Richard Barthelmess, Lew Cody, Conway Tearle and Bert Lytell). The studio, formed in 1917, was a growing concern with money behind it and a talented stock company: a good home for a young actor starting out. In 1925 it was bought by Warner Brothers, but continued producing and distributing under the First National banner.

Ben seemed to be good star material. He was tall and handsome, with dark hair and bright blue eyes. He had an amiable baby face, with a schoolboyish smile that gave him a youthful charm well into old age. Ben's career built slowly, with smallish supporting roles in Colleen Moore's *Flaming Youth* (1923), *Painted People* and *So Big* (both 1924), and Barbara La Marr's *The White Moth* (also 1924). He got star billing for the first time in 1925 with *The Necessary Evil, One Way Street* and *The Pace That Thrills*. He narrowly lost the leading role in *Ben-Hur* after it was decided he was a little too scrawny.

Through the mid-1920s, Ben costarred with most of First National's leading ladies (though he never teamed with either Talmadge sister, for some reason). He shared the screen with Blanche Sweet (*The New Commandment*), Anna Q. Nilsson (*One Way Street* and *Winds of Chance*), Mary Astor (*The Pace That Thrills*), Mary Brian (*High Hat*) and Billie Dove (*The Tender Hour*). He also appeared in Claudette Colbert's only silent movie, *For the Love of Mike* (1927), directed by Frank Capra. All agreed it was a dismal failure, and Claudette returned to Broadway.

By the time his five-year contract with First National was coming to a close, Ben Lyon was one of the screen's most popular "second-tier" actors. It was clear he would not become a major star, but his following was large and loyal, his talent and charm undeniable. Certainly Howard Hughes took notice. In late 1927 Ben was signed by Hughes for what was to have been a silent World War I epic, *Hell's Angels*—when the production shut down to convert to sound, Ben went to Germany and appeared in *Dancing Vienna* (1929).

It was about this time that he became involved with Bebe Daniels. The same age as Ben (they were born a month apart), Bebe

Bebe Daniels and Ben Lyon applying for their passports, 1932.

had been a film actress from childhood, when she played Dorothy in Selig's 1910 *The Wonderful Wizard of Oz* and costarred with Harold Lloyd in more than 100 two-reel comedies between 1915 and 1919. She went on to stardom in the mid-1920s with Paramount, and by the time she met Ben at a dinner party in 1928, she was one of Hollywood's brightest stars and most popular party girls— among her many admirers was writer and columnist Lucius Beebe, and one marvels that she gave up the chance to become Bebe Beebe. As Ben told one writer, "I spent my evening telling her about the films I had done and my work, and she thought I was the most egotistical man she'd ever met."

But Ben persisted, and the two began courting and soon got along swimmingly. They shared interests (he taught her to fly airplanes; she taught him how to play bridge). Bebe and Ben married on June 14, 1930, buying a house in Santa Monica. "If we didn't know each other well enough after 18 months to be as certain as we could be, then we guessed we never would," said Ben after their marriage. Their daughter Barbara was born in 1931, and they adopted a son, Richard, in 1937.

Ben had another seven films released in 1929 and '30, while *Hell's Angels* was still shooting or in lengthy post-production: in 1929 he took to the skies again in *The Flying Marine* and *The Air Legion*, and starred in *The Quitter*. In 1930 he appeared in four films, costarring for the first time with his wife, in the comedy *Alias French Gertie* (RKO). It was hardly a fitting vehicle for them, though; they had great chemistry onscreen but needed a better script.

Hell's Angels dragged on and on: out went heavily-accented leading lady Greta Nissen and in came newcomer Jean Harlow. Ben later claimed to have been the one to bring Jean to the producers' attention, but nearly everyone in Hollywood made that same claim—still, his later success as a producer and talent scout seems to give Ben legitimate bragging rights. *Hell's Angels* was finally released in November 1930 and proved to be a huge hit, financially and critically. Ben's performance as the weak-willed Monte Rutledge, who steals his brother's fiancée and turns yellow on the battlefield, assured him a place as one of the up-and-coming stars of talking pictures.

Ben's busiest year yet was 1931, as he appeared in ten films (mostly with First National and Warner Brothers). While many silent stars were struggling in early talkies and Broadway fledglings were carving out film careers, Ben worked nonstop. Some of his projects were low-budget quickies (*Aloha, Call of the Rockies*), but there were several bright spots that year. He costarred with Gloria Swanson in one of her better talkies, *Indiscreet*; was Marilyn Miller's leading man in her best film, *Her Majesty, Love*; costarred with Ona Munson in the delightful screwball comedy *The Hot Heiress*; appeared with daughter Constance and father Richard Bennett in the heavy-breathing *Bought*; saved *Night Nurse* Barbara Stanwyck from evil Clark Gable; and reteamed with his wife in the otherwise unremarkable *My Past*.

He made another six films in 1932, but none of them were terribly good, or heavily promoted. He was back with Constance Bennett in the three-hankie *Lady with a Past*, and appeared with her sister Joan in *Weekends Only*. He costarred with the pre-Astaire Ginger Rogers in *Hat Check Girl*, and with the ill-fated Peggy Shannon in the amusing whodunit *Girl Missing*. By 1933, it was clear that Ben's career was fading, despite the success of the crime thriller *I Cover the Waterfront*, with Claudette Colbert. His only other films that year were the low-budget *I Spy* and the MGM B-film *The Women in His Life* (who included acerbic blondes Una Merkel and Isabel Jewell).

It was just as well for their marriage that Bebe Daniels' career began a downslide at the same time. After her great success in the 1933 hits *42nd Street* and *Counsellor-at-Law*, she also found it hard to get good roles in A-films. Their happy marriage continued to make news, much to the Lyons' bemusement. "Despite the stories that went around about easy marriages in Hollywood and divorces, people were happily married there for years," Ben noted. Among their tricks for companionship, Bebe said, was, "when one of us wants to argue, the other shuts up. Nobody can argue with themselves."

It was in 1933 that the Lyons took their first joint trip to England, the country that was to become their second home. With their screen careers slowing, Bebe and Ben began making appearances on radio, both in the US and abroad (both had good singing voices), and toured the US and England on the vaudeville and music-hall circuit. When their nurse was implicated in a kidnapping plot in 1935 (not too long after the Lindbergh kidnapping), the Lyons decided to uproot themselves and move to England—Bebe also had a longtime stalker, a mental patient, whom she wanted to distance herself from. They took a house at 18 Southwick Street, in Paddington, which was to become their home base for the rest of their married lives. They appeared at the London Palladium and on BBC-TV as early as 1936 (when there were only 300 sets in all of London). They toured South Africa in 1937, and Ben found time to make a film, *He Loved an Actress* (with Lupe Velez and Harry Langdon, 1938).

Then came the war, during which Ben Lyon and Bebe Daniels went from being visiting American stars to heroes and goodwill ambassadors. They sent the children to Bebe's mother back in the US in 1939 and stayed in London ("The British have been so wonderful to us, we couldn't run out on them when they were in trouble," said Bebe). Their radio shows, *Hi, Gang!* and *Stars and Stripes in Britain*, cheered civilians and troops alike, and their stage shows, *Gangway* (which featured a teenaged Kay Kendall in the chorus) and *Haw-Haw*, were bombed out of theater after theater, always finding new venues and audiences. Bebe even had the honor to premiere the song "The White Cliffs of Dover" on their radio show—it, of course, went on to become a sentimental favorite.

When the US entered the war, Ben had to give up acting. He'd joined the US Army Air Corps back in 1931, and was now—at the age of 41—pressed into service, as a Major. While Ben spent the rest of the war on active duty (he was awarded the Legion of Merit in 1947), Bebe carried on her own fight, entertaining at field hospitals and on the front lines (she landed in Normandy only 15 days after the invasion). By the time the war ended, the Lyons were probably the best-loved American entertainers in England.

They returned home after the war, where Ben was made casting director at 20th Century-Fox and earned another footnote in movie history. One of his discoveries was starlet Norma Jean Dougherty, who turned up at a casting call in the summer of 1947. While it took another three or four years for her career to gain momentum, Ben Lyon thought enough of her to encourage her and even to change her name: "Marilyn" for his old costar Marilyn Miller, "Monroe" from the starlet's grandmother. While his discovery of Jean Harlow remains questionable, there does exist a 1950s photo of Ben with Marilyn Monroe, on which she inscribed, "You found me, named me, and believed in me when no one else did." Reminiscing about Marilyn, Ben later said, "She was the most conscientious youngster signed by the company. She devoted all her time to study, training, and exercise so that when an opportunity came she would be prepared. I have the greatest admiration for her."

In 1948 the Lyons returned to London, where Ben was named production chief at 20th Century-Fox's British office. In 1959, he

Still traveling, two decades later: Bebe and Ben in 1954.

joined the British TV company Associated-Rediffusion, as casting director. He and Bebe also became a sort of British Lucy and Ricky, or Ozzie and Harriet—their radio show, *Life with the Lyons*, proved so popular that it was moved to BBC-TV in 1950, where it ran until 1962 ("I liked the radio shows better than the TV shows," Ben admitted). It was Britain's first family sitcom, in which Bebe and Ben—and their children—portrayed themselves.

The Lyons coasted from war heroes to pop-culture icons through the 1950s, though their stars dimmed in the US (sadly, *Life with the Lyons* has never been seen in America and remains unknown over here). Bebe, who had written for Harold Lloyd back in the 1910s, contributed many *Life with the Lyons* scripts. There were also two feature-film spin-offs: *Life with the Lyons* (1954) and *The Lyons in Paris* (1956).

It all drew to a close in 1963, when Bebe suffered a crippling stroke. Ben cut back his workload and dedicated himself to nursing her back to a semblance of health. With time and effort, she rebounded to some extent; the Lyons gave interviews and socialized, though neither acted again. Bebe died on March 16, 1971, and Ben moved back to the US.

He recovered from his loss, and in 1972 married an old friend, recently widowed actress Marian Nixon (born in 1904, the pert blonde Nixon had never appeared onscreen with Ben; her own film career stretched from the early 1920s through the early 1930s). They stayed active, Ben being one of the more handsome and charming interviewees in Kevin Brownlow's documentary series *Hollywood*. Ben and Marian were on a round-the-world cruise when he died of a heart attack on March 22, 1979, while sailing past Honolulu. He was 78, and his second wife survived him by two years.

Bebe and Ben are still remembered fondly in Britain, long after so many American stars have been forgotten. Fittingly, the only two books on them were published in England: Ben's memoirs, *Life with the Lyons*, were published in 1953, and Jill Allgood's *Bebe and Ben* came out in 1975. Both books are long out of print and hard to find, but are well worth the search.

Jayne Mansfield

Jayne Mansfield had it all: looks, a slight but endearing and marketable talent, humor, a close-knit family and a studio contract. But she threw it all away; or, at least, it all slipped away from her with stunning speed. In 1957 she was the star of the moment, with three terrific films in theaters; by the time she died in 1967 (aged only 34) she was—literally—a figure from another age. A character in Edith Wharton's *The House of Mirth* says of its anti-heroine's self-destructive qualities, "Sometimes . . . I think it's just flightiness—and sometimes I think it's because, at heart, she despises the things she's trying for." Perhaps that was part of Jayne's problem in her quest for stardom—or maybe it was all just sheer bad luck and bad timing.

Ironically, the campest of the 1950s bombshells hailed from Bryn Mawr, Pennsylvania, on Philadelphia's old-money, quietly elegant Main Line. Vera Jane Palmer (she added the "y" later) was born to solidly middle-class parents on April 19, 1933. Her father died when Jayne was three; her mother remarried and the new family moved to Dallas, Texas, where everything grows bigger and bolder. Like Jean Harlow and Marilyn Monroe before her, Jayne married (Paul Mansfield) at 16. She gave birth to the first of what would be five children, enrolled in college, and eventually convinced her husband to move to Hollywood. She reportedly called Paramount and told the switchboard girl, "I want to be a star." "I'm sorry, we already have one" was the reply (the story is certainly apocryphal, but it is typical of Jayne's naïve, overwhelming ambition). Paul Mansfield returned home to Texas (the two divorced in 1958) and the newly bleached-blonde Jayne set out to conquer Hollywood.

In 1952 Jayne was signed by wildly inventive press agent Jim Byron, and began making appearances at publicity events and in newspaper and magazine spreads (notably, she stole the show at an event for the film *Underwater!*, in which she didn't even appear— her bikini top "accidentally" fell off while she was splashing about for photographers). With Byron's help, she was named Queen of the Chihuahua Show, Miss Texas Tomato, Miss Freeway, Miss Nylon Sweater, Miss Geiger Counter—turning down only Miss Rocquefort Cheese, "because it didn't sound right." Cute rather than beautiful, she had cotton-candy blonde hair, a little-girl voice (to which an ear-splitting squeal was frequently appended), and an eye-popping figure. Her measurements vary wildly from article to article, but averaged out at 41-18-36. With good posture, structured bras and corseting, she was hourglass to the point of looking damn near bisected.

A Warner Brothers' starlet contract resulted in small parts in several unremarkable films, all released in 1955: *Female Jungle* (a good bit as a gently bitter floozy), *Pete Kelly's Blues, Illegal, Hell on Frisco Bay.* She also filmed *The Burglar* that year, but it sat on the studio shelves till 1957. But success didn't come till Jayne was coerced into leaving Hollywood for Broadway, and a starring role in *Will Success Spoil Rock Hunter?*, which opened in October 1955. Playing a Marilyn Monroe-like bombshell in this comedy about stardom and advertising, Jayne spent nearly all of 1956 basking in her newfound fame and approval: magazine covers, interviews, a *Theater World* award and—when she left the show late that year— a seven-year contract with 20th Century-Fox, Monroe's own studio.

The next year was Jayne Mansfield's *annus mirabilis*; had she died late in 1957 she would be remembered as one of the mid-1950s' brightest, most sparkling and promising performers; it seemed she could do no wrong. Her first starring film was the delightfully camp, candy-colored *The Girl Can't Help It* (written and directed by former Warner Brothers animator Frank Tashlin). Presented as a live-action cartoon, Jayne played a sweetly talentless moll molded into a star by agent Tom Ewell (the middle-aged, ferret-faced Ewell, oddly, also romanced Marilyn Monroe in *The Seven Year Itch*). Jayne's wiggling strut down the street, to the film's

The quintessential Jayne Mansfield, 1957.

title song yelped by Little Richard, became an instant pop-culture touchstone (the scene was memorably parodied by Divine in *Pink Flamingos*).

Next came a sweet, understated dramatic performance in *The Wayward Bus*, based on the John Steinbeck book. As a shy pin-up model trying to hide her past from possible suitor Dan Dailey, Jayne gave Marilyn Monroe a run for her money (Monroe was promoting herself by 1957 as a serious dramatic actress). In the summer of 1957 came the film version of *Rock Hunter*, costarring Tony Randall and showcasing Jayne's finely-honed comedic skills.

And then, somehow, it all went horribly wrong. Intimations that something may have been a bit off-kilter with the new star appeared in April 1957, when Jayne was a guest at Romanoff's at a dinner for Sophia Loren. Wearing a white satin spaghetti-strap gown, she leaned *way* over Loren for the photographers. Later, sitting next to Loren and a gob-smacked Clifton Webb, Jayne briefly popped out of her dress (a memorable photo caught Loren's raised-eyebrow reaction).

Then came a series of dreadful movies. Certainly, every star has to suffer through some stinkers (around the same time, Monroe had *The Prince and the Showgirl*; Audrey Hepburn had *Green Mansions*; Kay Kendall had *Quentin Durward*). But Jayne's *Kiss Them for Me* wasn't just bad; it was bad with raisins on top. It looked okay on paper: a World War II romantic comedy/drama starring Cary Grant and introducing supermodel Suzy Parker in her first acting role. But the result was unwatchable. Next, Jayne was shipped off to England for the labored Western comedy *The Sheriff of Fractured Jaw* (1958), with British star Kenneth More.

While Jayne's professional life floundered, her personal life took on a bright tabloid happiness: in January 1958 she married Mickey Hargitay, the Joe DiMaggio to her Marilyn Monroe. The two made an eye-popping couple: "Mickey has a 52-inch chest expansion, and I measure over 40 inches, and we both have short arms," said Jayne. "All this makes dancing difficult." The Hungarian-born Hargitay was a former Mr. Universe and a muscleman in Mae West's nightclub act when he and Jayne met. It was a real love match, and Hargitay provided a much-needed stabilizing influence in Jayne's life for as long as she let him. A genuinely nice, uncomplicated fellow, Hargitay went along where Jayne's ambitions took them, but was happier working as a builder and contractor. He remodeled their home into a Pink Palace of delightfully stunning bad taste (it was, sadly, demolished in 2002).

Jayne befriending a dog on the set of *The Wayward Bus*, 1957.

Critics, reporters and the public certainly didn't "respect" Jayne by the end of the 1950s, but she was also impossible to dislike. Utterly lacking in pretension, she was by most accounts a warm-hearted, friendly woman without a mean bone in her body. She could be childishly temperamental and petulant at times, but her better nature always shone through. Indeed, it was this childlike enthusiasm and failure to think through the big picture that often got her into trouble and proved her undoing.

The 1960s were not kind to Jayne. She only made one more film for 20th Century-Fox, a mish-mash about the 1896 Olympics called *It Happened in Athens* (released in 1962). The rest of her films—many of them shot overseas—were produced and released through independent companies, and they ranged from "interesting" to jaw-dropping. In England, she filmed two crime dramas, *The Challenge* and *Too Hot to Handle* (both released in 1960); she played the Betty Grable character in the biopic *The George Raft Story* (starring Ray Danton, 1961). Her most hilariously awful film of that time was the Italian-made *Loves of Hercules* (1960). Costarring Mickey Hargitay as Hercules (with Jayne as the Loves), it featured unconvincing dragons, Mickey in a skimpy toga, Jayne in an array of wigs, and characters being strangled by evil trees.

Jayne appeared frequently on TV through the 1960s: game shows, talk shows, series (*Alfred Hitchcock Presents, Burke's Law, The Jack Benny Show*). And she earned the bulk of her money through live performances, often with Mickey: Las Vegas, nightclubs, even regional theatre (productions of *Bus Stop, The Rabbit Habit* and others). What must be remembered when looking at Jayne's lamentable résumé is that she was a freelancer scrambling for a living. With no studio contract, no health plan or insurance, a growing family, a mortgage and a star's public image to maintain, she had to accept every piece of crap that was offered, if the money was right. She even cut ribbons at grocery-store openings in exchange for free food. It's sometimes said that she turned down the role of Ginger on *Gilligan's Island* because she thought it was beneath her. Actually, she turned it down because sitcoms paid peanuts back then, and a nightclub tour earned her ten times what that show would have paid.

Even fashions turned against her. As the hourglass shape of the 1950s gave way to the bouffant hair and perky little suits of the Jackie Kennedy years, Jayne looked top-heavy with her huge bosom and ribcage and skinny little bird-legs. Later in the decade, she gamely tried for the mod look: miniskirts, increasingly elaborate wigs, go-go boots. Though she was still young, the look aged her (Jayne's then-teenage daughter, Jayne Marie, looked much more comfortable in the new fashions).

Divorced but still friends, Mickey Hargitay and Jayne, ca. 1966.

The films got worse and worse through the 1960s: the German-made musical drama *Homesick for St. Pauli* (1963); the bedroom comedy *Promises! Promises!* (with an embarrassed Mickey, and a headline-making topless scene by Jayne, 1963); the Italian-made soft-core porn comedy *Primitive Love* (1964); the nasty, dark crime comedy/drama *Dog Eat Dog* (1964); and three cringe-making, juvenile comedies: *The Fat Spy* (1966, with a very pregnant Jayne in a bad wig making love to insult comic Jack E. Leonard); *The Las Vegas Hillbillys* (1966, an equally pregnant Jayne sharing the screen with Mamie Van Doren and a painful series of backwoods comics); and the big-budget, all-star leer-fest *A Guide for the Married Man* (1967). She had a nice little role in the Evelyn Waugh black comedy *The Loved One* (1965), which wound up being cut.

A few of her later projects held either promise or a few enchanting moments: in the frantic comedy *Panic Button* (1964), Jayne appeared with Maurice Chevalier, and in her final film, the experimental indie drama *Single Room Furnished* (released in 1968), she played three characters and had a few moments of real dramatic intensity.

She also appeared—sometimes without her approval or even knowledge—in a number of feature-length documentaries. *Spree* (also called *Las Vegas By Night*) included footage of Jayne's nightclub act, filmed in the early '60s and released in 1967. *Mondo Hollywood* (1967) included footage of Jayne, as well as of Sonny and Cher, Ann-Margret, Brigitte Bardot, Princess Margaret, and hairdresser/ Manson victim Jay Sebring. But the maddest of these compilations was the posthumously-released *The Wild, Wild World of Jayne Mansfield*, which has become a cult sensation. Composed of clips of Jayne touring Europe and "visiting" (thanks to highly unconvincing editing and doubles) strip clubs and drag parties, it was narrated in breathless, lunatic quotes by actress Carolyn De Fonseca, doing an excellent Jayne imitation (a small sampling at random: "It made me think of other toes—and other times." "Sometimes I think fish are so lucky, especially when the sun is shining on them." "After all, dwarves and midgets need sex, too!").

As Jayne's career tumbled, so did her private life. She became increasingly fragile, had affairs with the wrong men, had problems with her weight and with alcohol. She and Mickey had three children (Mickey, Jr., Zoltan, and Mariska) and had a nasty, shattering divorce in 1964. (Jayne and Mickey stayed close to the end, though—he was one of the last people she spoke with before her death, and right till his own death in 2006, he never said a bad word about her.) She was married to director Matt Cimber from 1964-66, and had a son, Tony, with him. At the end, she was dating married attorney Sam Brody, who has (possibly unfairly) been labeled an abusive monster by her family and fans.

The end came, of course, in the early morning hours of June 29, 1967. She, Brody, and driver Ronald Harrison were en route from a ticky-tacky club date at Gus Stevens' Supper Club in Biloxi, Mississippi, to a TV show appearance in New Orleans. Their Buick Electra slammed into the back of a truck on Highway 90 in Slidell, Mississippi. The three adults in the front seat were killed (one hopes) instantly; the three children asleep in the back seat were relatively unharmed. Rumors still persist that Jayne had been decapitated: actually, her wig caught on the windshield and gave photographers a grim trophy.

After years of struggling in bad TV series and B-movies, Jayne and Mickey's daughter Mariska Hargitay hit the big time with the crime series *Law & Order: Special Victims Unit*, and is now an Emmy- and Golden Globe-winning performer her mother would be proud of. Mickey, Jr., runs Hargitay Plants, a successful landscaping firm started by his father.

The question remains: was Jayne Mansfield a canny actress portraying an idiot, like Gracie Allen, or was she really an idiot? Some of her remarks are too fluff-headed not to be scripted: "I can cook turkeys," she told a *Life* reporter. "They're so good when they're cooked, you know." Returning from Spain, she squealed, "The people there are so *Spanish!*" Conversely, her mishandling of her personal and professional lives hardly indicates the 163 I.Q. her press releases bragged of. If Jayne Mansfield wasn't a dumb blonde, she so consistently and effectively played the part that it eventually overtook her and became her legacy.

Marilyn Miller

Marilyn Miller was one of Broadway's brightest musical comedy stars in the late 1910s and '20s. Still young and vibrant at the dawn of the talkie era, she nonetheless failed in her bid for screen stardom and retired from the fray after only three films. Like Sophie Tucker, Fanny Brice and other great stage stars, she was not fated to translate well to film.

She was born Mary Ellen (soon shortened to Marilynn, then Marilyn) Reynolds on September 1, 1898, into a working-class family in Evansville, Indiana. When Mr. Reynolds left the family, Marilyn and her three siblings took to the stage. Soon they were trouping in vaudeville (with a new stepfather, thus the Miller surname). It was a rough-and-tumble childhood, touring the US and England, and Marilyn developed the hard shell she needed to survive in the business.

The slim, petite actress had golden-blonde curls, small, sparkling blue eyes, and a thin-lipped, girlish smile. Not classically beautiful, she was pert and cute in a style that proved popular in a Mary Pickford way. Theatrical producer Lee Shubert spotted the 16-year-old singer and dancer and signed her for his *Passing Show of 1914*, her Broadway debut. A brilliant and versatile dancer (ballet, eccentric dance, old-fashioned tap hoofing) with a sweet soprano voice, she was an instant success and appeared in the 1915 and 1917 *Passing Shows*, as well as *The Show of Wonders* (1916-17) and *Fancy Free* (1918).

Marilyn was snatched away from the Shuberts by Florenz Ziegfeld for his *Follies of 1918*, in which she had several well-received numbers. There were then—and are still—rumors that Marilyn and

Broadway star Marilyn Miller in *Fancy Free*, 1918.

Ziegfeld were romantically involved. It's known that Ziegfeld had affairs (or at least romances) with other showgirls, including Lillian Lorraine and Olive Thomas, but his exact relationship with Marilyn Miller remains unclear. Certainly he did not approve of her 1919 marriage to musical-comedy actor Frank Carter (who died in a car accident in 1920, a loss Marilyn never really got over).

After the *Follies of 1919*, Ziegfeld starred his new acquisition in a show of her own, the rags-to-showgirl musical *Sally* (1920-23). The grieving widow became the biggest new star on Broadway. Her number "Look for the Silver Lining" became a lifelong theme for Marilyn (as well as the title of her lackluster 1949 biopic, starring June Haver). In 1922, during the run of *Sally*, Marilyn married Jack Pickford, Mary's brother. Charming, irresponsible, talented, and already an alcoholic (he also earned the nickname "Mr. Syphilis" from Lilyan Tashman), Pickford had already been married to Ziegfeld Girl Olive Thomas, who had died under very mysterious circumstances while the couple was in Paris in 1920. Certainly, Marilyn and Jack had recent grief in common; soon they also shared an alcohol problem.

Marilyn's Broadway career bloomed through the 1920s: after a disappointing revival of *Peter Pan*, she went on to great success with *Sunny* (1925-26, in which she sang the now-standard "Who?"), and the George Gershwin/Sigmund Romberg operetta *Rosalie* (1928). She divorced Pickford in 1927 (he died in 1933, at the age of 36). No moss grew on Marilyn, who enjoyed flings with the delightful and handsome Jack Buchanan and Ben Lyon. Her personality varies, according to what account one reads: she had long-term friendships with Fred and Adele Astaire and Mary Eaton, but could also be temperamental and difficult to work with. According to one book, she was capable of being "rude and cruel," and Patricia Ziegfeld (Flo's daughter) recalled catching Marilyn in the throes of a dressing-room tantrum: "I had never seen anything that beautiful that angry."

It was in 1929, after *Rosalie* closed, that Marilyn Miller arrived in Los Angeles to begin her film career, with a First National version of *Sally*. It seemed like a sure hit: musical films were popular, and everyone knew what a hit Marilyn had been in the show. For an added kick, it was partially filmed in what Beatrice Lillie called "Primeval Technicolor." But somehow, everything went wrong: First National took a Broadway hit and removed everything that had made it successful. Only two songs remained from the stage show and the complex plot was showcased instead, and the role played by showgirl Dolores was axed entirely. Marilyn's romantic lead was the handsome but colorless Alexander Gray. Marilyn hated filming under the hot studio lights, with no audience feedback.

But when *Sally* opened in December 1929, it still met with some success. Today, it's hard to explain why, except for audience curiosity about the star. Marilyn Miller herself comes off well in *Sally*: she looks lovely, her acting is only slightly stagy, and her voice, while a little weak, is charming. But it's her dancing that sets the film on fire. The only time *Sally* is truly riveting is when Marilyn takes to her toes. The fact that she was never teamed with her friend Fred Astaire is one of the tragedies of cinema.

The first glimpse of Marilyn in *Sally* is of her dancing feet, as she slings hash in a diner. Her next number, the famed "Look for the Silver Lining," is sung with Gray; later, she and Joe E. Brown do a knockabout comic song-and-dance version of the same tune. After a dull love duet with Gray comes one of the film's high points, Marilyn's remarkable "All I Want to Do is Dance." That sequence alone saves the film (despite a rather unattractive feathered and sequined costume). Another enjoyable production number follows as Sally impersonates a socialite at a garden party ("Wild, Wild Rose"). Musically, the film goes downhill from there: another ballad, a faux-Russian dance, and a Land of the Butterflies number which may have been a knockout onstage but which *dies* here.

Sally was enough of a hit to guarantee a continuation of Marilyn's First National contract, despite her own misgivings. Her next vehicle, *Sunny*, was filmed in 1930 and released late in the year. Based on her stage hit, it told the convoluted story of a circus performer in love with a childhood friend, and the "comedy couple" (Joe Donahue and the wonderful wisecracker Inez Courtney) who help them out. Again, the male lead (Lawrence Gray—no relation to Alexander, but equally colorless) added little to the proceedings. Marilyn was swamped in the plot and again, many of the songs that had made *Sunny* a hit were dropped from the film.

Marilyn was becoming accustomed to filmmaking, and *Sunny* was not as traumatic an experience as *Sally* had been. It shows in her performance, which is a bit looser and more comfortable than in her first film. Again, it is her dancing which holds the eye, though there is less of it to see. She sings "Who?" with Gray, then (in male drag) sings a love ballad and does a delightful clog-style tap dance. Not—and this can throw modern audiences—the graceful light-as-air style of Fred Astaire or Eleanor Powell, but the old-fashioned

Back on Broadway, in *As Thousands Cheer*, 1933.

"hoofing" of Ruby Keeler and James Cagney. Back in skirts, she dances to "When We Get Our Divorce" with Joe Donahue (though, sadly, the song's hilarious lyrics were cut). Later, the two execute another athletic tap dance; finally, she dances alone (in riding habit) a rather flat production number.

Sunny did not do as well as *Sally* at the box office. Marilyn returned to Broadway, now in her early thirties, starred in the flop *Smiles* (with the Astaires, 1930-31) before crawling back to First National with her tail between her legs to make her third and final movie. *Her Majesty, Love*, released late in 1931, was by far her best film, but her biggest failure.

Based on a German stage play and film, it was directed by William Dieterle, whose knowledge of cinematography, lighting and timing was far superior to that of her previous directors, John Francis Dillon and William Seiter. Her costars included the brilliant comic actors W.C. Fields, Leon Errol, Ford Sterling and Chester Conklin—and, just as important, her leading man was the charming and personable Ben Lyon, a former boyfriend of Marilyn's (by now happily married to Bebe Daniels).

The plot—a wealthy playboy weds a barmaid, to his snooty family's horror—was strong and simple enough to hold its own without songs. This is just as well, for the musical numbers (except for the delightful opening) were pretty dismal, and Marilyn, recovering from a leg injury, only danced briefly. But she really shines as an actress in *Her Majesty, Love*, playing her role almost as ably as Claudette Colbert might have. It's a charming, lightweight little film, with many bright spots—though why the filmmakers opted to set it in Germany is puzzling, as none of the cast attempted accents and it could just as well have taken place in the US. While not as enjoyable as the 1931 releases that have gone on to become classics (*The Public Enemy, Monkey Business, Dracula,* etc.), there's no reason why *Her Majesty, Love* shouldn't have been a modest hit. But it wasn't: *Her Majesty, Love* was a tremendous box-office disappointment. Marilyn cancelled her film contract and returned to New York, her professional future in grave doubt.

Marilyn Miller still had one hit left in her—the Broadway revue *As Thousands Cheer* (1933-34), costarring Clifton Webb, Ethel Waters, and Helen Broderick, and written by Irving Berlin and

Moss Hart. Also in the cast was 24-year-old chorus boy/stage manager/choreographer Chester O'Brien. Twelve years Marilyn's junior, he became her third husband in 1934. The marriage was rocky (and friends dismissed him as a trophy husband), but the two stayed married till Marilyn's death.

Sadly, that was not far off. Marilyn had long suffered from sinusitis and migraines. In 1935 she underwent an operation, which, according to her biographer, was badly botched. Her condition grew worse, and she was hospitalized with a raging infection. When she was treated with insulin (antibiotics were still in their infancy in the 1930s), she lapsed into a coma and died on April 7, 1936. She was 37 years old.

Marilyn Miller leaves a slim legacy: her three films (still extant but rarely seen and unavailable on video or DVD); Warren G. Harris' 1985 biography, *The Other Marilyn*, and—for New Yorkers—an obscure presence in Times Square. In 1925 the I. Miller Shoe Building was redesigned on the northeast corner of 46th Street and Broadway. Known as The Show Folks' Shoe Shop, the 46th Street frontage was decorated with bronze statues, in niches, of the day's four leading actresses: Mary Pickford (cinema), Rosa Ponselle (opera), Ethel Barrymore (drama), and Marilyn Miller (musical comedy). Today, half-hidden behind a billboard, Marilyn Miller can still be seen by alert New Yorkers, dressed as Peter Pan, keeping vigil over Times Square.

Carmen Miranda

In 1909 (or thereabouts), three baby girls were born, in Warsaw, Mexico, and Portugal. All three came to Hollywood when they grew up. All three found fame as fast-talking foreign bombshells, then fell prey to typecasting and early deaths. The Polish girl, Lyda Roberti, turned in a number of brilliant comic portrayals before dying of a congenital heart condition in 1938. The Mexican, Lupe Velez, proved herself as a comedienne and dramatic actress before committing suicide in 1944. And the Portuguese girl grew up to be the most famous of all: Maria do Carmo Miranda da Cunha, better known as Carmen Miranda. To this day, her image can be summoned with just a fruit-laden hat, broad smile, and a flip of the hands.

Unlike Roberti and Velez, Carmen Miranda was a big star before hitting the American shores. She was born in Portugal, on February 9, 1909, but when she was still an infant her family relocated to Rio de Janeiro, Brazil. Carmen grew up in a large, working-class family; her father was a barber in a waterfront neighborhood and her mother ran a boarding house. Carmen attended a Catholic school, but left at 15 to work as a salesgirl. It was then she met her first boyfriend, Olympic rowing champion Mario Cunha. Later he recalled that even as a teenager, she was star-struck and ambitious to become a singer. Overtly sexual in a playful way, Carmen Miranda was not a classic beauty. Short and curvy, with a headful of black wavy hair (later hidden by her famous headdresses), she had a Bob Hope ski-slope nose, a huge, endearing grin, and eyes like "green headlights" (painted out in her publicity shots was a large brown spot on the white of one eye).

Her sister Aurora (younger, prettier, but not so famous) noted that composer and musician Josué de Barros discovered Carmen singing at a party and helped launch her career. She began recording in 1929, and almost instantly became a sensation with her lilting, lively voice. She could also sing tongue-twisting songs faster than Ann Miller could tap-dance. On tour (accompanied by her father), her star rose in Brazil. "A good bowl of soup and the freedom to sing" was all she wanted, she said at this time. She teamed with composer Laurindo Almeido in 1935. "Carmen was truly genuine," he recalled for filmmaker Helena Solberg. "There was nothing false about her." Intensely patriotic about her adopted homeland of Brazil, she was idolized by the record-buying masses.

The Bando da Lua began accompanying her in 1934, and she remained true-blue to them, insisting they share her every job and every success. She sang sambas, tangos and paeans to her country. She also adopted the costume of the Bahiana, which was to become her trademark. The "Bahiana look" was derived from the costume of Brazilian women who carried produce on their heads to market. Carmen's early version was simple and fairly straightforward: a modest fruit-bedecked turban, midriff-baring ruffled blouse, and flouncy skirt. After a few years, Hollywood costume designer Yvonne Wood had elaborated on this theme to a delirious extent. Carmen was weighed down with jewels and increasingly hilarious hats; her skirts and blouses incorporated lamés, brocades, pompoms and lace, and her platform shoes grew to crippling heights. It was a look which came to define, and eventually, to confine, Carmen.

Carmen had made her film debut in 1932 with the musical *O Carnaval Cantado No Rio*, and went on to appear in such popular fare as *A Voz do Carnaval* (1933), *Aló, Aló Brasil!* and *Estudiantes* (both 1935), *Aló, Aló, Carnaval* (1936), and *Banana-da-Terra* (1938). As popular as they may have been south of the border, none of these films made an impression in the US. It was her nightclub work which proved to be her ticket to Hollywood.

In 1939, producer Lee Shubert spotted Carmen in Rio and signed her for his Broadway show, *The Streets of Paris*. She insisted on taking her Bando da Lua with her, and the lot of them arrived in New York that spring. She was thrilled with her good fortune and gave interviews in the halting English which would soon become both her trademark and her downfall. Decked out in her Bahiana outfit, she sang four numbers in *The Streets of Paris*, two of which ("South American Way" and "Mamãe eu Quero") became hits. The show, and Carmen, became the biggest sensations of the summer of '39. Immediately, imitators sprang up, and the Carmen Miranda look was adopted by both fashionable society ladies and cutting-edge drag queens.

Down Argentine Way (1940) introduced the American film-going public to Carmen Miranda (it was also Betty Grable's first starring hit, after ten years as a bit player). Carmen's two songs were filmed in New York on the *Streets of Paris* set. The film, a light-as-air trifle, was a charming success, as were Grable and Miranda. The latter was added to the 20th Century-Fox stable; the grooming process began, and executives tried to figure out exactly what to do with their unusual new acquisition. Publicity releases and interviews played up Carmen's amusingly fractured English: the same thing had already happened to Lupe Velez and Lyda Roberti. Carmen played along, and though she was quite fluent in English after a few years, to the end of her life she was quoted, and acted, in broken, highly-accented baby talk.

In the summer of 1940, Carmen returned to Rio de Janeiro. There was a huge reception, enormous crowds. But there was also a strong undercurrent of hostility, which hurt the sensitive and patriotic actress. There was a feeling that Carmen had sold out and gone Hollywood. Some felt that she presented a cartoon-character version of Brazilians to the US. When Carmen returned north to pick up her movie contract, she was somewhat chastened by this dual reaction from her homeland.

She returned to 20th Century-Fox for her series of cotton-candy wartime musicals. She appeared in four home-runs right away, delightfully bizarre and light-hearted films that epitomize the escapist fare of the war years. Carmen bought a Beverly Hills home (complete with swimming pool) and moved much of her family in with her. A friendly, outgoing and unpretentious woman, she quickly became one of the most popular members of the movie colony. "She certainly was a family girl," said costume designer Yvonne Wood in an interview with this writer. "Her sister Aurora, Aurora's husband, her mother, her band, their wives and babies.

Carmen Miranda doing her stuff, in *That Night in Rio*, **1941.**

Every time there was a celebration, our holidays or their holidays, she gave a party. She loved to entertain."

The first film under her new contract, *That Night in Rio* (1941), was a remake of the 1935 film *Folies Bergère*. This was Alice Faye's first film with Carmen, and the two became great pals. Carmen played a fiery nightclub performer, and this time she had a real role. Carmen proved herself a great comic foil, spitting out her lines at breakneck speed. No showbiz neophyte, she had great comic timing and stole every frame of film from her costars. She also had several songs, including two of her biggest hits, "Chica Chica Boom Chic" and "Yi Yi Yi (I Like You Very Much)."

Carmen had an even bigger role in *Weekend in Havana* (1941), as a singer romancing her manager (Cesar Romero) while sparring with Alice Faye and John Payne. She even got a few romantic scenes with Payne, which seemed a step in the right direction. Her songs included the title number and "When I Love, I Love," both of which were far better than anything Faye was given.

It was during the filming of this last movie that scandal nearly sidelined Carmen's career. She was called to do a photo shoot after filming wrapped. She and Cesar Romero hit a few dance poses, including one shot of Carmen doing a high kick. She'd neglected to put on underpants, and when the film was developed, Carmen had totally revealed herself South of the Border. The studio managed to contain most of the prints, though some circulated underground for years. Not only didn't it hurt her career, but she added her footprints to Grauman's forecourt on March 24, 1941.

Carmen returned to Broadway for the second and last time once more after filming wrapped on *Weekend in Havana* in late 1941. She provided musical and comedic support to Olsen and Johnson in the knock-about revue *Sons o' Fun*, which was a great hit and ran through early 1942. She even had time, somehow, to make a series of records for Decca and to appear at President Roosevelt's birthday ball on January 30. Then it was back to Hollywood to fill the rest of her movie obligations.

Springtime in the Rockies (1942) was another sheer delight, with Carmen and Cesar Romero playing comedy couple to Betty Grable and John Payne. Carmen also had some great scenes with Edward Everett Horton, and sang a fractured version of the hit "Chattanooga

The rarely-seen hair of Carmen Miranda (or an approximation of same), 1943.

Choo-Choo." She had as good an on- and off-screen relationship with Grable as she'd had with Faye. "She was a real lady, a lot of fun," recalled Wood, and Ann Miller remembered being brought home and taught Portuguese recipes.

The last of her great Fox musicals was *The Gang's All Here* (1943), costarring Alice Faye, Charlotte Greenwood and Edward Everett Horton. There was little plot (show folks put on a benefit for the troops), but that wonderful cast and some hummable songs: "Brazil," "Paducah," "No Love, No Nothing," and Carmen's most famed production number, "The Lady in the Tutti-Frutti Hat." This Busby Berkeley fantasy included a sky-high hat, half-naked chorus boys, suggestive six-foot bananas and very catchy lyrics. It also turned out to be Carmen's swan song, in a way.

After a cameo appearance in the all-star war film *Four Jills in a Jeep* (1944) came Carmen's first top-billed role, in *Greenwich Village*. But this was not the prize package it might have seemed; indeed, Fox was quietly ushering Carmen out the door. *Greenwich Village* was a silly musical about a nightclub owner (Carmen) and a hopeful songwriter (Don Ameche) in the Bohemian New York of the 1920s (a very 1940s-looking 1920s). Starlet Vivian Blaine was given the ingénue role. Today, the film is mostly notable for the performers cut from it: the musical comedy group The Revuers (Judy Holliday, Betty Comden and Adolph Green), who can be spotted in the background of a party scene.

Carmen finished out her Fox contract with three more films, all of them again costarring Vivian Blaine. Blaine was a chirpy kid, but no Alice Faye or Betty Grable, and Carmen's leading men were no John Paynes or Don Ameches. *Something for the Boys* (1944, with Michael O'Shea) had a "help the soldiers" theme; in *Doll Face* (1945, with Dennis O'Keefe) she and Blaine were burlesquers; and *If I'm Lucky* (1946, with Perry Como) was a political musical. Carmen did her best in all these films, but her musical numbers were becoming repetitive, and her characters had frozen into that same fast-talking comic sidekick. One of her most delightful numbers, "She's Always True to the Navy," was censored from *Doll Face* and only recently resurfaced.

On January 1, 1946, the 37-year-old Carmen was let go from 20th Century-Fox. Of course, it must be noted that many actresses who had enjoyed spectacular screen success during the mid-1940s found their careers in a tailspin when the war ended. Alice Faye, Betty Grable, Rita Hayworth, Veronica Lake, Hedy Lamarr; the reasons were many, but all of these ladies were considered has-beens by the late 1940s. Carmen began doing more nightclub work (in the US, Europe and Latin America), and by the early 1950s was also appearing on TV.

One frustration which Carmen noted to Yvonne Wood was that "she was getting a little sick and tired of some of the dialogue that was written for her. 'I don't speak English like that anymore!' She had one helluva vocabulary. But the scriptwriters still wrote things like 'stripsqueeze,' and the audience didn't know any different; they thought she was cute as a bug."

Carmen's first film after her Fox contract ended was the rather dispiriting *Copacabana* (United Artists, 1947), which costarred Groucho Marx as her boyfriend/agent. The whole film looks rather shabby today, with its black-and-white camerawork and cast of has-beens, hopefuls, and endearingly talentless Copa Girls. But *Copacabana* is not a total loss. There are a couple of typical and rather uninspired "Carmen Miranda numbers," but she also got to sing some French ballads in a blonde wig and veil, as "Mlle. Fifi." She also appeared several times, startlingly, hatless and in a simple house dress. It was a glimpse of versatility which she had never been allowed before, and, sadly, was never allowed again. Two films at MGM followed, in which Carmen had only supporting roles. The leading ladies in *A Date with Judy* (1948) were youthful Elizabeth Taylor and Jane Powell; Carmen (as a dance teacher) romanced chubby, middle-aged Wallace Beery, of all people. She played local color in the bright little trifle *Nancy Goes to Rio* (1950). And that was essentially the end of Carmen Miranda's film career.

It was back to nightclub work, television, and making a home with film editor David Sebastian, whom Carmen had married in March 1947. Sebastian does not come off well with Carmen's biographers ("I only met him once, and that was enough," said Wood). He seems to have been opportunistic, but the two stayed married; they had no children, though Carmen suffered a miscarriage in 1948. Her last film was the unwatchable Dean Martin-Jerry Lewis comedy *Scared Stiff* (Paramount, 1953), in which Lewis also does

Carmen enjoys a moment of quiet good taste, 1948.

an imitation of her. Carmen looked overweight and tired. "Oh, zose boys, zey drive you nuts!" she said in a press release. She never appeared on film again.

Carmen suffered a nervous breakdown in 1953 ("zose boys" evidently had driven her nuts indeed), and in 1954 she returned to Rio to recuperate. In newsreels, she looks haggard and tired; her dyed red hair pulled haphazardly back, her smile forced. She traveled the world: Italy, Hawaii, Sweden, Denmark, Rome. By 1955 she was back in the US. She should have been rested by this time, but, actually, Carmen was struggling with her weight, alcohol, tranquilizers, and age (she had a facelift around this time; she had already had two fairly unnoticeable nose jobs in the '40s). After some dates in Havana in July 1955, she flew to Los Angeles to appear on Jimmy Durante's popular TV show on August 4. As usual, the show was hilarious: Carmen and Durante were superb together, making one wish they'd been teamed on the big screen. While being spun by Durante during a number, Carmen suffered a heart attack: she dropped to one knee, got up, and said, "I'm out of breath." Durante took her lines, and the show went on. By the finale, with Carmen swishing happily out the door, waving goodbye, all seemed well again.

She went home to her husband and family (most of whom lived with the Sebastians) and went up to bed around 2:30 in the morning. Carmen was felled instantly by another heart attack while preparing for bed. She was discovered by her husband the next morning. On August 13 she had a huge public funeral in Rio; she lay in state while sobbing crowds passed by; the throngs in the streets were reminiscent of Valentino's passing thirty years earlier. Her last performance was aired on October 15, but her legacy has never dimmed. Carmen's death has been viewed as a tragedy, but—except for its occurrence at the too-early age of 46—it was quick and merciful: she died at home, after a party, and right after appearing on TV with Jimmy Durante, a passing many of us would be lucky to suffer.

Marilyn Monroe

In the nearly 50 years since Marilyn Monroe died (good lord, is it really that long ago?!), she has become as much a mythic figure as Robin Hood or The Lady of Shalott. The actual facts of her life have become less important than her image: the ultimate 20th-century glamor girl, Hollywood's broken butterfly, "the last love goddess and the first love child," in the words of biographer Fred Lawrence Guiles. But Marilyn Monroe was first and foremost an actress. All of her films—from a walk-on in *Scudda-Hoo! Scudda-Hay!* to the aborted *Something's Got to Give*—are available to us, and they reveal a woman who was a talented though somewhat limited comedienne, and an underrated dramatic actress and singer.

The facts of her life have been hashed over ad nauseam, but they boil down to a simple chronology. She was born on June 1, 1926, in Los Angeles, the daughter of twice-divorced film cutter Gladys Baker Mortensen and an unknown man. There are many candidates for the father of Norma Jean (sometimes spelled "Norma Jeane"), but no one can be singled out with any real accuracy. Her childhood was pretty terrible in spots, but not the all-out horror she later claimed. Gladys was often unemployed, in and out of psychiatric hospitals, so Norma Jean lived with a variety of caregivers. She spent seven years with the Bolenders, a stable and loving family, and another few years with a woman named Grace McKee. It was then, in the mid-1930s, that Norma Jean's acting ambitions began blossoming.

Her body began blossoming, too, and in 1942, at 16, she married a neighbor, the good-natured, uncomplicated Jim Dougherty. By the time they divorced in 1946, Norma Jean's career as a model had begun. While working in a wartime factory, she was spotted and signed by the Blue Book Agency. When she first walked onto a film set in 1947, she was no naïve unknown; she was one of the nation's most promising models. Her first two films were nothing worth putting on a résumé: she had one line in the silly hick comedy *Scudda-Hoo! Scudda-Hay!* (1948) and a walk-on as a waitress in the delinquency drama *Dangerous Years* (1947). Some Marilyn scholars also put her in such late-1940s films as *The Shocking Miss Pilgrim, You Were Meant for Me,* and *Green Grass of Wyoming.*

Her first big chance came in a 1948 B-film called *Ladies of the Chorus*—by this time, she had rechristened herself Marilyn Monroe (Marilyn after Marilyn Miller, at Ben Lyon's suggestion; Monroe from her grandmother). She is utterly delightful in *Ladies of the Chorus,* a cheesy musical about a chorine engaged to a high-society playboy. She bore more than a passing resemblance to Betty Grable and showed some musical gifts—there is some controversy as to whether or not her singing voice was dubbed in this film (costar Adele Jergens was dubbed by Virginia Rees). But one B-film from Columbia does not launch a star, and the 1950s started shakily for Marilyn.

She was reduced to a sexy walk-on in *Love Happy* (1950), one of the Marx Brothers' lesser films; she was only a chorus girl in *A Ticket to Tomahawk* (1950); she had small bit parts in the minor dramas *The Fireball* and *Right Cross* (both 1950). But—with the help of her boyfriend, agent Johnny Hyde—she landed a small but vital supporting role in the *noir* gangster film *The Asphalt Jungle* (1950), directed by John Huston. She was only eleventh-billed, but made quite an impression as the innocent, teeny-bopper mistress of mobster Louis Calhern. Already some of the Marilyn schtick was in place, including the breathy voice and half-closed eyes. Later that very busy year came another small but impressive role, as a hopeful starlet ("Why do they always look like unhappy rabbits?") in *All About Eve,* one of the best films of that—or any other—year. Terrified at working with Bette Davis and George Sanders, Marilyn was already showing signs of the insecurities that would make her both endearing and infuriating to her coworkers.

A sophisticated Marilyn Monroe in 1950.

But these two good showcases were followed by larger roles in smaller pictures through 1951: *Hometown Story, As Young As You Feel, Love Nest, Let's Make it Legal.* She was handed another good role early in 1952: as Peggy, a tuna-factory worker, in the Barbara Stanwyck drama *Clash By Night.* Based on a Clifford Odets play and directed by Fritz Lang, it was a welcome change from the B-comedies Marilyn had been doing of late. This role gave her the chance to be more than a prop; she played a headstrong girl who Stanwyck tries to keep on the straight and narrow. Less gaudily turned-out than usual, Marilyn showed signs of real talent in this drama; her career might have gone in a totally different direction had she not signed with 20th Century-Fox early in 1952.

But sign she did, at $500 a week, and she would stay with Fox (except for a few loan-outs) for the rest of her life. She finished out 1952 in a series of motley films: the weak comedies *We're Not Married!* and *Monkey Business*; the anthology *O. Henry's Full House*, and the thriller *Don't Bother to Knock.* In this last drama, Marilyn played a demented babysitter, obsessed with her long-lost fiancé. It was a chance to shine again in a drama, but the script and Roy Ward Baker's direction gave her no help. Though she tried hard, any contract player could have done as well. Also problematic was her next drama, *Niagara* (1953), though this film helped ratchet up her stardom. Looking fabulous in Technicolor (and a sexy wardrobe by Dorothy Jeakins), Marilyn was once again a whispery villainess; her performance came nowhere near to matching her appearance. She did shine in one scene: singing along to record of "Kiss" while jealous husband Joseph Cotten fumes, she was lovingly filmed by cinematographer Joe MacDonald, and looked every inch a star.

Marilyn's real star-making vehicle was *Gentlemen Prefer Blondes* (1953, based on the 1949 Broadway musical, rather than the 1925 novel or the 1926 play). Marilyn's was the ultimate Lorelei Lee for the 1950s, and for the first time, she really came across with a happy, perfectly-timed comic performance. It's all there, classic Marilyn: dreamy eyes, breathy voice, deadpan takes—and it all works. It was also the first time Marilyn's singing voice had been really showcased, and (with some help from Marni Nixon for the highest notes), she did an expert job.

A 1958 snapshot of Marilyn.

One hit followed another: later in 1953, Marilyn costarred with Lauren Bacall and Betty Grable in the witty, stylish *How to Marry a Millionaire*. The movie carried on the grand old tradition of the "good-hearted girls on the make" genre, which had existed at least since the 1919 play *The Gold Diggers*. As the nearsighted Pola, Marilyn acquitted herself well, though it was another of the dumb blonde roles she was already tiring of.

Along with her movie stardom came an increasingly public life: Marilyn married retired baseball star Joe DiMaggio in January 1954; they separated in the autumn of that same year and divorced in 1955, though they later became close friends again.

Troubles between Fox and Marilyn had been brewing for some time, and she was put on suspension in 1954 after making the silly musical Western *River of No Return*. She turned down several other projects, tired of spinning her wheels in what she felt were second-rate comedies; her contract was finally revised to give her $100,000 a film and a little more creative control—not bad for a 28-year-old who had been a money-making star for only a year. Still, her next film was a disappointment: the overblown musical *There's No Business Like Show Business*. Despite a cast that included Ethel Merman, Dan Dailey, and Donald O'Connor, and a score of Irving Berlin tunes, the film was little more than loud and brassy. Marilyn's role was small (a dumb hat-check girl-turned-singer) and her big number, "Heat Wave," was a classic of bad-taste choreography. She fared better singing "After You Get What You Want, You Don't Want It," but her enunciation was so odd in the number "Lazy" that she seemed to be singing about "a great big valeeshful of booksh to read where it'sh peashful."

Her singing voice was not to be dismissed, however. Marilyn cut some records in the mid-1950s, and they reveal a light, untrained but lovely voice. With a little coaching, she could easily have been a successful singer, though not in the ranks of Julie London or Rosemary Clooney—still, nightclub work or musical TV shows might have provided an outlet for her talents.

Her next project, *The Seven Year Itch* (1955, based on a Broadway hit) is seen as a charming, innocent romp today, but Marilyn was not happy to be cast as the nameless sexpot tootsie living upstairs from middle-aged horndog Tom Ewell. Filming took her to New York, where the famous skirt-blowing scene was filmed on Lexington Avenue, on the site of today's Citicorp Building—it was then that her marriage to DiMaggio really hit the rocks. New York opened a whole new world for Marilyn. She started hanging out with "serious" performers, writers, intellectuals. Uneducated but very bright, she was drawn to anyone who might take her seriously as an actress. She latched on to the respected (and self-consciously artsy) Actors Studio, being all but adopted by its leaders, Lee and Paula Strasberg. Marilyn reportedly showed great talent in staged class performances of *Rain* and *Anna Christie*, and the Strasbergs began making noises about a stage career. But, sadly, everyone recognized that Marilyn did not have the professional temperament for the theater, where one must show up letter-perfect and on time every night.

Her next film was probably her personal favorite: William Inge's *Bus Stop* (1956), in which she played a white-trash nightclub singer who finds redemption with a dumb, good-hearted cowboy. Marilyn brought her New York training to the role and turned in a quiet, heartfelt performance. She agonized over her Southern accent, and insisted on take after take, to the frustration of her director and costars. Amazingly, Fox did not even put her up for an Oscar that year, though her performance stands up well against nominees Susan Hayward, Katharine Hepburn and Anna Magnani.

Marilyn's third and final marriage was to playwright Arthur Miller; the two wed in 1956, and split up during the disastrous filming of *The Misfits* in the summer of 1960 (they officially divorced in 1961). Unlike Dougherty and DiMaggio, who were discreet and gentlemanly in their later treatment of her, Miller wrote a self-justifying play about their marriage, *After the Fall* (1964). He called Marilyn "highly self-destructive . . . all my energy and attention were devoted to trying to help her solve her problems. Unfortunately, I didn't have much success."

In the glow of their new marriage, Marilyn and Miller (her name turned out to be Marilyn Miller after all!) took off for London to make *The Prince and the Showgirl* (1957), with Laurence Olivier. The film was a disaster for all concerned. Olivier had no patience with Marilyn's now-famous eccentricities; Marilyn was paralyzed with fear; Terence Rattigan's script did not translate well onto the screen. She looked lovely, and her light comic style worked much better than Olivier's sledge-hammer hamminess; but the film was a flop.

Marilyn's eccentricities were getting more pronounced by the late 1950s, but she was by no means the helpless basket-case she's often portrayed as. No one can maintain a twelve-year film career without having something on the ball. Street-smart and very tough when she had to be, Marilyn's biggest problems were insecurity (both professional and intellectual) and insomnia—all this led to constant lateness, and her alcohol and sleeping-pill addictions. But, as many friends will attest, Marilyn at her best was canny, self-deprecatingly witty, and very wise in the ways of show business.

She really didn't want to do the comedy *Some Like It Hot* (1959), now generally perceived to be her best film. Again, not a happy set: she and costar Tony Curtis cordially detested each other, and she miscarried during filming. Irritated at playing another dumb blonde role and at the black-and-white format of the film, she was grumpy and ill-prepared. But, remarkably, her performance was light as air and shows none of her unhappiness.

Next came possibly her worst film, the musical comedy *Let's Make Love* (1960), with French star Yves Montand. Ostensibly about a satirical off-Broadway show and its unwilling target, the film was a barrage of unbearable be-bop numbers, cringe-making celebrity impersonations, and an unconvincing romance between the leads (despite the actual spooning going on between Marilyn and Montand). Not even director George Cukor could make anything of this hash, which remains downright painful viewing.

All of Marilyn's offscreen problems found a perfect breeding ground in the horror that was *The Misfits* filming. Written for her by Arthur Miller, the film was a character study of an unhappy divorcée (Marilyn) and three washed-up cowboys (Clark Gable, Montgomery Clift and Eli Wallach—hardly The Happiness Boys themselves by 1960). Gable was dying of heart disease, Clift and Marilyn were floating in and out of chemical hazes, the Miller/Monroe marriage was shattering, and director John Huston was in no mood for any of it. The finished product was overly long, rambling and occasionally incoherent, but it did contain a few flashes of brilliance and one of Marilyn's best-sustained dramatic performances.

During her lifetime, Marilyn Monroe was underrated as a dramatic actress, and this rightly rankled her—but she was also overrated as a comedienne. Of her most successful dramas, Peggy (*Clash by Night*), Cherie (*Bus Stop*) and Roslyn (*The Misfits*) are each separate, well-defined characters. There's no mixing them up: each was well thought-out and painstakingly created by an intelligent actress. But

Marilyn in the unfinished _Something's Got to Give_, 1962.

as charming as her comic portrayals were, they are all the same
person: Miss Casswell in _All About Eve_, Lorelei Lee in _Gentlemen
Prefer Blondes_, Pola in _How to Marry a Millionaire_, Sugar in _Some
Like it Hot_. They all have the same dreamy eyes, breathy voice,
"Marilyn walk," and basically the same personality. It was cute as
hell, but any good Marilyn Monroe impersonator could have phoned
it in.

Back at Fox, Marilyn started work on another fluffy comedy, *Something's Got to Give*, in which she played a long-shipwrecked spouse returning home—it was a remake of the 1940 comedy *My Favorite Wife*, which in turn was inspired by Tennyson's 1864 poem *Enoch Arden* (Marilyn's character was named Ellen Arden). At age 36, she had never looked better. Whisper-thin (due to a gall-bladder operation and subsequent diet), she had left the zaftig 1950s look behind for a more sophisticated, pared-down style. Her hair platinum and pouffed, her makeup petal-light, she looked an entirely different woman than she had five years earlier. Outtakes reveal that she was also giving a superb performance, despite a sitcom-silly script. The scene where her character sees her children for the first time in years is a moment of silent acting worthy of Lillian Gish or Greta Garbo. With age, she was developing into a much more deft comic actress.

Fired from the film for frequent absences, she was soon rehired and was set to go back to work in mid-August. As everyone knows, Marilyn Monroe died sometime during the night of August 4 or the morning of August 5, 1962. Almost immediately, the conspiracy theories started: the Kennedys had her killed; her doctor or her live-in nurse accidentally killed her; the Mafia killed her; she died at a hospital and was whisked back home; everyone but the Gabor sisters has been accused of killing her. The most boring theory is probably correct: she simply took too many pills, either on purpose or accidentally.

Marilyn Monroe has enjoyed an afterlife generally associated with religious figures. She's certainly as popular today as she was during her lifetime; countless biographies have been published (at least one new one a year, like clockwork); biopics, posters, postcards, dolls, websites, YouTube tributes and clips, DVD reissues . . . She would have turned 80 in 2006. Part of the fascination is guessing what would have become of her. Would she have become a fabulous ruin like Elizabeth Taylor? A blowsy character actress like Shelley Winters? An eccentric recluse like Brigitte Bardot? Marilyn Monroe died at her loveliest, just at the cusp of a new career—or possibly at the beginning of her downslide. As sad as her death was, it was also a good career move—it insured her an immortality yet to be equaled by any other star.

Renate Müller

Two of the most popular actresses in late 1920s Berlin were the sexually sophisticated Marlene Dietrich and the perkier, more wholesome Renate Müller. Dietrich, of course, was beckoned by Hollywood in 1930, and went on to a half-century career of international stardom. Renate, after her breakthrough hit in *Die Privatsekretärin* (*The Office Girl*, 1931) went on to appear in a number of successes in Germany and—being multi-lingual—in British and French releases as well. Her films were often shipped to the US a year or two after their German release, either shown subtitled or in German-language movie theaters. But Renate neither embraced the growing Nazi regime—as did her fellow stars Kristina Söderbaum and Paula Wessely, among others—nor did she flee, like Dietrich. And in this situation lay her undoing and her mysterious, violent end at the age of 31.

Renate Müller came from a family steeped in culture, and not short of money. She was born on April 26, 1906, in Munich. Her mother, who was born in South America, was a painter; her father was editor-in-chief of several major newspapers. The family moved, as he was transferred to successively better jobs, to Munich, Danzig and, finally, Berlin. During Renate's early childhood, the family lived in Emmering, a wealthy suburb of Munich, where they owned a home on the Ammer River. Her studio biographies describe Renate as a top student, who wrote "passionate and free" poetry, sang with the choir at Danzig's City Theater, and had her coming-out party at 16 aboard a British Naval ship.

One year short of high-school graduation, Renate got her parents' permission to leave school and study acting at the renowned

Reinhardt-Schule. She attended for only one year before getting her first professional jobs, in the summer of 1925. One of Renate's professors, director Erich Pabst, hired her to appear in a season at the Harzer Bergtheater in Thale, the German equivalent of summer stock. Her performance as Helena in *A Midsummer Night's Dream* brought her first notice from the critics, and soon she was playing small roles with various theater companies. Her career took a turn for the *avant-garde* when she joined an experimental theater collective under the direction of Joe Sherman. In the brief time before the company's sheer weirdness caused its financial disintegration, Renate appeared in the absurdist productions *Brigitte* and +++.

Through the late 1920s, Renate Müller established herself as one of Berlin's busier and more versatile young stage newcomers. She appeared in light drawing-room comedies, Shakespeare (*Love's Labor Lost*), in Georg Kaiser's tragic *Zweimal Oliver*, and Wedekind's *Franziska*. She played a tough peasant girl in *Des Kaisers Soldaten* (*Soldiers of the Kaiser*), and a modern young flirt in *Arm wie eine Kirchenmnaus* (*Poor as a Churchmouse*).

By 1929 she was one of the leading lights of Berlin's Staatstheater, and the film studios were taking note of her, as well. Popular light comic actor, director and writer Reinhold Schünzel cast Renate in her first movie, the 1929 silent comedy *Peter der Matrose* (*Peter the Sailor*). Renate went over well with movie audiences and critics alike, and she was highly amused when one reviewer called her film debut "the best movie of her career so far." She was signed by the Erich Engel company to appear in the silent films *Teure Heimat* (*Dear Homeland*) and *Drei Machen ihr Glück* (*Third Time's a Charm*). A third silent, *Revolte im Erziehungshaus* (*Boarding School Revolt*), caused something of a censorship scandal. Held up in post-production for many months while the studio and the government censors fought over it, by the time it was released, there was little left but "pieced-together shreds of the original . . . Yet it sufficed to showcase Renate's abilities" (from a 1930s studio bio).

According to her recent biographer, Uwe Klöckner-Draga, Renate suffered from a bout of ovaritis around this time that was so painful it affected her work; she was allegedly prescribed morphine for the pain, and may have fallen into the pain-prescription cycle that sucked in Wallace Reid, Pearl White and other film stars.

Renate Müller in *Die Privatsekretärin*.

By the turn of the decade, Renate was getting so many film offers that she somewhat reluctantly gave up her berth at the Staatstheater and threw her lot in with the film industry, which was—like

America's—just converting to sound. Renate's status as one of the most promising young actresses of Germany's fledgling talkie industry was established by 1930, with five films under her belt. Already she was known for playing the kind of roles taken in the US by Claudette Colbert, Nancy Carroll and Jean Arthur: pert, apple-cheeked girls, wholesome and cheerful, but with a twinkle of naughtiness and big-city sophistication showing through. In 1930, the 24-year-old appeared in the sensational boxing story *Liebe im Ring* (*Love in the Ring*), a part-talkie directed by Reinhold Schünzel and starring Max Schmeling, fresh from winning America's heavyweight championship. *Der Sohn der Weissen Berge (In the Alps)* was a typical outdoorsy mountain film, the kind that had made Leni Riefenstahl so famous in the late 1920s. It was filmed by an Italian production company and directed by popular director and matinée idol Mario Bonnard. *Das Flötenconzert von Sans-Souci* (released in the US as *The Flute Concert of Sans-Souci* in 1931) "swept triumphantly through half of Europe," according to one contemporary account: "Critics gave [Renate] the highest of praises." In this 18th-century comedy, Renate played the flirtatious wife of one of Frederick the Great's courtiers, constantly trying to evade detection by her husband.

Liebeslied (*Love Song*) was shot in Rome, the first German-language talkie to be made there. Directed by Constantin J. David, it costarred Gustav Frölich (who, according to a contemporary press release, "recalls with fondness their work together under the sunniest skies of Europe"), but was held up for a year in complicated dual-country post-production. And in *Liebling der Götter* (*Darling of the Gods*), Renate had the toughest of her assignments so far: playing the wife of a temperamental tenor, played by the temperamental Emil Jannings, just fresh from his role opposite Marlene Dietrich in *Der Blaue Engel*. That film had made Dietrich a star, but Jannings felt it had been stolen from under his nose by an upstart actress and her besotted director. Never easy to work with, on *Liebling der Götter*, Jannings was a horror.

It was in 1931 that Renate's stardom was cemented, with the title role in the light, sexy comedy *Die Privatsekretärin* (*The Office Girl*), directed by Wilhelm Thiele, who later came to America and, as William Thiele, directed a handful of B-films and the TV series *The*

Lone Ranger. Playing the kind of snappy, flirtatious but essentially innocent secretary looking for love and success in the office (seen in many a pre-Code American film), Renate's was one of the breakout performances of the year. A contemporary entertainment writer noted that "Wilhelm Thiele, aided by an excellent cast, gave the work . . . an original treatment . . . with a stunning pace . . . [Renate Müller] reached the top of the ladder of success and fame. Everywhere in Europe was repeated the almost never-before-seen response to the cheery tale of the little stenotypist." Renate filmed an English-language version of the movie, titled *Sunshine Susie* (her German lead, charming comic actor Hermann Thiming, was replaced by aging British dreamboat Owen Nares). Directed by Victor Saville (*Hindle Wakes, Green Dolphin Street*), this version reached the US and England in 1933.

She made two other films that year as well: *Der Kleine Seitensprung* (*The Little Escapade*), written and directed by Reinhold Schünzel, was a sophisticated marriage and divorce comedy, with Renate as the wife of lawyer Hermann Thimig. This was her first film for the production company Universum Film Aktiengesellschaft (UFA), which made an offer to sign Renate to a long-term contract. After she'd fulfilled her obligations to the German/Austrian company Felsom-Film with *Die Blumenfrau von Lindenau* (released in the US in 1932 as *Storm in a Water Glass*), she moved to UFA. *Die Blumenfrau von Lindenau* was mostly notable for being the fourth film of Viennese starlet Hedy Kiesler, a year before she shot to fame in *Exstase* (*Ecstasy*) and changed her name to Hedy Lamarr.

Renate made three films in 1932, all of them light, sexy comedies. *Wie Sag' Ich's Meinem Mann?* (released in the US in 1934 as *How Shall I Tell My Husband?*) was again directed by Schünzel. *Wenn die Liebe Mode Macht* appeared in the US (also in 1934) as *When Love Sets the Fashion; Mädchen zum Heiraten* (*Girls for Marriage*) was directed by Wilhelm Thiele, and costarred cherubic character actor S.Z. Sakall, who later gained an affectionate following in the US as "Cuddles" Sakall.

Then, just as Renate's career was reaching its height, all hell broke loose in Germany. In early 1933, Adolph Hitler became chancellor, his National Socialist party won the Reichstag elections, and we all pretty much know what *that* led to. Along with all the other aspects of life, show business and the film industry were affected by the new regime, as well. Joseph Goebbels was appointed minister of propaganda in the Nazi government. He ruthlessly and enthusiastically interfered with all forms of the arts: literature, painting and sculpture, radio, music, stage and films. Goebbels was also a notorious skirt-chaser, and Renate Müller was one of many actresses who found herself pursued by him.

Some of Hitler's biographers have suggested that the Führer was obsessed with Renate as well, perhaps because of her startling resemblance to his niece, Geli Raubal, who committed suicide in 1931. But German film historian Cinzia Romani writes in *Tainted Goddesses: Female Film Stars of the Third Reich* that Renate was romantically involved with a Jewish actor, Georg Deutsch, who had wisely fled to France. She was helping to support him, and traveling to see him at every opportunity. This did not sit well with Hitler or Goebbels, but Renate was apparently unwilling to either give him up to or to leave Germany.

Renate starred in three films in 1933, two of which came and went pleasantly, without creating much of a wave: *Walzerkrieg* (*The Waltz War*) was an historical romance starring Anton Walbrook (still billed as Adolf Wohlbrück) as Johann Strauss. The very modern Renate was dolled up in 19th-century frills and danced to waltzes and polkas. And Renate accompanied her frequent collaborator Reinhold Schünzel to France, where they made *Idylle au Caire* (*Season in Cairo*).

But her third 1933 entry was something else altogether. If *Die Privatsekretärin* had rocketed Renate to stardom, then *Viktor und Viktoria*, written and directed by Schünzel, cemented her place in film history, and remains her most famous and influential vehicle. Renate starred as Susanne Lohr, an out-of-work actress who takes over for Viktor Hempel, a female impersonator sidelined by laryngitis. A chorus girl (the bubbly Friedel Pisetta), a society woman (Hilde Hildebrand) and a playboy (Anton Walbrook) all fall for her, and the expected double-entendre zaniness ensues. The film costarred the delightfully intense and over-the-top Hermann Thimig as Viktor, and the stars' byplay is marvelous. Schünzel's direction brings to mind Rouben Mamoulian's *Love Me Tonight* (1932), with the dialogue half-spoken, half-sung. While Renate wasn't remotely

Renate in the mid-1930s.

believable as a man (she looked oddly like Regis Toomey with too much lipstick on), her comic performance, timing and singing are impeccable, and the film—and Renate—remain an absolute treasure.

Critics and audiences alike went wild over *Viktor und Viktoria*: "We haven't seen Renate Müller so radiant and high-spirited since the days of *Die Privatsekretärin*," said one paper. *Der Licht-Bild-Bühne* added, "It is Renate Müller's finest film to date; we cannot praise her too highly!" Released in the US in 1935, the film has been remade several times: in England as *First a Girl* (1935) with Jessie Matthews, then as *Victor/Victoria* (1982), with Julie Andrews. Andrews also went on to appear in the 1990s Broadway version, her role later being taken over by actresses as varied as Liza Minnelli and Raquel Welch.

Renate was now one of Germany's most popular stars, and her fame was spreading to England, France and the US, as well. A fan booklet published about her at this time noted that her personal appearances brought out throngs of fans, that "everywhere she met with an enthusiastic reception and heartfelt displays of appreciation . . . Flowers were constantly showered on her. German [radio] stations have broadcast stories on her work and future developments. Her picture appears in newspapers around the globe. In every corner of the world where a projector whirs, her next film is eagerly anticipated." But even so, Renate found her career running into trouble, as the German film industry spiraled into chaos, its greatest talents absconding for safer countries and its studios beginning to discourage creativity, making only government-approved films.

She made only one film in 1934, but it was both successful and fun to make, being directed by her champion Reinhold Schünzel: *Die Englische Heirat* (*The English Marriage*) is a light comedy poking fun at the upper-class British lifestyle. Two more films followed in 1935: *Liebesleute* (released in the US as *A Pair of Lovers* in 1936), and *Lisolette von der Pfalz* (released overseas as both *Lisolette of the Palatinate* and the more descriptive *The Private Life of Louis XIV*), the kind of escapist historical romance so popular in the early Nazi era.

Renate made another two films in 1936, both filmed at UFA's Babelsberg studios. *Allotria* (released in England as *Hokum*) was a delightful light comedy, directed by Willi Forst (a multi-talented Viennese star, director, writer and producer). *Allotria* was a pleasant, innocuous film about two zany couples (played by Renate, Anton Walbrook, Jenny Jugo, and Heinz Rühmann). Her penultimate production was *Eskapade* (released in England as *His Official Wife*).

One of the writers was Renate's friend Thea von Harbou, famed for her work on the *Dr. Mabuse* series and *Metropolis*. Formerly married to director Fritz Lang, von Harbou was an enthusiastic supporter of the Nazi party and used her influence with Renate to pressure her into cooperating with Goebbels, who wanted her in propaganda films.

Renate's life and career began to spin out of control in 1937, as the political situation darkened and people in the arts felt more pressure to either buckle under or get out. Renate Müller was German-born and bred, and loved her country. She was just old enough to remember the horrors of the First World War and the years of hardship that followed. Like too many others, she just could not believe the current situation would worsen, and she could not bring herself to abandon her homeland. Making Renate's situation more difficult was what happened on March 6, 1937: Marlene Dietrich became an American citizen. The German press had been pillorying her, while government officials and film producers had been begging her to return to Germany all through the 1930s. With this slap in the face, Germany's once-biggest star aligned herself with "the Hollywood Jews." It became more imperative that Germany keep its resident stars in line, and Renate's career looked more constrained than ever.

Despite the fact that her UFA contract gave her script approval, she finally agreed to the demands of the government and her friend Thea von Harbou, and starred in her first and only propaganda film. In *Togger* (1937), directed by Jürgen von Alten, Renate played a newspaper reporter who helps expose the Jewish/Bolshevik control of the German press. One reviewer approvingly noted the plot: ". . . the seizure of power of national socialism and in the concrete action by the simultaneous success of the clearing-up work of an . . . idealistic reporter. The [Jewish-owned] Reuter company is exposed and comes on the dock, and Togger [the leading character, playing Renate's father] sees himself shown to his life's work, the newspaper." Despite this one bit of praise, *Togger* was an overall critical and financial failure.

The mystery of Renate's death begins in late September 1937. In one version of the story, she had checked into a Berlin hospital, ostensibly for knee surgery. Goebbels later released statements that she was actually being treated for morphine and alcohol addiction, but Cinzia Romani says that "these were false charges . . . in order to smear the reputation of an actress beloved by the public, and who, even dead, continued to be a thorn in the side of the regime." In this version of her death, Renate was due to be released from the clinic when, on October 1, she jumped, fell or was pushed from a third-story window. She died instantly (if rumors were to be believed, before she even landed). But in the recent biography, *Renate Müller, Ihr Leben ein Drahtseilakt,* Uwe Klöckner-Draga writes that Renate had fallen out of a window at her home and was taken unconscious to the Augsberg Sanitorium, where she was diagnosed with a knee injury and—more worrying—a possible concussion. She seemed to be on the road to recovery, receiving visitors and talking of future film projects, but suffered a seizure (related perhaps to brain injuries suffered in the fall) and died—in her hospital bed, not out on the sidewalk—on October 7.

Goebbels ordered that no one from UFA attend Renate's funeral, but her coworkers Lillian Harvey, Willy Fritsch, Sibylle Schmitz and Hans Brausewetter bravely showed up to pay their respects. Thea von Harbou was also on hand, to give an emotional tribute. Renate's death was hushed up in the press, but was the talk of the film industry. Renate certainly had reasons to jump: she saw her country spiraling into chaos, and she saw no more *Privatsekretärin*s or *Viktor und Viktorias* in her future, only more *Toggers*. The government had an equal number of good reasons to have her killed: Renate was unenthusiastic about the regime, was linked to a Jew, and was perilously close to "pulling a Dietrich" and abandoning Germany for a film career elsewhere. There was never any investigation into her death, and so many millions of deaths followed that the mysterious demise of one actress seemed unimportant.

Jack Oakie

He was hardly a matinée idol: a little short, a bit pudgy, with a grinning moon-face and tiny, sparkling eyes. But Jack Oakie was one of the most likable players of the 1930s and '40s. Indeed, he was rarely out of work: Oakie made nearly 90 films, including 44 in the 1930s and 21 in the 1940s. Whether in big-budget comedies, B-westerns or football flicks, Jack Oakie was always a bracing breath of fresh air.

Jack Oakie wasn't really an "Okie." He was born Lewis Delaney Offield in Sedalia, Missouri, on November 12, 1903. But he was raised in Muskogee, Oklahoma, leading to the nickname which stuck for life ("Jack" was from an early stage role). His father is a shadowy figure: he died when Jack was young and is barely mentioned in interviews or memoirs. His mother, however, was a remarkable woman. Mary Evelyn Offield founded several schools and taught psychology at Columbia University in New York. Mother and son were devoted to each other (she can be spotted playing Oakie's mother in the 1933 film *Too Much Harmony*).

While in New York, the teenaged Oakie worked as a runner on Wall Street, narrowly escaping death in the 1920 terrorist bombing of the Treasury Building. A natural mimic and wisecracker, Jack began appearing in amateur variety shows, making his professional debut as a chorus boy in George M. Cohan's *Little Nellie Kelly*. He learned his trade in a handful of musicals: *Sharlee* (1923), *Innocent Eyes* (1924), the revue *Artists and Models* (1925), *Peggy-Ann* (1927). While with *Innocent Eyes*, Jack briefly dated fellow chorister Lucille LeSueur, who shortly thereafter decamped for Los Angeles and became Joan Crawford.

But it was in vaudeville that Jack really came into his own. "It was the happiest and most instructive time of my career," he later said. He toured the country with comic Lulu McConnell ("there was no funnier woman onstage, ever"). They did up to six shows a day, finally playing the Palace in New York. By 1927, Jack felt he had gone as far as he could go onstage and determined to crash the movies.

Unlike many stage players, Jack hit Hollywood in mid-1927, before the talkie craze. He had done a few bits in silents, but no billed roles. At a party, he met director Wesley Ruggles, stepped up to him and brashly inquired, "What are you doing for a comic?" Ruggles hired Jack for his first real film role, in *Finders Keepers* (1928). He made another four silents, *Road House, Sin Town, The Fleet's In* and *Someone to Love.* Jack's style depended largely on verbal humor, so the new popularity of talking films provided him with a shot in the arm.

He signed with Paramount in 1928 (staying there through 1934), debuting as a supporting player in the crime drama *The Dummy* that same year (playing "Dopey" Hart). He made ten films in 1929, including Clara Bow's *The Wild Party* and the musical *Close Harmony,* and shared star billing with Jeanette MacDonald in *Let's Go Native.* In the college comedy *Sweetie,* he teamed with Helen Kane and sang the jaw-dropping school song parody "Alma Mammy." Clara Bow was one of Jack's favorite costars, and they remained friends till she died in 1965. He regretted that "the little girl's magnificent red hair and purple eyes were lost on the screen" in the days of black and white, and he was impressed by her acting talent. "The Redhead was one of the greatest emotional actresses, ever," he wrote, also remembering her many kindnesses when he was a newcomer and she was the biggest star at Paramount.

By the time the 1930s dawned, Jack Oakie was obviously a comer. From the start, he was a scene-stealer. While the stars would carry the plotline, Jack would be doing his already familiar double- (and triple-) takes, bellowing out his lines shamelessly. Like fellow vaudevillians Jimmy Durante, Helen Kane, Joe E. Brown and Bert Lahr, Jack was not a classical actor; he didn't create characters, he simply said his lines as Jack Oakie. That was what directors and audiences wanted: the same reliably funny Jack Oakie from film to film.

The quintessential Jack Oakie, 1935.

Early in his career, Jack was teamed with fellow vaudevillian Richard "Skeets" Gallagher, a blond, laconic and sleepy-eyed comic. Though the two never clicked like Laurel and Hardy, they costarred in six films between 1929 (*Close Harmony*) and 1933 (*Alice in Wonderland*, both unrecognizable in costume and make-up). Like the ill-advised teaming of Jimmy Durante and Buster Keaton at MGM, this eventually fizzled out.

Within a few years of his arrival in Hollywood, Jack was known as The World's Oldest Freshman, due to his appearance in such collegiate films as *The Wild Party, Sweetie, Touchdown, College Humor, College Rhythm* and *Collegiate*. "I played football for State for over ten years," he laughed, "advancing from a coach in the first one to a freshman in the last." In that last film, *Rise and Shine* (1941), the 38-year-old portrayed an 18-year-old ("Linda Darnell was 17 and she played a senior," he noted).

But it wasn't only college boys Jack was playing through the 1930s. He was a brush salesman turned Olympics scout in the hilarious screwball farce *Million Dollar Legs*, an unwilling gangster in *Dancers in the Dark* (both with Lyda Roberti, 1932); Clark Gable's gold-mining pal in *Call of the Wild* (1935); a radio-station owner in *The Big Broadcast of 1936* (again with Roberti); a manic press agent in *The Affairs of Annabel* (1938). This last film, costarring Lucille Ball, was followed up with *Annabel Takes a Tour* later that same year.

If Jack Oakie had a dark side, he kept it hidden. "When you see him on the screen, you really know him," said friend and costar Richard Arlen. "He's never at a loss for a wisecrack. Most of his lines in his pictures are his own. He's one of those people who can step onto the set and fire away without any worry and without tripping up." The only hint of personal problems came in 1938, when Jack's first wife, actress Venita Varden, sued him for divorce, citing him with being "jealous, quarrelsome and abusive." (That marriage had lasted two years; Varden later died in the same 1948 plane crash that killed theatrical producer Earl Carroll and showgirl Beryl Wallace.)

But to his friends, Jack was an inveterate socializer ("No matter how hard I work all day I could always find a party to go to"). He kept his dressing-room door open, inviting all in for a drink or a joke between takes. This resulted in lifelong friendships with such coworkers as Clara Bow, Lucille Ball, Joseph Mankiewicz, Bing Crosby, Robert Benchley and Gregory Ratoff. He socialized with non-professionals as well (ironically, one friend, Joseph Kennedy's oldest son, Joe, Jr., nicknamed Jack "Jackie O" in the early 1940s). But Jack was no push-over. In his posthumously published memoirs, he recalled walking off the lot when they refused to make him a

Jack and Venita Varden en route to their Yuma wedding, 1936.

tuxedo for *Paramount on Parade* (1930), and fighting with many cameramen over the years about screen makeup (Jack refused to wear any).

His Paramount contract ending with *Murder at the Vanities* (1934), Jack was free to appear on radio, and he had his own WABC show from 1936-38, hosting such stars as Judy Garland, Benny Goodman, Eddie Cantor and Alice Faye. The 1940s began auspiciously for Jack, with Charlie Chaplin's political satire *The Great Dictator*. Jack's role as Benzini Napaloni, Il Duce of Bacteria, was a brilliant, broad and very thinly disguised slam at Mussolini, and earned Jack a Best Supporting Actor Oscar nomination. He later said that "working with Charlie Chaplin was the highlight of my career. He also made it one of the happiest periods of my life." Jack understood the film's mixed reception, though. "By the time the picture was released," he admitted, "Hitler was no longer a funny little clown to be laughed at."

Jack's follow-up, *Young People* (1940), was a charming little show-business tale with Shirley Temple and Charlotte Greenwood; but his third film that year, *Little Men*, turned out the be a cloying adaptation of one of Louisa May Alcott's lesser books. Happily, Jack found a berth at 20th Century-Fox, where he made a handful of thoroughly enjoyable wartime musicals. He played second banana to (and handily stole scenes from) Alice Faye, Betty Grable, John Payne, Sonja Henie, Victor Mature and June Havoc in such bright, silly and feather-light films as *Tin Pan Alley* (one of his best, 1940), *The Great American Broadcast* and *Song of the Islands* (both 1941), *Iceland* (1942), *Wintertime* (1943), *Hello, Frisco, Hello* (another winner, 1943), and *Sweet and Low-Down* (1944).

He never became more than a well-liked supporting player, but if that bothered him, he never let on. "The pictures I made were called the bread and butter pictures of the studio," Jack wrote. "They cost nothing and made millions, and supported the prestige productions that cost millions and made nothing. Paramount had me working twenty-four hours a day, seven days a week, and when there was a lull they loaned me out to other studios."

Jack continued working steadily through the 1940s, though his weight ballooned alarmingly. "I looked like a walking blimp," he admitted. "I was even too fat for the big screens." He finished out the decade in a handful of Westerns (*Northwest Stampede*, *Tomahawk*). Among Jack's later high-profile films were the Betty Grable/Dan Dailey musical *When My Baby Smiles at Me* and the fast-moving gangster film *Thieves' Highway* (both 1948).

In 1950 he wed actress Victoria Horne and settled down to the life of a gentleman farmer in the San Fernando Valley. Jack had no money worries; he'd invested in AT&T and General Electric "when they were American Smoke Signals and General Candle." Also active in real estate, Jack took up dog breeding, gardening and "loafing."

But he never really retired from acting. Jack had begun appearing on TV as early as 1950, and turned up on such shows as *Kraft Television Theater* and *Studio One* (both 1958), *The Real McCoys* (1962) and *Bonanza* (1966). His last professional appearance was on a 1972 Johnny Carson special, with fellow old-timers Bette Davis, Ethel Waters, Jerry Colonna and Eddie Foy, Jr. Trimmer than he'd been in years, he boasted a shock of thick white hair. He also turned up in films from time to time, including a cameo in *Around the World in 80 Days* (1955) and roles in *The Wonderful Country* (1958), Debbie Reynolds' *The Rat Race* (1960) and *Lover Come Back* (his swan song, 1961).

Jack's sudden death from an aortic aneurysm on January 23, 1978, came as a great shock to his family and friends. He'd been in great spirits and apparently great health right to the end, socializing and giving interviews. More than 300 people attended his funeral; the eulogy was given by Charles "Buddy" Rogers. Chaplin's death a month earlier was noted, and *The Great Dictator* was prominently mentioned in Jack's obituaries. But to most fans, Jack's best moments were in cheesier, bouncier films, using his triple-take to steal scenes from Betty Grable, Alice Faye, Clara Bow or Lucille Ball.

Lyda Roberti

Few things are as uncertain or transient as fame. A handful of performers shine for decades, thanks to the semi-permanence of film, video, DVD—yet many more are forgotten as new stars emerge. Pickford, Valentino, Garbo, Gable, live on in the public mind. But for every Gable there's a Phillips Holmes; for every Pickford a Florence LaBadie—middling-successful yet still talented performers whose names are remembered mainly by people who buy books like this. Such is the case of Lyda Roberti, a delightful musical comedienne who rose with meteoric brilliance in the early 1930s, to be almost completely forgotten ten years later.

No one really knows when—or even where—Lyda Roberti was born, or what her birth name was. Most sources state the place as Warsaw; the date as May 20, and the year as sometime between 1906 and 1909. This may have been an actress-like coyness on her part, but she claimed that she was born into a traveling circus family, there were no records, and that even her parents disagreed on the year. Lyda had a brother, and a sister, Manya, who later appeared in several films and looked (and sounded) like a brunette version of Lyda.

Accounts of her childhood read like the most dubious of press releases—and, indeed, may solely consist of fanciful invention. She was born—the story goes—the daughter of Roberti, a German circus clown, and his Polish bareback-rider wife. The family traveled through Russia, Egypt, China, France, Germany and Turkey. One of the more implausible stories she related was set during the Russian Revolution: according to a newspaper article cited by the marvelous website *glamourgirlsofthesilverscreen.com,* "The maddened revolutionists of Russia set fire to the circus. Her father locks her and her sister in a dressing room fearing they might be harmed if discovered by soldiers. He doesn't think of fire. One of the soldiers, who rushes into the flames to get the prize circus horse as loot, releases the girls from their apparent doom." *Hmmm.* Well, *maybe.* This might have happened to *someone;* why not Lyda and Manya?

We next pick up the Roberti girls in the mid-1920s; their circus gone broke, their family broken up, the sisters performing in nightclubs in Shanghai: the thought of how exactly two lovely teenaged sisters might have earned their keep in Shanghai nightclubs would best have a curtain drawn across it. In any case, sufficient cash was raised for steamer tickets to San Francisco, where Lyda landed a job singing, dancing and clowning in a Fanchon and Marco vaudeville show (among other stars who began their careers as "Fanchonettes" were Cyd Charisse, Joan Crawford, Dorothy Lamour, and Doris Day). In the late 1920s she also appeared in a Larry Cebellos revue which was filmed as a Vitaphone short: recently released on DVD, it does Lyda no favors. She sings and dances a bit, backed by six chorus boys; the number does nothing to show off her talents or her voice.

Lyda worked her way east, and around 1930 was working as a stooge at the Paramount Theater in Brooklyn: keeping the audience entertained between newsreels and features, and when the projector broke down. She was spotted there by comic Lou Holtz, who grabbed her for his upcoming Broadway show: in January 1931, Lyda opened at the 46th Street Theater in the Harold Arlen college musical *You Said It.* "Giddy, giggling Miss Roberti amiably submits to a great deal of gross mistreatment," wrote *Time* magazine, and she all but stole the show with her rendition of Arlen's jazzy "Sweet and Hot." Columnist O.O. McIntyre wrote, "Lyda Roberti, the platinum haired Polish girl, is a new toast of Broadway. And deservedly." Another paper added that "Lyda sizzles it so naïvely that it is worth walking miles down the aisles to see. The boys in the orchestra trenches called for so many encores that Lyda was embarrassed. Lyda looks so cute when she is embarrassed."

Lyda's appeal—still apparent in her films and even in still photos—is in her effervescence. With her platinum-blonde sex appeal, mischievous slit eyes, mile-wide grin and impenetrable accent, it's like Jean Harlow and Carmen Miranda had a baby. One acquaintance described her as "a cool glass of soda on a hot day," and this feeling still bubbles through. Her two-month stint at the Palace Theater on Broadway broke records, and in early 1932 she signed a contract with Paramount and headed west, along with countless other stage performers hopeful about talking pictures. She made her Paramount debut as a torch singer (and comic relief) in the gangster film *Dancers in the Dark*, starring George Raft, Miriam Hopkins and Jack Oakie, who became a lifelong friend: "One reason that we got along so well was just that we both liked laughs," he said.

Lyda hit the jackpot with her second film: *Million Dollar Legs* (released in the summer of 1932) was one of the funniest screwball comedies of the era, equal to the best of the Marx Brothers' Paramount films. Zipping along at a little over an hour, *Million Dollar Legs* is the story of the kingdom of Klopstokia (run by W.C. Fields), which enters the 1932 Olympics, spurred by trainer Jack Oakie. Lyda, in a delicious parody of Garbo's *Mata Hari*, played "Mata Machree, The Woman No Man Can Resist," stealing every frame she was in. Singing "It's Terrific When I Get Hot," vamping the entire Olympic team, and "only being resisted between four and six in the afternoon," Lyda established herself as one of the most brilliant—and sexy—comics of the year.

Next, she was loaned to Goldwyn for the Eddie Cantor comedy *The Kid from Spain* (released in March 1932), with Lyda and Robert Young cast as the world's unlikeliest Hispanics. It's not a bad film; Lyda and Cantor, as the "comedy couple," worked well together, and it did very well at the box office. But after *Million Dollar Legs* (which did not do nearly as well financially), anything is a let-down.

In early 1933, Lyda returned to Broadway for the Gershwin musical *Pardon My English*, which opened and closed like a camera shutter (a total of 43 performances). She sang the title song, as well as "My Cousin in Milwaukee," "Where You Go, I Go," and joined in the finale, "He's Not Himself." The Gershwin brothers were not

Lyda Roberti in her greatest role, as Mata Machree, The Woman No Man Can Resist, in _Million Dollar Legs_, 1932.

themselves, either; the show was quickly forgotten and Lyda's costars, Jack Pearl and George Givot, returned to middling film and stage careers.

In the summer of 1933, Lyda appeared in what was to be her only other really classic film, after *Million Dollar Legs*. The screwball comedy *Three-Cornered Moon* followed the efforts of the *nouveau pauvre* Rimplegar family of Brooklyn to earn a living in the Depression: dizzy matriarch Mary Boland, spoiled daughter Claudette Colbert, and her three brothers. Lyda played unglamorous Swedish cook Jenny, who understood not a word of English and furiously refused to be fired or ousted from her kitchen. It's a small role, but in a brilliant film.

It was pretty much downhill from there; undemanding supporting roles in indifferent films. She appeared again with Colbert in the odd melodrama *Torch Singer* (released shortly after *Three-Cornered Moon*). Both actresses played unwed mothers, but Colbert starred and Lyda had only a brief—though underplayed and touching—bit part. It showed what she was capable of as a dramatic actress, a talent she was never allowed to develop.

Then there was the silly *College Rhythm* (1934), with her pal Jack Oakie—football games, school mascots, huge production numbers, and radio stars Joe Penner and Lanny Ross, making tries at film careers. It was cute and pleasantly innocuous, and Lyda, at least, got to sing the title song, as well as "Take a Number from One to Ten" (both of which she also recorded for Columbia Records). The ups and downs of Hollywood can be read into this film as well: faded silent screen stars Franklyn Farnum and Mary Brian have small roles, while Ann Sheridan and Jane Wyman are uncredited bit players.

Lyda's last lunge at Broadway turned lucky for her: she had a large supporting role, as Clementina Scharwenka, in the hit Jerome Kern musical *Roberta*, about romance and swindling at a dress-design house. Appearing with future film stars Bob Hope, Sydney Greenstreet, Fred MacMurray, and George Murphy, and the great old-timer Fay Templeton, Lyda was in clover. She sang "Something's Got to Happen" with her partner in crime Hope, and soloed "I'll Be Hard to Handle." It ran from late 1933 into the summer of 1934. But when *Roberta* was made into a movie in 1935, Fred Astaire and Ginger Rogers were given the Hope and Roberti roles (Rogers did an infuriatingly good impression of Lyda).

Back in Hollywood in late 1934 with a one-picture Fox contract, she took an apartment at the famed Ravenswood Apartments, home to such stars over the years as Mae West, Burns and Allen, Clark Gable, George Raft and Ava Gardner (in 1936, Lyda moved into her own hilltop home, with a breathtaking view of Los Angeles and a wild, multi-colored design scheme). That Fox film was the unremarkable *George White's 1935 Scandals*, in which she and Cliff Edwards played the comedy couple to leads Alice Faye and James Dunn. It was cute and forgettable, except for one dance number ("The Hunkadola," in which dancers flung around dummy "partners" in a bizarrely sadistic and amusing way).

In the summer of 1935, Lyda was hospitalized for an appendectomy, and met fellow patient Hugh "Bud" Ernst, a tall, dark and handsome pilot and radio executive, laid up after a car accident. The two sparked quickly, and on June 25, 1935, they eloped to Yuma, Arizona. "It is such a change to come home to my apartment and find someone here, someone with whom I can talk over everything, and laugh a little at things that have occurred during the day," Lyda told a reporter shortly after her marriage. "'How can a movie actress be lonely in Hollywood?' I have been asked many times. That is simple. It takes a long time to make good friends and without good friends, one is lonesome." The marriage was a stormy one, with accusations of brutality (Lyda appeared at one event with a black eye). The couple was separated by the spring of 1936, but Lyda put off filing for divorce.

Paramount's *The Big Broadcast of 1936* (released late in 1935) was, at least, an A-film, with Bing Crosby, Burns and Allen, Ethel Merman, Jack Oakie, Bill "Bojangles" Robinson, and Lyda as a temperamental countess dangling her bank account over the head of radio producer Oakie. It was another *College Rhythm* or *George White's 1935 Scandals*—a by-the-book musical with a game cast, a few good songs (notably Ethel Merman's "It's the Animal in Me" and the dreamy classic "Goodnight Sweetheart," sung by the equally dreamy Al Bowlly). Lyda's two songs were forgettable, and so was the script. Lyda's days in features were coming to an end, so she wisely turned to short subjects.

In early 1936, Lyda stepped in to fill the shoes of Thelma Todd, who had died in December 1935, while costarring in a series of

Honeymooners Lyda and Hugh "Bud" Ernst on the S.S. Santa Elena, July 30, 1935.

comedy shorts with Patsy Kelly (the final Kelly/Todd short was released in January 1936). Lyda might have been more cautious: Patsy Kelly was murder on blondes. In 1933, she'd been the passenger in platinum-blond comic and emcee Jean Malin's car when it plunged off the Santa Monica Pier, killing him and injuring Kelly. Then Thelma Todd was found dead in her garage from carbon monoxide poisoning. Blondes should have been steering clear of Kelly by this time.

But Lyda appeared in two silly, inconsequential shorts with her, released in April 1936: *Hill-Tillies* (in which the girls go camping) and *At Sea Ashore* (in which recent immigrant Lyda gets pal Patsy in trouble). Patsy Kelly, of course, played the wise-cracking tough gal, while Lyda was the enthusiastic, bubble-headed blonde, her accent heavier than ever. This was one of producer Hal Roach's many attempts to create a female Laurel and Hardy: ZaSu Pitts and Thelma Todd; Patsy Kelly and Thelma Todd; Patsy Kelly and Pert Kelton, Patsy Kelly and Lyda Roberti. But none of these talented ladies could overcome the indifferent writing and directing of these efforts.

Still, Roach costarred Lyda and Patsy in a full-length (though obviously low-budget) feature, *Nobody's Baby* (released in April 1937). The fact that it had many of the same staff and crew as the shorts hints that it was merely another two-reeler, stretched out to 68 minutes. The film is not bad: the girls play nurses in training (lots of slapstick) who care for an abandoned baby in their shared apartment (lots of heart-tugging). Both Lyda and Patsy get some good moments, but *Nobody's Baby* would have worked better cut into two snappier, separate shorts, about nurses and bachelor mothers. The *New York Times* review called Lyda "the Lionel Stander of soubrettes," which one hopes she took as a compliment.

By now, both Lyda's career and health were fading. After five years at Paramount, Goldwyn, Fox, and MGM's Hal Roach offshoot, she still had not starred in an A-feature. At about 30, she was suffering from what appears to have been a congenital heart problem. At this late date there is no telling what her ailment was: endocarditis, arrhythmia, myocarditis, cardiomyopathy—the possibilities are many, and in the 1930s, treatment was basically minimal, surgery or transplant unthinkable. All that we do know is that Lyda steadily

The mile-wide smile of Lyda Roberti, 1935.

grew weaker through 1936 and '37, which hardly helped her film career (in mid-1936, she had to drop out of the Paramount feature *Wives Never Know* because of illness). No studio was going to sign an uninsurable actress to a longterm contract.

In early 1937, Lyda's estranged husband, Bud Ernst, returned to his ailing wife, and stayed with her to the end. (After Lyda's death, Ernst married Mary Pickford's niece, Gywnne, and then starlet and future TV journalist Betty Furness; neither marriage worked out, and Ernst committed suicide in 1950.)

Hal Roach gave Lyda a cameo in the Patsy Kelly feature comedy *Pick a Star*, released in May 1937. The story of a small-town rube (Rosina Lawrence) trying to hit it big in Hollywood, it featured a scene in which "Dagmar, the great foreign star" (Lyda) is shooting a musical number on a soundstage. Wearing a Gainsborough-inspired gown and huge hat, she looked great and gave the number all her accustomed hotcha. But—considering her health problems—the lyrics are more than a little disturbing:

> *I don't need a physician, he can't do me no good—*
> *Still, I'm in a bad condition, let me make myself understood . . .*
> *Oh, what an ache, and I think my heart will break,*
> *And I'm so afraid I'll need first aid—*
> *Oh, ho, I got it bad!*

It was Lyda's next-to-last movie appearance. Columbia hired her for the Joe E. Brown comedy *Wide Open Faces*, released in April 1938. She was fourth-billed, in a crime caper about a soda jerk (Brown) trying to help out his girlfriend (ingénue Jane Wyman). Lyda looked thin and drawn in her few scenes, trying to give her comic vamp as much oomph as she could still summon. In one publicity shot, she appears to be holding onto a chair for support.

She was dead before the film was released. Somewhere, somehow, a rumor started that Lyda died of a heart attack "while bending over to tie her shoes," one of the odder Hollywood urban legends. She suffered heart failure on the night of March 12 (shoelace involvement is anyone's guess). Her doctor was summoned but there was nothing he could do: Lyda's husband was at her bedside when she died. The end of her life is as clouded in mystery as the beginning. One source has her buried at Forest Lawn Memorial Park as Lyda Roberti Ernst; but according to the website *findagrave.com*, she was cremated and the location of her ashes, "given to a family or friend," is unknown.

Norma Shearer

"Sure, Norma gets all the good parts," groused Joan Crawford. "She sleeps with the boss." Joan had a point. Norma Shearer's position as the wife of MGM's vice president and production supervisor Irving Thalberg certainly got her dibs on some of the best scripts. But (and even Joan might have grudgingly admitted this), Norma carried those films on her own merits. Sometimes being the protégée of a well-placed benefactor can be a double-edged sword. Marion Davies—one of the sprightliest actresses of her day—was derided as just the lucky mistress of William Randolph Hearst. The offspring of Douglas Fairbanks, Lon Chaney and others had to fight for recognition in their own right. And Norma Shearer has often been brushed off as just Mrs. Irving Thalberg, the First Lady of MGM. But the availability of Norma's films on TV and DVD reveals that she was a talented actress, much less mannered and pompous than posterity will have it. She played a wide array of roles—classic and modern, comic and tragic—with impressive force and intelligence.

Norma Shearer was born on August 11, 1902, in Montreal, the third child of Edith (Fisher) and Andrew Shearer. Norma's brother Douglas later followed her to Hollywood and became head of MGM's sound department, winning 12 Academy Awards and revolutionizing many aspects of talking film production. Her sister was saddled with the unfortunate name Athole (one can *imagine* the childhood teasing). Not surprisingly, Athole's life was not as productive as those of her siblings; at one time the wife of director Howard Hawks, she suffered from emotional problems and alcoholism.

Andrew Shearer ran the James Shearer Lumber Company (founded by his father) until it failed shortly after World War I. Dropping from the upper- to lower-middle class, Edith determined to make stars of her daughters. Ambitious, intelligent and personable as a child, Norma fell right in with her mother's plans. The three female Shearers moved to New York in 1920, leaving their menfolk behind.

Showing an impressive amount of gall, the teenaged Norma wangled an introduction to Broadway's "glorifier of American girls," Florenz Ziegfeld. Not surprisingly, she got nowhere with him. Norma Shearer, it must be admitted, was no great beauty, and not till the late 1920s did she develop the glamorous shell which would overcome her plain appearance. She had a strong chin, long nose, and Mrs. Patrick Campbell once accurately purred about her, "such *pretty* little eyes—and so close together, too!" A minor cast in one eye, and rather chubby legs, did not put Norma in the Ziegfeld Girl category.

Not discouraged one bit, Norma managed to get extra work in the 1920 films *The Flapper* (quite visible, as one of Olive Thomas' school friends), *The Restless Sex*, and D.W. Griffith's *Way Down East*; she had featured roles in the B-romance *The Stealers* and the two-reel *Torchy's Millions*. Then nothing, for a whole year, at which point she got a role in Universal's boxing serial *The Leather Pushers* (1921). Suddenly she found herself working in film after film for Universal, most of them cheap programmers made on the east coast and quickly forgotten. But she studied her craft: smart and a quick learner, Norma caught on to the art of film acting and also became an expert in makeup, lighting, and camera angles. In 1922 and '23, she acted in *The Man Who Paid, Channing of the Northwest, The Devil's Partner, The Bootleggers, A Clouded Name* (in which Edith Shearer appeared with her daughter), and *Man and Wife*. By early 1923, she was an up-and-coming starlet, and other studios tried to lure her away from Universal. Her roles and films there had been unremarkable, and she was willing to be lured.

Recognizing that the future of the film industry lay in Los Angeles, Norma accepted an offer from Louis B. Mayer Productions and headed west in April 1923. Her first day in the studio, she met a darkly handsome, puppy-eyed young man whom she took for an office boy: he was, of course, 24-year-old Irving Thalberg, himself a recent émigré from Universal and now Mayer's production manager. The two did not hit it off right away, though each admired the other's talent and drive (it had been Thalberg, in fact, who had suggested hiring Norma). But her first Mayer film was actually made on loan to First National, and did not show much promise: in *The Wanters* (1923), she played second fiddle to the effervescent Marie Prevost. She had the lead, as a flapper, in *Pleasure Mad,* then was loaned again, to Warners, for *Lucretia Lombard.*

Nineteen-twenty-four was Norma's make-or-break year, as she had not yet risen above the "slightly promising starlet" rank at Mayer. She made eight films that year (during which her studio morphed into Metro-Goldwyn-Mayer). On loan to Fox, she appeared in *The Wolf Man* (about alcoholism, not lycanthropy, with John Gilbert). At her home studio, she was built up slowly through *The End of the World, Broadway After Dark,* and *Blue Waters* (as an unlikely Indian maiden), then *He Who Gets Slapped* and *The Snob,* both again with John Gilbert (in the first, she was a circus rider loved by Lon Chaney; in the second a small-town girl).

She also had her first serious affair, with Victor Fleming, who directed her in *Empty Hands.* Thalberg, at the time, was pursuing an affair with Constance Talmadge (who was herself more interested in hanging around with her pals Billy Haines and Jimmy Shields). By this time, Thalberg and Norma were friends, accompanying each other to red-carpet events. He took a more active interest in her budding career, and in 1925 she appeared in another six films, only one on loan-out (*Waking Up the Town,* costarring and directed by Jack Pickford).

Norma's glamorous side began coming out in some of her 1925 films: as a honeymooner in the romantic comedy *Excuse Me,* as a *Slave of Fashion,* and as a showgirl in *Pretty Ladies* (which also featured ambitious young newcomers Joan Crawford and Myrna Loy). Norma costarred for the second time with Lon Chaney in *The Tower of Lies,* an odd film about Swedish villagers. And she showed her versatility in *Lady of the Night,* playing both a shy deb and her lookalike, a tough moll. Playing the back of Norma's head in the two-shots was Joan Crawford, who never quite recovered from the experience.

By 1926, Norma Shearer was firmly placed as one of MGM's leading younger stars, complete with stacks of fan mail, magazine covers, publicity and a good salary coming her way. Mae Murray and Lillian Gish were on their way out the studio's door by then, and Greta Garbo and Joan Crawford were just barely getting started. Norma's main competition at MGM for romantic leads were Marion Davies, Renée Adorée, and Eleanor Boardman. Norma made only three films in 1926, and none of them were huge hits (*His Secretary, The Devil's Circus* and *The Waning Sex*)—but the studio had long-term plans for her, and the last year of the silent era was to be an important one for her, both professionally and personally.

She got a new five-year contract in 1927, which would eventually raise her salary from $1,000 a week to $5,000. Her four 1927 films were also a step up. *The Demi-Bride, Upstage* and *After Midnight* all did well and got good notices, and in *The Student Prince in Old Heidelberg* Norma had her first real hit. Costarring with Ramon Novarro, Norma played a girlish waitress to his boyish heir apparent. The two were terrific together, and the film was in MGM's best late-silent style: romantic, funny, beautifully shot and scripted, *The Student Prince* was one of that year's best films.

By the end of 1927, Norma was also Mrs. Irving Thalberg. The two married on September 29 at Thalberg's home (Norma converted to Judaism shortly before the marriage). The two workaholics took a week's honeymoon and returned to the studio (their children, Irving, Jr., and Katherine, were born in 1930 and 1935). While the Thalbergs gave dinners and parties, they never became society leaders like Mary Pickford and Douglas Fairbanks; nor were they a "fun couple" like Ben Lyon and Bebe Daniels, or Lilyan Tashman and Edmund Lowe. Anita Page recalled that Norma was too much the Great Lady to get familiar with: "You didn't just walk up and say hello to Norma Shearer," she said.

There was, of course, talk that Norma had married Irving as a cool-headed career move. Certainly a woman as ambitious as Norma cannot have ignored the good he did her career. But Irving Thalberg was quite a catch on his own merits: handsome, intelligent, funny. Whether or not Norma loved him, she proved to be a terrific, protective wife and made him very happy. The Thalbergs, now living at their Santa Monica beach house, played host to F. Scott

Fitzgerald, who later portrayed them in his story *Crazy Sunday* and his book *The Last Tycoon*. Norma also spent much time guarding her husband's health, trying to keep him from overworking and shielding him from unnecessary annoyances.

Silent films were in their death throes in 1928, and Norma made only two films that year, *The Latest from Paris* and *The Actress*. The Thalbergs also took a trip to Europe: partly for fun, partly to scout for performers and directors, partly for Thalberg's health (it was already known that his heart was weak and his life expectancy limited). It was a risky time for even the biggest stars, but Norma's voice tests went well and her career was safe. After a part-talkie, *Lady of Chance* (1929), she fought like a tigress for the lead in *The Trial of Mary Dugan*, an all-talkie adapted from a Broadway hit. Norma's quiet, well-thought-out performance still stands up well, and the film was a hit. That same year, she did a funny little *Romeo and Juliet* parody with John Gilbert (shot in color) in *The Hollywood Revue of 1929*.

But good talkies were hard to come by in those first couple of years, even for MGM's First Lady. *The Last of Mrs. Cheyney, Their Own Desire, Let Us Be Gay* (all 1930) and *Strangers May Kiss* (1931) were stagy teacup dramas, all but unwatchable today. The only interesting part of *Let Us Be Gay* is in the early scenes, where Norma, as a drab housewife, allowed herself to be filmed without any makeup (she looks amazingly like Beatrice Lillie). But even MGM's new stable of glittering actresses had their flops in those earliest talkie years: Joan Crawford's *Untamed*, Garbo's *Romance*, Marion Davies' *Not So Dumb*.

Norma glamorized herself further with help from studio portrait photographer George Hurrell and won the role of *The Divorcée* (1930), a racy pre-Code film about a loose-living, two-timing couple (Norma and Chester Morris). The role won Norma a Best Actress Oscar (her competition, of course, groused that it was just a popularity contest—which, to be fair, the Oscars have *always* been). Just as big a hit was *A Free Soul* (1931), with Norma as a slutty rich girl involved with gangster Clark Gable (both Gable and Shearer come off much better than Lionel Barrymore, who does his "crotchety Lionel" schtick). Norma was sexy and sleek in the role, her Adrian gowns and softer hairdo showing her at her loveliest.

Norma Shearer, the personification of art deco, ca. 1932.

Less happy was *Private Lives* (1931). Noël Coward's brittle, witty comedy dragged onscreen, and Norma and costar Robert Montgomery were too young and not nearly sophisticated or comedically adept enough for their roles. Only slightly more interesting was *Strange Interlude* (with Gable again, 1932). Adapted from Eugene O'Neill's rather forced (and already much-parodied) drama, it involved a tragic, long-term love affair—the asides that made the stage version so talked-about (and so *long*) were wisely done as voice-overs in the film. Norma had the first of her great tear-jerking period pieces in *Smilin' Through* (1932), a terrific four-hankie melodrama about a murdered Victorian bride who is reborn a generation later, looked over by the ghost of her older self. It's silly and sentimental and over-the-top, but thoroughly enjoyable, and Norma seems to take the goings-on very much to heart. Audiences loved it, shopgirls crying so hard they swallowed their gum.

It was 1934 before Norma made another film: she took time off to nurse her husband through a heart attack. They took a trip to Havana and then Germany (where they were alarmed by anti-Jewish demonstrations) and then Paris. On his return, Thalberg's health was not helped by having to fight Louis B. Mayer, who was trying to oust him from MGM. A guarded truce was arranged, though Thalberg was no longer head of production.

Norma next appeared in *Riptide*, another teacup drama, which was not an easy shoot, as Lilyan Tashman (who played Norma's sister) was dying of cancer. From 1934 on, Norma made fewer films per year than most MGM stars, and they tended to be huge prestige productions. They cost a fortune, took forever to shoot and flopped in small towns, but they made MGM look good and satisfied Thalberg's desire for "important" films. Norma's first was *The Barretts of Wimpole Street* (1934), from the Broadway hit starring Katharine Cornell. Norma gave a terrific performance as poetess Elizabeth Barrett, and Charles Laughton enjoyably chewed the scenery as her thoroughly dreadful father. Sadly, Brian Aherne (Broadway's Robert Browning) turned down the part, which was played onscreen by a rather chilly Fredric March.

Norma looked after her husband's health and fretted over her sister's while preparing for her next film, which was not released till 1936. It was at this time that she famously arrived

Norma Shearer and Irving Thalberg returning from a 1933 vacation.

at Carole Lombard's "White Ball" in a red dress, earning Lombard's
enmity and possibly inspiring a similar scene in the film *Jezebel*.

In retrospect, *Romeo and Juliet* was probably a mistake; everyone was too old for their roles: Norma at 34, Leslie Howard (Romeo) at 43, John Barrymore (Mercutio) at 54. Norma had no Shakespearean background, and faced classically-trained costars Howard, Barrymore, Edna May Oliver and Basil Rathbone. Still, she worked her tail off, and did better than her enemies hoped. She seemed to understand her lines (no small feat with Shakespeare) and there was a minimum of starry-eyed twinkling. The film premiered on September 2, 1936, and Irving Thalberg died on the 13th.

Many thought that Norma's career would end with the death of her husband. But she owned MGM stock, still had box-office pull, and had a very big film in mid-production. In 1936, she signed a new three-year contract, giving her $150,000 per film. That next very big film was *Marie Antoinette*, not released till 1938, after more than two years in production. It might have been terrible, but was instead a triumph, helped by the script, Adrian's 18th-century gowns and Sydney Guilaroff's towering wigs, Cedric Gibbons' sets, and the fact that Norma, Robert Morley (Louis XVI) and Tyrone Power (Count Axel Fersen) eerily resembled their real-life counterparts. Norma gave perhaps her best performance as Marie Antoinette, aging from a giddy princess ("Think of it, Mamma, I am to be Queen of France!") to an imperious Queen to a haggard, defeated victim of revolutionary terror. Her last scenes were remarkable and commendably underplayed. Predictably, the film did well in big cities, but business quickly fell off in smaller towns. *Marie Antoinette* lost money for MGM but it remains one of the era's most satisfying and impressive period pieces.

Much smaller but just as enjoyable were Norma's two 1939 films, *Idiot's Delight* and *The Women*, both adapted from recent Broadway hits. In the former, she took Lynn Fontanne's part as a role-playing opportunist (in a bizarre art-deco wig) who meets former vaudeville partner Clark Gable just as war is overtaking Europe. The film works right up till the last moments, when playwright Robert Sherwood's tragic finale is watered down.

The Women was Norma's last great film, and one of her best—also, perhaps, her only successful comic performance. She tended to go all arch and try too hard in comedy, but director George Cukor toned her down and reined her in here. *The Women* starred nearly

A chic Norma in her next-to-last film, *We Were Dancing* (1942).

every actress on the lot: Norma as a noble, wronged wife; Joan Crawford as her gold-digging rival; Rosalind Russell as a backstabbing gossip; Joan Fontaine as a naïf; Paulette Goddard as a brassy showgirl; Mary Boland as a giddy dowager; and Marjorie Main as a rough-edged innkeeper. Clare Booth Luce's script was only slightly toned-down for the screen, but it's still an engagingly funny and smart catfight (the 1956 remake was ghastly, as was the "what were they thinking?" 2008 version).

In 1940, Norma starred in *Escape*, a war drama (with all the Judaism carefully excised from the source book). Though the great Alla Nazimova gave a brilliant performance as the woman Norma and Robert Taylor try to smuggle out of Germany, the film failed to make a mark in those pre-Pearl Harbor days. Norma turned down *Mrs. Miniver* and *Gone With the Wind* (she would have been terrific in the former and terrible in the latter). Her last two films were the dated society comedies *We Were Dancing* and *Her Cardboard Lover* (both 1942). "On those two, nobody but myself was trying to do me in," she later admitted. Norma looked great: at 40, she had an auburn, fluffy hairdo, flattering gowns and makeup, and looked like a lovely sophisticate on the verge of a promising middle age.

MGM's three biggest female stars, Norma Shearer, Greta Garbo and Joan Crawford, slunk away from the studio almost simultaneously. Only Crawford's career would rise from the ashes. But Norma Shearer surprised everyone by finding personal happiness. There were later rumors about her having had affairs with Robert Taylor, Tyrone Power, Maurice Chevalier, even Mickey Rooney, though no one will ever know the truth at this late date. After six years as The Widow Thalberg, Norma married 28-year-old ski instructor Martin Arrougé. She never looked back. Everyone gave the marriage a year at most, but the Arrougés stayed married till Norma's death and were apparently quite happy. Norma made noises about returning to the screen from time to time, but never seriously considered any offers.

The Arrougés had some thirty good years together, but Norma Shearer was denied a happy ending. By the mid-1970s she was exhibiting signs of what was probably vascular dementia or Alzheimer's (she began calling her poor husband "Irving," which he bore with good grace); her eyesight was failing as well. She'd been a recluse for several years when she finally entered the Motion Picture Country Home in 1980. She was well-cared-for, but her physical and mental health declined quickly, and she died of pneumonia on June 12, 1983. Though she had been out of the public eye for 40 years, Norma Shearer got the kind of obituaries usually given to dowager empresses and First Ladies.

Barbara Stanwyck

There were giants striding the screen in the 1930s and '40s: four actresses so talented, hardworking and versatile that they became laws unto themselves. Joan Crawford and Bette Davis have also become high-camp figures of fun, as they both had such wildly theatrical offscreen lives, and their performances could sometimes veer into self-parody. But Barbara Stanwyck and Claudette Colbert stand the test of time in each and every film: our memories of them are not overshadowed by scandals or vituperative daughters. One rarely sees a Stanwyck or Colbert drag queen. But these ladies were fully the equal—sometimes the superior—of Davis and Crawford. Barbara Stanwyck, in particular, was peerless in everything from high and low comedy to drama to musicals to *film noir*. She never took a false step.

Barbara Stanwyck ("Missy" to her friends, never "Babs"), was born Ruby Stevens on July 16, 1907, in Brooklyn. It was a tough childhood: her mother was killed in a streetcar accident when Ruby was four; her father deserted her and her four siblings. Ruby lived with neighbors and foster families, and left school at 13 to take entry-level jobs in department stores and offices. Tall, smart and pretty by age 15, she became a chorus girl in New York nightclubs and speakeasies. Her older sister Millie was already in show business and acted as Ruby's sponsor. Through the mid-1920s, Ruby hoofed, fought off overly-friendly customers, and learned the ropes of show business (she roomed with Mae Clarke, another dancer who would go on to Hollywood fame). She danced and acted in a few sketches in *George White's Scandals, Keep Kool* and *Artists and Models* (all 1923), *Innocent Eyes* (1924—other choristers included Joan Crawford and Jack Oakie), the 1924 touring edition of Ziegfeld's 1923 *Follies*, *Gay Paree* (1925), and in vaudeville.

Ruby hit the legit with *The Noose*, a 1926 Broadway drama which required a dancing actress for a small part. She was soon promoted to a larger role, and chose this time to change her name. Her story was always that she saw an old poster or program advertising "Jane Stanwyck in *Barbara Frietchie*," but there is no evidence that an actress named Jane Stanwyck existed, let alone one who appeared in *Barbara Frietchie* (the cast lists for the 1899 and 1901 Broadway versions of that show do not have any Janes or Stanwycks in them). Whatever its origin, though, the name stuck.

The Noose also inaugurated Barbara's love life—she and the play's star, Rex Cherryman, began a serious affair. The married Cherryman, a 30-year-old actor who had appeared in a handful of movies (including Alla Nazimova's 1921 *Camille*) and Broadway shows, was involved with Barbara for two years. The affair ended with Cherryman's death from blood poisoning in mid-1928. Cherryman was only the first of the famous men whom Barbara Stanwyck would romance. In 1928, probably on the rebound after Cherryman's death, she married 31-year-old emcee and Broadway actor Frank Fay, then at the height of his fame. His career—and their marriage—quickly went downhill despite (or perhaps because of) the son they adopted in 1932. Barbara and Frank divorced in 1936. Her only other marriage—and, as far as can be ascertained, her only other love—was actor Robert Taylor, four years her junior. They met while costarring in *His Brother's Wife* (1936) and married in 1939. They divorced in 1951 (Taylor later married actress Ursula Thiess), but remained close friends till his death in 1969. If she had any other heartbreaks or love affairs, Barbara kept them to herself.

From her supporting role in *The Noose*, Barbara was advanced to leading lady in *Burlesque* (1927-28), a showbiz drama starring Hal Skelly—producer Arthur Hopkins praised Barbara's "rough poignancy," as good a description of her charms as was ever voiced. The film industry had already shown some interest in the fast-rising actress. She was a bit player in her only silent, *Broadway Nights*, in 1927, but hated the experience.

But then talkies arrived. In 1929 Barbara and Frank Fay headed

A tough but chic Barbara Stanwyck in 1931.

west for film contracts—hers with United Artists, where she starred in the remake of Norma Talmadge's *The Locked Door* (1929). After another programmer (*Mexicali Rose*), a savior arrived in the person of 33-year-old director Frank Capra, who cast her as a good-hearted, tough-talking "party girl" in *Ladies of Leisure* (1930). Capra quickly guided Barbara through three more signature roles: she portrayed a fraudulent preacher in *The Miracle Woman* (1931), had an affair with a married politician in *Forbidden* (1932), and was courted by a Chinese warlord in *The Bitter Tea of General Yen* (1933). "She knew nothing about camera tricks," Capra later recalled, "how to 'cheat' her looks so her face could be seen, how to restrict her body movements in close shots. She just turned it on—and everything else on the stage stopped." The director teamed with the star only once more, for 1941's *Meet John Doe*, in which Barbara played a scheming, cynical newspaper reporter.

For *Ladies of Leisure* (1930), Barbara signed with Columbia, and spent the next few years being exchanged back and forth between that studio and Warner Brothers. In 1935 she signed an unusual nonexclusive contract with RKO, and pretty much freelanced for the rest of her career.

Through the early 1930s, Barbara Stanwyck established her reputation in a field overflowing with other young Broadway starlets: Bette Davis, Miriam Hopkins, Katharine Hepburn, Claudette Colbert, Joan Blondell. Barbara was lower-keyed and less mannered than Davis and Hepburn; less glamorous than Colbert. She was "real," and she also proved to be the personification of no-nonsense professionalism, making her popular with directors and coworkers alike. The hard-to-please Cecil B. DeMille (who directed Barbara in *Union Pacific* in 1939) said of her, "I have never worked with an actress who is more cooperative, less temperamental and a better workman, to use my term of highest compliment."

She starred in 16 films from 1930-34, and of course not all of them were choice projects. But Barbara brought a freshness and tough honesty to even minor fare like *Ten Cents a Dance* (1931), *Gambling Lady* (1934) and *The Woman in Red* (1935). Some of her early projects remain delights: she was a menaced *Night Nurse* (1931), the citified mail-order bride of farmer George Brent in *The Purchase Price* (1932), a bank robber in *Ladies They Talk About* (1933) and—

in one of the most notorious films of the pre-Code era—an amoral climber in *Baby Face* (1933).

The careers of many of her contemporaries hit snags in the late 1930s (the infamous "Box Office Poison" tag), but Barbara Stanwyck's star only continued to rise. Her 17 films from 1935-40 included some of her best. Some of these were offbeat "prestige" productions the actress fought for: *A Message to Garcia* (1936, a Spanish-American War drama), the Sean O'Casey play *The Plough and the Stars* (1936, directed by John Ford), and Clifford Odets' *Golden Boy* (1939, costarring her lifelong friend William Holden). There were also the rousing historical Westerns *Annie Oakley* (1935) and *Union Pacific* (1939), and a handful of screwball comedies, in which Barbara proved herself fully the equal of Carole Lombard and Claudette Colbert. In particular, *The Mad Miss Manton* (1938, as a crime-solving debutante) is the funniest of her early roles. And she got her first of four Oscar nominations for *Stella Dallas* (1937), Olive Higgins Prouty's evergreen mother-love weepie. As the annoying yet sympathetic Stella, Barbara brought a gaudy trashiness to a part that would have been easy to overplay.

By 1940, the 33-year-old star was at the top of her game, and married to one of Hollywood's handsomest leading men. The 1940s proved to be her defining decade, during which she aged from a zany young cutie (Preston Sturges' comedy/drama *Remember the Night*, 1940) to a whining harridan stalked by her husband's paid killer (the harrowing *Sorry, Wrong Number*, 1948, and another Oscar nod). She appeared in some of her best comedies during this decade: Preston Sturges' *The Lady Eve* (1941), as a con artist after millionaire Henry Fonda; Howard Hawks' *Ball of Fire* (1941), in which she was on-the-lam stripper "Sugarpuss" O'Shea; and the charmingly home-spun *Christmas in Connecticut* (1945). She turned on a dime to drama with Capra's *Meet John Doe* (1941, with Gary Cooper), the episodic *Flesh and Fantasy* (1943) and the *noir* classic *The Strange Love of Martha Ivers* (1946).

She played her most iconic role in the 1940s—it was also one of her least typical. Decked out in a blonde wig, Barbara was the most evil of *film-noir* antiheroines in Billy Wilder's *Double Indemnity* (1944). Based on James M. Cain's novel (but ditching the devil-worship subplot of that work), *Double Indemnity* featured

Barbara Stanwyck in 1944, the year she made *Double Indemnity.*

Barbara as the conscienceless murderess Phyllis Dietrichson, and placed her in the pantheon of such glamorous villainesses as Rita Hayworth's Gilda, Mary Astor's Brigid O'Shaughnessy (*The Maltese Falcon*) and Gene Tierney's Ellen Berent (*Leave Her to Heaven*). Making her star turn even more amazing is that her gimlet-eyed Phyllis was bookended by a bump-and-grind queen (*Lady of Burlesque*) and the warm-hearted magazine writer of *Christmas in Connecticut.*

Time caught up with Barbara Stanwyck in the 1950s, and good leading roles became harder to come by. Still, she appeared in 22 films through that decade, a good many of these being Westerns. Barbara's tough-gal persona transferred well to the Wild West and she rode horseback and handled guns and whips like a female John Wayne in such horse operas as *The Furies* (1950), *Cattle Queen of Montana* (1955), *The Maverick Queen* (1956) and *Forty Guns* (1957). There were a few good, tense melodramas as well: in Fritz Lang's *Clash By Night* (1952, with Robert Ryan and a young Marilyn Monroe), she played a bitter man-hater; she sailed on the *Titanic* (1953) with Clifton Webb; she was a hard-driving executive in the all-star *Executive Suite* (1954). She also brought a professional sincerity to such wheel-spinners as *The File on Thelma Jordon* (1950), *The Moonlighter* (1953), *Crime of Passion* (1957), and other 1950s projects.

By the time she was in her early forties, Barbara's hair had begun to show white streaks. Remarkably for stars of her (or our) era, she elected to go natural. Through the early 1950s, her hair lightened from dark brown to a brilliant, flattering silver (except for a few films in which she wore wigs). By the time of *The Violent Men* (1955), the 48-year-old sported the short, slightly bouffant white hairdo that became her latter-day trademark.

Barbara made only three more theatrical-release films after 1960: the bizarre lesbian/whorehouse drama *Walk on the Wild Side* (1962), the Elvis Presley vehicle *Roustabout* (1964), and the William Castle horror flick *The Night Walker* (1965), which she made only because her ex-husband Robert Taylor costarred. The rest of her films were early 1970s TV releases, all rather silly.

As with many performers of her vintage, television offered more in the way of variety (and frequent paychecks) than did film. Barbara made her TV debut on *The Jack Benny Program* in 1952, and went on to make guest appearances through the decades on such shows as *Zane Grey Theater, Wagon Train, The Untouchables* and *Charlie's Angels*. TV proved a successful medium for the now mature actress. Like Loretta Young, she starred in and hosted an anthology series, winning an Emmy as Best Actress. *The Barbara Stanwyck Show* ran only one season (1960-61), airing 39 half-hour episodes on NBC. Her biggest small-screen success was with the

The latter-day, silver-haired Barbara, in *The Night Walker*, 1964.

hour-long Western series *The Big Valley*, which aired on ABC from 1965-69; Barbara played Victoria Barclay, the gun-toting matriarch of a California ranch in the 1870s. After appearing in several episodes of the nighttime soap *Dynasty*, Barbara was given her own spin-off, *The Colbys* (ABC, 1985-87). She only stayed with the show through the first season. Her last great hurrah was *The Thorn Birds* (1983), a four-part ABC miniseries that proved to be a huge ratings hit. Barbara, then 76, won an Emmy for her performances as an Australian sheep rancher in love with a much-younger priest (Richard Chamberlain).

The end of her life was as hard as the beginning had been. The seemingly indestructible actress was suffering from recurring lung problems by the mid-1980s (she gave up smoking in 1986), and in 1981 she was badly beaten during a break-in robbery at her Beverly Hills home. She was a semi-invalid for her last few years, telling her friend, costume designer Nolan Miller, "How could this happen to me? I always thought I'd be trampled by a wild stallion or run down by a stagecoach. But never *this*." Hospitalized with a slipped disc, she died from congestive heart failure on January 20, 1990, at 82. Barbara's ashes were scattered over the California mountaintops by her publicist, who said, "She had seen too many of what is termed 'Hollywood funerals,' and she didn't want one."

Inger Stevens

Maybe it's something in the water, but Stockholm has provided Hollywood with two of the most beautiful, talented and perpetually depressed actresses of the 20th century. Greta Garbo's roles fit her personality perfectly: glum, tortured and tragic. Inger Stevens, however, seemed the very picture of level-headed cheeriness onscreen. In her TV series, *The Farmer's Daughter*, and in a dozen films she made between 1957 and 1969, she appeared to be a forthright and untroubled young woman. Yet compared to Inger Stevens, Garbo was Pollyanna the Glad Girl.

Stevens was born Inger Stensland, on October 18, 1934. Shortly after the birth of her younger brother, Carl, their parents (both of whom were professors) split up; her father, Per, moved to the US to study under a Fulbright scholarship. He remarried and moved to Kansas in 1946, sending for his children. Inger and Carl arrived in New Orleans on a freighter and were cared for by the Traveler's Aid Society until they could be shipped off, unchaperoned, to Kansas. She felt like a rube and later recalled a policeman who laughed at her ragged shoes. "After that I burnt the shoes and walked five blocks out of the way to avoid that cop."

Soon, Inger ran away from home: "Most everybody does at 15 . . . It was normal adolescent rebellion." What wasn't so normal is that Inger took a burlesque job in Kansas City, under the name Kay Palmer. Corralled back home, she held down more usual after-school jobs: waitress, library aid, cashier, record-store clerk. At 18, in 1952, she used her savings to move to New York.

Tall and blonde, a dimpled Grace Kelly lookalike, Inger quickly got modeling jobs and TV commercials; she studied at the prestigious Actors Studio while breaking into show business via summer stock and live television. She was briefly a showgirl at the Latin Quarter ("Couldn't dance a step," she later admitted). With the help of a talent agent, Anthony Soglio, she began appearing on such mid-1950s TV anthologies as *Kraft Television Theater, Studio One, Playhouse 90* and *Robert Montgomery Presents*. She and Soglio married in 1955.

In 1956 she made her Broadway debut, in the aptly-titled comedy *Debut*—it failed after five performances. "The theater was closed," Inger recalled the following year, "but my name remained in lights on the marquee until the theater reopened six months later." By a sad coincidence, her next Broadway play, the Sidney Sheldon-scripted *Roman Candle* (1960), also lasted five nights. She only appeared on Broadway once more: in 1962, she briefly replaced Barbara Bel Geddes in the Jean Kerr comedy *Mary, Mary*.

Inger's big break came with a 1956 episode of *Playhouse 90*, directed by John Frankenheimer, which included a ten-minute dramatic monologue. Paramount signed her to a long-term contract, promptly loaning her to MGM for a leading role in *Man on Fire* (1957), a divorce/child custody melodrama in which she played the romantic lead to Bing Crosby. Filming started on a bad note: two days into production, she was rushed to the hospital for an emergency appendectomy. Then she began a torrid affair with her 54-year-old costar. That same year, Crosby married Kathryn Grant, and Inger was visibly distraught. "I thought he loved me," she later said, "I went into a state of shock. I actually became physically sick from all the distress."

By this time she and Soglio were separated, and Inger filed for divorce in 1957. "I can't figure it out," said her unhappy ex-husband. "I married her and worked my head off. I used every contact, every person of importance I knew. I got her offers from every studio in Hollywood . . . Now she wants a divorce. I tell you I'm crushed. I can't understand what's happened to her."

Later that same year, 1957, while filming the thriller *Cry Terror!*, Inger had yet another brush with death. While filming in a New York/New Jersey tunnel near Hoboken (through which today's PATH trains run), she and ten other crew members, including costars James Mason and Rod Steiger, were felled by carbon monoxide fumes. She was confined to bed for several days. The

Inger Stevens in her first movie, *Man on Fire*, 1957.

film, when released in 1958, was a tidy little drama, but Inger remained unsatisfied professionally. Also in 1958, she appeared in the pirate adventure *The Buccaneer*, and had a romance with the director (and noted ladies' man), Anthony Quinn. "He is the perfect embodiment of the virile male that all women unconsciously seek," Inger told a reporter.

It's unclear what pushed her over the edge: romances with Crosby, Quinn, or someone else; perhaps the loneliness of Hollywood or unhappiness with her screen roles. But Inger made a violent suicide attempt in New York, on the last day of 1958. She attended a New Year's party with NBC executive David Tebet, who took her home early. He later phoned Inger's Gramercy Park apartment and got no answer. Police found her in bed, in a coma from sleeping pills washed down with caustic ammonia. Given only a 50% chance of survival, she lingered in the hospital for two weeks before recovering. Talking of the incident in later years, she said tersely, "I don't recommend it to anyone. I was in love. It ended. I tried to end myself. It solves nothing. I did find out you have to like yourself."

Her most interesting film to date, while not a totally successful one, was *The World, the Flesh and the Devil* (1959). A terribly earnest and rather naïve sci-fi melodrama, it starred Inger, Harry Belafonte and Mel Ferrer as the only survivors of a nuclear holocaust. Shot in off-hours in Manhattan, the film gave Inger a chance to develop a real character: her Sarah Crandall is headstrong but uncertain young woman who is forced to choose between the last two men in the world (one black and perfect in every way; one white and pretty much a complete jerk).

But she was still unhappy, both in her private and professional lives. She turned down a role in *Key Witness* in 1959, telling reporter Joe Hyams that "Everyone here seems to feel that the important thing is to be in big, successful films. They just don't understand that there comes a time when a performer has to feel she is making a contribution, too. That gives an actress as much a feeling of success as money . . . I'm not knocking money, but in the final analysis it's me who's on the screen, and I have to be happy with what I do." Paramount certainly wasn't happy with Inger's attitude, and put her on suspension: she didn't make another film till 1964, and never worked for Paramount again.

She moved to New York, and was not unhappy to leave Hollywood: "Out there I wasn't me," she said. "I was a stranger, living for a lot of people who don't care a hang about you." She elaborated to reporter Dickson Terry that "Just to be a star doesn't interest me. I just want to do good work. So many people who come out to Hollywood feel they have to take the first thing that comes along. And it is hard to turn it down. But my contract allows me a certain amount of freedom. I can do plays, I can do some television."

Inger did return to TV: *Bonanza, Zane Grey Theater, Route 66.* One of her best-remembered guest appearances was on *The Twilight Zone*, in the classic 1960 episode "The Hitch-Hiker." She claimed another brush with death in real life, saying that she survived a plane crash in Lisbon in 1961, jumping off just before it burst into flames, but this account is both unverified and somewhat unlikely.

Late in 1961 Inger married actor and musical arranger Ike Jones in Mexico: the problem was (in the 1960s, anyway) that Jones was black and Inger about as white as you could get. Jones talked about the secret marriage after Inger's death. "We mutually agreed to keep our marriage unpublicized since it was the opinion of many that public knowledge of our relationship would have adversely affected my wife's career. May I add that the differences in race was not our personal problem, but the problem of the world around us. We were simply two human beings in love with each other, which is private."

It's unclear just how long—or how often—Inger and Jones lived together. She had "bachelorette pads" on both coasts and at her death was rooming with Emmy-winning makeup artist Lola McNalley in Laurel Canyon. Reports after Inger's death stated that she and Jones shared a Malibu home, but that they had separated in 1969. But despite broad hints in the press from columnists Jack O'Brien and Marilyn Beck, the marriage was kept under-cover. For the rest of her life, Inger danced around the question, telling reporters that "I'd like very much to get married again" and "For the time being I've sort of built a wall around myself, not ruling out men, but at least being as happy and carefree as I can until another man—perhaps the right one—comes along."

Inger at Dulles Airport in 1963.

In 1963 Inger won the role that enshrined her in the Baby Boomer hall of fame. For three seasons, she played Katy Holstrom, governess for the children of Congressman Morley (William Windom), in the ABC sitcom *The Farmer's Daughter*. Loosely based on the Loretta Young film, the show was a huge hit and made Inger financially independent. Her press interviews, however, gave ABC nightmares: "I believe it is a heartwarming, honest series," she said in September 1963, just as the show premiered. "But I won't predict whether it will be a success. I just do the best job I know how. I am never overly optimistic. If a thing doesn't work out you can always do something else." Later, she said that in 1964 "we opened badly with a two-part show which we shouldn't have started with," and noted that "nobody thought it would last more than eight weeks." One can almost see the press agent frantically signaling her.

The Farmer's Daughter gave Inger the freedom to work on other projects. She filmed a documentary on Sweden for TV in 1964 (aired in '65), and that same year returned to the big screen in the medical soap opera *The New Interns*. She talked wistfully about leaving the acting profession and going back to school to become a child psychiatrist. She began working with the California Council for Retarded Children, and was on the advisory board of UCLA's Neuro-Psychiatric Institute. She also volunteered at a community health center in Watts. "I live my whole life on television," she told the *New York Times* in 1965. "The hours are long—five in the morning till 8:30 at night, five days a week—and there's not much time to do anything except learn your lines and keep healthy." She was probably relieved when *The Farmer's Daughter* went off the air in 1966.

Inger made a three-film comeback in 1967, beginning with the Civil War-era Western *The Long Ride Home* (also released as *A Time for Killing*). Her role wasn't very deep: she was the kidnapped fiancée of Glenn Ford. That summer she also costarred in the smarmy "swinging" comedy *A Guide for the Married Man*, directed by Gene Kelly. Inger played the perky, perfect and utterly personality-free wife of Walter Matthau, who is aching to have an extramarital affair. Today, it's an almost unwatchable film, trying desperately to be hip.

She also starred with Don Murray in the TV movie *The Borgia Stick* in 1967, then played Richard Widmark's wife in the above-average police film *Madigan* (1968). After filming a cameo in the James Stewart/Henry Fonda Western *Firecreek*, she headed for Durango, Mexico, to costar in *Five Card Stud* (1968), a Dean Martin Western (according to rumor, she and Martin were an item at the time). She lingered in the Old West for *Hang 'em High*, a much better film, with Clint Eastwood playing one of his typical loners bent on vengeance. Inger's final feature film was the odd little drama *A Dream of Kings* (1969), starring her ex-lover Anthony Quinn as a Chicago man who wants to take his ailing son to Greece. Inger, as a widow attracted to Quinn, gave a superb performance, quiet and warm, and garnered terrific reviews. The film itself, though, was not commercial and did indifferent business.

She made two last TV-movies, both aired in 1970. *The Mask of Sheba* was a romantic adventure costarring the aging Walter Pidgeon, while *Run, Simon, Run* was a crime drama starring Burt Reynolds (again, an affair was rumored). At 35, Inger was at the top of her game and the height of her beauty, and was signed to begin filming a new series, *The Most Deadly Game*. She made one episode and was giving hopeful interviews about the new show in the spring of 1970, and on the evening of April 29 chatted on the phone with roommate Lola McNalley, who was away from home.

On the morning of April 30, McNalley arrived to find Inger unconscious on the kitchen floor. By the time the ambulance arrived and got her to Hollywood Receiving Hospital, she was dead from an overdose of barbiturates. Considering her past history, no one doubted it was intentional. Her lifelong dissatisfaction, her feeling of "not fitting in," her romantic misadventures, her own lack of self-esteem, caught up with her at last. Though she felt lonely, Inger had a lot of friends. "I had more fun taking Inger out on a date than any girl I remember, and I've been out with a million," said one anonymous young man. "Inger can talk on any subject. But she'll shut up all night when somebody has something to say." Anthony Quinn said sadly that "Inger didn't belong here. She should have stayed in Sweden and married a truck driver and had eight kids."

Inger's ashes were scattered over the Pacific Ocean. A month after her death, the news hit that Inger's widower, Ike Jones, had stepped forward and asked to be named administrator of her $200,000 estate. Inger's brother Carl appeared in court and supported his brother-in-law, who in August was awarded half the estate. Jones promptly turned the money over to children's charities and mental-health organizations.

Sharon Tate

In the late 1960s, she was one of the most promising starlets in Hollywood. Breathtakingly beautiful, hard-working and genuinely well-liked, Sharon Tate had a future easily as bright as fellow newcomers Raquel Welch, Faye Dunaway and Candice Bergen. But a handful of homicidal cult members changed all that, and Sharon became better known as one of the century's most famous murder victims. She only made nine films, but Sharon had been on her way to becoming a promising actress as the 1970s dawned.

She was born in Dallas, on January 24, 1943, the daughter of Major Paul Tate and his wife, Doris. Already a beauty at six months, she won a Miss Tiny Tot contest. Sharon and her two younger sisters had peripatetic childhoods: their father, working with Army Intelligence, spent much of the 1950s moving the family from Dallas to Tacoma, Houston, El Paso, and San Francisco. In 1959, when Sharon was 16, they moved to Verona, Italy, where she attended high school and become multilingual.

It was in Italy that she began considering an acting career. Richard Beymer was making a film near Sharon's school, and introduced her to his agent. Nothing came of this, but Beymer had put a flea in her ear. She came back to the US in 1963 and began seriously looking for work. "I was shy and bashful when I reached Hollywood," she said in 1965. "I only had just enough money to get by and I hitchhiked a ride on a truck to the office of an agent whose name I had."

An audition for the TV series *Petticoat Junction* didn't work out, but her test was seen by Martin Ransohoff of Filmways Productions.

Impressed, he put her under a seven-year contract and set out to develop her in the old-fashioned Hollywood manner. Ransohoff sent Sharon to New York's Actors Studio, and to classes in dancing, singing, body-building and modeling. "I'm sure the three years I spent in training to be an actress will pay off," Sharon told the *New York News* in 1966.

By that time, she had gotten her first few jobs. She can be spotted briefly guesting on *The Man from U.N.C.L.E.*, *Mister Ed*, and as Mr. Drysdale's secretary in several episodes of *The Beverly Hillbillies*. She did TV ads, including one for cigarettes which nearly did her in: "The commercial required many takes," Sharon recalled. "Just when they were ready for the final one, I passed out from taking too many puffs on my first attempt at smoking."

Ransohoff wangled her small roles in *The Americanization of Emily* (1964) and *The Sandpiper* (1965) to get her accustomed to filming. Her first real part was in the pretentious British-made thriller *Eye of the Devil* (1966), also known as *13*. The film starred David Niven and Deborah Kerr as a middle-aged couple living in a French chateau. Sharon—ironically, playing a homicidal cult member—was thrilled to be in such company, even in a less-than-sterling project. All she had to do was wander about looking hollow-eyed and spooky and saying ominous things. It made no impact on Sharon's career, but the wily Ransohoff took advantage of location shooting to produce a one-reel promotional short, *All Eyes on Sharon Tate*.

Sharon was an odd duck in the swinging Hollywood of the mid-1960s. Strictly brought up, she was sweet and innocent in a town that was neither—one actor called her "one of the toughest lays in town. Strictly a one-man woman." She reportedly had an unhappy relationship with a French actor, then was briefly engaged to the handsome celebrity hairstylist Jay Sebring. The two broke up, but remained good friends. Then, at a London party in 1966, she met Roman Polanski.

The 33-year-old director and actor was already famous for his dark films *Knife in the Water* (1962) and *Repulsion* (1965). He also had quite an offscreen reputation: one ex-girlfriend described him as "the quintessential male chauvinist pig. He treats women like objects, like toys, like his latest pet car. It can be fun to share his

Sharon Tate in the late 1960s.

limelight for a while, but ultimately it becomes boring." Ransohoff loaned Sharon to Polanski for his horror comedy *The Fearless Vampire Killers* (1967), filmed on location in the Italian Alps and England. Sharon and Polanski became involved, despite their obvious differences in cultural background and personality. Polanski later said, "It took the longest time for me to get her to go to bed with me. She was not someone who went easily to bed with a man." They moved to a house in London's Belgravia district, and Sharon learned to love the Swinging England of the late '60s: "There are so many talented young people with fantastic, original ideas here," she said in 1967. "The Mod look, the long, straight hair for girls and long hair for boys, miniskirts . . . it all started here and eventually got to America. Americans are too inhibited but they are slowly coming around to realizing what a swinging world we live in." But the fact was that Polanski and his crowd were too swinging for her. According to Mia Farrow, Sharon experimented with pot and LSD, didn't care much for them and never really got into drugs.

Sharon's only film with Polanski turned out something of a disappointment. Visually it was a stunning replication of 19th-century Eastern Europe in the dead of winter. But the performers were given little to do. *Vampire Killers* veered between bad sitcom dialogue and gory thrills, and never really settled on a style. Sharon, in a long red wig, looked beautiful but somewhat detached. The film did not do well in the US, and Polanski tried to help it along by shooting nude photos of Sharon for the March 1967 issue of *Playboy*. Aside from raising questions of taste and exploitation, this did nothing for the film or for Sharon's career.

Sharon's first mainstream, big-budget film was MGM's beach comedy *Don't Make Waves* (1967), starring Tony Curtis. Sharon had a small but showy role as Malibu, a sky-diving beach bunny who Curtis steals from her body-building boyfriend. The film was fairly dreadful, but critics noted Sharon's combination of beauty and deadpan humor. She did not share their enthusiasm: "It's a terrible movie," she accurately noted before it had even been released, then admitted that "sometimes I say things I shouldn't. I guess I'm too outspoken."

Next came her most famous project, the movie which—for better or for worse—will be her legacy. *Valley of the Dolls* (1967), based on the Jacqueline Susann novel, is one of those wonderfully camp "so bad it's good" extravaganzas. The most vigorous scenery-chewing was handled by Patty Duke (as a drugged-out Judy Garland manqué) and Susan Hayward (in a role originally planned for the drugged-out Judy Garland). Sharon turned in a quiet, touching performance as Jennifer North, a sexpot-turned-"nudie" actress—in a movie crammed with hilarious dialogue, she was given such lines as, "Mother, I *know* I don't have any talent, and I *know* all I have is a body, and I *am* doing my bust exercises!"

No one was more surprised than Sharon when she was offered the role by director Mark Robson. "Since the book was a runaway best-seller, I was sure the leading roles would go to big-name stars," she said in late 1967. "You know, like Natalie Wood or somebody like that. But I was just thrilled to get the role. I liked Jennifer as I read the book. I think she is the most sympathetic girl in the group. She's sweet, unspoiled and unselfish. She doesn't mean anyone any harm, and yet terrible things keep happening to her."

Sharon might have been describing herself; everyone in Hollywood remarked about how "sweet, unspoiled and unselfish" Sharon was. Roman Polanski said, "When I first met Sharon, I expected her to be nothing more than just another beautiful and not-too-bright American girl. But she surprised me—she turned out to be rather remarkable. In a way she was naïve. But she also had this tremendous unaffectedness and sense of decency and loyalty that really impressed people. She never bad-mouthed anyone and was completely free of any of the neurotic ambition which one usually associates with actresses."

Sharon worked hard on *Valley of the Dolls*. "I learned a great deal about acting on this film," she told *The Sunday News*. "Particularly in my scenes with Lee Grant. She knows what acting is all about and everything she does, from little mannerisms to delivering her lines, is pure professionalism." The film was widely panned when it opened, but Sharon got away with less fire than her costars. Discussing the nudity in this film and in her project with Roman Polanski, she told a reporter in 1967 that "if it's important to the story that I appear nude, then by all means I'll do it." Explaining what *did* unnerve her, she said that "I've made movies and appeared on television, but I have never appeared onstage and I don't know if I ever will. Live audiences frighten me to death."

She and Polanski were back in London for Christmas 1967. They married on January 20, 1968, honeymooning in the Swiss Alps. Sharon had been longing for marriage since they had met, though Polanski admitted that "She never asked me, never said a word about it. So I finally said, 'I'm sure you would like to get married,' and she said she would. So I said, 'We'll get married, then,' and we did. By that time I wasn't nervous about it at all." Polanski almost immediately began having affairs, according to his biographers. He and Sharon returned to the US, where she cooled her heels in California, mulling various film offers, and Polanski flew to New York to film *Rosemary's Baby*. With an eye to future projects together, Sharon bought back the rest of her contract from Martin Ransohoff and Filmways.

The Wrecking Crew (1969) was the fourth (and last) film starring Dean Martin as the James Bond parody Matt Helm. An almost Austin Powers-like film in its self-aware, self-mocking grooviness, it benefited from Martin's amiably laid-back style and Sharon's superb turn as his klutzy, near-sighted assistant. While Elke Sommer, Nancy Kwan and Tina Louise filled the sexpot "Helm Girl" roles, Sharon showed real promise as a comedienne, proving to be the most memorable woman in the film. One scene sticks in the mind for the wrong reason: Martin passes a bloody corpse and tells Sharon, "That could have been you," to which she replies, "*Never*—never, never, never."

She seemed determined to downplay her eyelash-batting, clothes-shucking past. For most of *The Wrecking Crew*, her hair was hidden under a hat, her eyes behind large, comic glasses, and her figure in a high-buttoned dress. Only in one scene does she let down her hair (or, rather, her red wig), put on a micro-mini and shake her backside in Martin's face. "I don't think I'm a sexpot at all," Sharon said. "Honestly, I think I'm just normal." She even pointed out her tiny flaws to one reporter, including three all-but-invisible facial scars. "I suffered the big scar when I fell on a piece of corrugated tin when I was five. I wouldn't dream of having the scar removed. I am very proud of it. It's me." Her ambition, she added, was to become "a light comedienne in the Carole Lombard style." (Lombard, whether Sharon knew it or not, also had a facial scar,

Sharon and Roman Polanski at a 1968 party.

from a 1926 auto accident.)

Sharon discovered that she was pregnant in December 1968. In the spring of '69, while she still had her girlish figure, she flew to Rome and made her last film, the frantic comedy *12 + 1*. Costarring with Orson Welles, Vittorio Gassman and Vittorio de Sica, Sharon played a gold-digging American girl who, with the rest of the cast, chases an antique chair (supposedly stuffed with a fortune) around Europe. Filmed in Italian and dubbed into English for US release, *12 + 1* bombed when it opened in May 1970.

Early in 1969, Sharon and Polanski rented a Benedict Canyon house at 10050 Cielo Drive from agent Rudi Altobelli. The airy, pleasant house, which was built in 1944 for actress Michèle Morgan, had also been rented by the Gish sisters, Cary Grant, Henry Fonda and, more recently, Doris Day's music-manager son, Terry Melcher. It became a gathering place for Sharon's friends and for Polanski's (two rather distinct social sets). The couple went to London in the early summer, where she dubbed *12 + 1* and he worked on various projects. She sailed back home in mid-July to await the baby's birth, while Polanski, to her dismay, stayed in London.

Friends of Polanski's, Voityck Frokowski and Abigail Folger, were staying at the Cielo Drive house, and Sharon invited her ex-boyfriend, Jay Sebring, to keep her company on the night of August 8. Nearly everyone in Hollywood (way too many to squeeze into the place) later claimed that Sharon had also invited them to stay that night, but they all had, happily, other plans. Sometime that night, Sharon, her houseguests and a passerby were shot and stabbed to death by four followers of cult leader Charles Manson. Even in her crime-scene and morgue photos, Sharon looks lovely, a slight smile on her face. Sharon—wearing a Pucci-print minidress—was buried with her baby son, posthumously named Paul. Los Angeles was thrown into a panic until the killers were arrested and sentenced to death (a fate overturned by the brief abolishment of capital punishment). Roman Polanski suffered further personal setbacks, fleeing from the US in 1977 to avoid charges of statutory rape.

That is how Sharon Tate is remembered: the most famous victim of a band of murderous hippies. The night of the killing is played over and over again, while Sharon's promising career (except for the lurid *Valley of the Dolls*) is pretty much forgotten.

Thelma Todd

Thelma Todd is another one of those unfortunate performers—like Sharon Tate and Vic Morrow—who is better known for her death than for her life. That's especially sad for Thelma, who was a brilliant comic actress with a respectable career in both silents and talkies. She was born in Lawrence, Massachusetts, on July 29, 1905. Her father, John, was a police lieutenant; her mother, Alice, an ambitious clubwoman. Thelma attended the Lowell State Normal School and in 1925 began teaching at the Hood Practice School. That same year, her ten-year-old brother William died in a farm accident while on vacation.

Thelma had done some modeling during summer breaks, and a friend entered her in a beauty contest—one thing led to another, and Thelma was crowned Miss Massachusetts of 1925. A contract with Paramount was offered, and accepted. Thelma Todd was pretty, but in an off-kilter way. Her blonde hair, bright smile and big blue eyes typed her as a typical cutie. But her pugnacious chin and tough, down-turned nose set her apart from the crowd of starlets; she was just different enough to have real star potential.

She was part of the "youth invasion" of the mid-1920s. As the first generation of silent stars was fading into middle age, a veritable platoon of flappers and jazz babies in their teens and early 20s hit town: Janet Gaynor, Clara Bow, Joan Crawford, Carole Lombard, Myrna Loy, and scores of others. Early in 1926, Thelma began work at Paramount, where she spent the next two years appearing in seven films. They were all big-budget productions: *Fascinating Youth* (her first, with Charles "Buddy" Rogers and Clara Bow), *Rubber Heels* (Ed Wynn's film debut), and *Nevada* (with Gary Cooper and William Powell). And she had supporting roles, not just walk-ons. Still, Paramount dropped her option in late 1927.

She picked up work at First National (*The Noose, Vamping Venus*), where she was spotted by Milton Sills, and he insisted she be cast as his leading lady in *The Crash* (1928). Despite making a good showing in the film, Thelma never signed a long-term contract with another studio. Perhaps her experience with Paramount had made her wary; perhaps her agent or advisor convinced her she'd do better on her own; perhaps she was just never offered a studio contract. Thereafter, she worked at nearly every studio on the west coast, from majors (Paramount, First National, Universal, Fox, United Artists) to the minors (Tiffany, Sono Art-World Wide, Monogram, Equitable). Her longest association was with Hal Roach Studios, which released her many comedy shorts through MGM. Freelancing certainly didn't help Thelma's career in the long run. No studio was going to spend money building up a star with publicity that would just be cashed in on by someone else. With no long-term investment in her, studio heads took no real interest in Thelma's career.

Things were looking up, though, at the dawn of the talkie years. Thelma appeared in seven features in 1928—however, she rarely starred, and most of these films sank without a trace. She appeared in half-a-dozen features in 1929, but more importantly, she began her career in comedy shorts. In 1929 alone, Thelma appeared in *Unaccustomed as We Are, Hurdy Gurdy, Snappy Sneezer, Hotter Than Hot, Look Out Below, Crazy Feet,* and *Stepping Out* (her costars included such accomplished comics as Laurel and Hardy, Edgar Kennedy, Charley Chase and Harry Langdon). With Hal Roach in charge and Leo McCarey writing and directing many of them, these shorts were generally bright spots on any evening's program.

For the rest of her career, Thelma would intersperse her feature films with these short comedies: a dozen with Charley Chase, four with Laurel and Hardy (as well as appearing in their full-length films *The Devil's Brother* and *The Bohemian Girl*), seven with Harry Langdon. But in 1931, Hal Roach decided to try something different: he teamed Thelma with the wispy, fluttery ZaSu Pitts in a series of "girlfriends" comedies, starting with *Let's Do Things*. Over the next two years, Thelma and ZaSu made 18 of these two-reelers: *The Soilers* (as door-to-door saleswomen), *Sneak Easily* (Thelma as a

ZaSu Pitts (left) and Thelma Todd in the comedy short *Hot Dogs*, 1931.

lawyer), *Red Noses* (a Turkish bath comedy), *Maids a la Mode* (crashing a costume party), *The Old Bull* (tramping through the country), *Asleep in the Feet* (as taxi dancers), *Alum and Eve* (faking sick in a hospital to avoid a traffic ticket). It was very Lucy and Ethel/Laverne and Shirley: the boisterous, madcap Thelma dragging poor hand-wringing ZaSu into her harebrained scrapes.

In 1933, Hal Roach felt that the Thelma Todd/ZaSu Pitts team had gone as far as it could, and paired Thelma with brash, tough-talking comic Patsy Kelly. This provided a whole new onscreen relationship, and a new character for Thelma. Her character became more madcap and wily, as the down-to-earth Patsy Kelly practially blew steam out of her ears in reaction to the team's zany predicaments. Thelma and Patsy released 21 shorts between 1933 and 1936 (when the posthumous *All-American Toothache* appeared in theaters). These shorts, still seen on TV (though not, as of yet, compiled on DVD), include such lightweight, amusing titles as *Twin Triplets* (as reporters), *Top Flat* (Thelma tries to make Patsy think she lives in the penthouse where she works as a maid), *The*

Horse Farmers (the girls buy a country home), *The Tin Man* (a mad scientist romp), *The Misses Stooge* (as incompetent burlesque dancers), *Bum Voyage* (on an ocean liner with a gorilla) . . . None of these 20-minute comedies were *It Happened One Night*, but their fans loved them, and they kept Thelma and Patsy in money while they both made feature films.

On July 18, 1932, Thelma married Pat DiCicco, a man who—in light of Thelma's death—has come down in history as being a lot more shady and menacing than he probably really was. Rumors cast DiCicco as Charles "Lucky" Luciano's "right-hand man in Hollywood," a gambler and drug dealer. The marriage lasted till March 1934. Thelma's next love was director, writer and producer Roland West, who directed her in the 1931 drama *Corsair* (she was billed as Alison Loyd, an odd and unsuccessful attempt to either change her image or avoid responsibility for *Corsair*). West had been in films since 1916, but was now also dabbling in restaurant management.

All through the 1930s, while making her shorts for Hal Roach, Thelma Todd was still making the rounds of the studios and appearing in feature films; some of them were absolute delights. The best-known today are those she made with the Marx Brothers: she's a gun moll in the shipboard comedy *Monkey Business* (1931) and the "college widow" in *Horse Feathers* (1932). Her talent as a comic really comes to light in these films. Just watch how she interacts differently with the four brothers: she trades quips at lightning-quick speed with Groucho, deadpans as a straight woman for Chico, stares goggle-eyed at Harpo, and flirts vampishly with Zeppo. Thelma was no mere decorative blonde; her training in comedy shorts had given her a smart, professional air that should have carried her farther in films.

Among the other highlights in her career were in *The Hot Heiress* (a wonderful 1931 romantic comedy, though Thelma was only in support to stars Ben Lyon and Ona Munson); the 1931 *Maltese Falcon* (with Thelma in the Gladys George role to Ricardo Cortez's Sam Spade); as Clara Bow's slutty, tough-talking rival in the delirious *Call Her Savage* (1932); as a client of John Barrymore's marvelous *Counsellor-at-Law* (1933); playing straight woman to Jimmy Durante in *Speak Easily* (1932) and *Palooka* (1934), and to Wheeler and Woolsey in the 1934 *Cockeyed Cavaliers* and *Hips, Hips, Hooray!*

Thelma Todd shortly before her death in 1935.

By 1935, the thirty-year-old Thelma had been in films exactly ten years. She was still not an A-star, like Harlow or Lombard, and at this rate she never would be. Not giving up on her career, she nonetheless wisely decided to diversify, and opened a restaurant in the Castellammare neighborhood of Pacific Palisades, Thelma Todd's Sidewalk Café, at 17575 Pacific Coast Highway. Roland West was her business partner (West was between wives—he married actresses Jewel Carmen and later Lola Lane). Later, authors Kenneth Anger and Andy Edmonds claimed that Pat DiCicco and Lucky Luciano were also involved in the café, and that Thelma had refused their demands to turn it into an illegal gambling club—but no evidence has ever turned up that DiCicco or Luciano had any dealings with Thelma at this time (or, indeed, that Thelma and Luciano ever met).

On the morning of December 16, 1935, Thelma was found by her maid, dead in the front seat of her car in a closed garage belonging to Roland West and Jewel Carmen, at 17531 Posetano Road, in Pacific Palisades. She looked lovely, in an evening gown and fur coat, with perfectly coiffed hair, slumped over face-down. Rumors immediately started flying, and they have not stopped yet: Thelma was killed by Luciano and/or DiCicco in revenge for not cooperating with their plans for the café (or, in some versions, for turning down their sexual advances). Roland West had killed her accidentally or on purpose, beating her up and locking her in the garage. West's estranged wife, Jewel Carmen, had her taken care of. Thelma's poor mother, shrieking *"murder"* at the top of her lungs from day one, did little to quiet conspiracy theorists.

But the L.A. police, after thorough investigation and endless interviews, decided Thelma's death was probably an accident—and that really does seem to be the most likely (if the most boring) scenario. Thelma, tired after a late night out at a party at the Trocadero (and with a blood alcohol level of .13), simply fell asleep in her car, on her way to spend the night at West's, and never woke up. The coroner ruled her death as carbon monoxide poisoning.

Thelma's viewing and funeral were packed (thanks to the information superhighway, the morbidly curious can find photos of Thelma looking lovely in her coffin and not so lovely at the coroner's). Thelma's mother kept her ashes with her at home till her own death; the two are interred together in Bellevue Cemetery, in Thelma's hometown. Hal Roach spoke for her coworkers: "She was a favorite with everyone on the lot," he said, "from the lowest employee to the highest. She was always joyous and happy and seemed thoroughly to enjoy her work. She was well-loved, and we will miss her."

As for Thelma's legacy, it's challenging for fans to innocently enjoy her in *Monkey Business*, as Groucho Marx tells her, "You're a woman who's been getting nothing but dirty breaks. Well, we can clean and tighten those brakes, but you'll have to stay in the garage all night."

Judy Tyler

It's particularly frustrating when a promising performer's career ends abruptly after only a handful of films. James Dean comes to mind, of course, along with earlier novices like Dorothy Dell, Robert Williams, and Clarine Seymour. Totally forgotten today is the "Cinderella Girl" of the mid-1950s, musical comedy actress Judy Tyler, who starred in only two films before her death.

She was born Judith Mae Hess in Teaneck, New Jersey, on October 9, 1932. Her father, Julian Hess, was a trumpet player who retired to become a building contractor. Her mother, the former Lorelei Kendler, claimed to have been a Ziegfeld Girl and understudy for Marilyn Miller (though no stage could hold all the women who claimed to have been "Ziegfeld Girls"). Judy was stage-struck from an early age. She took voice, dancing and acting lessons, and quit school at the age of 15 to become a Harry Conover model. Conover—considered a shady character even for the modeling business—gave her the choice of "Taylor" or "Tyler" as a new last name, and she was off and running. Conover had the teenager named "Miss Stardust of 1949."

Judy, with her cat-like face and jet-black hair, became a successful junior model. She moved to an apartment in Manhattan and auditioned at the Copa. As she later told it, "I just walked over there and they said, 'Do you dance?' and I said, 'Yes, I'm a dancer!' So they said, 'Oh,' and threw somebody else out. Of course, to call it dancing was entirely ridiculous. It was hardly walking." The pianist at the Copa was 26-year-old Colin Romoff, who soon became Judy's teacher. "As a vocal coach, there ain't nobody better," Judy later said. "He told me I was the worst singer he ever heard."

Judy Tyler, in a headshot from *Bop Girl Goes Calypso*, 1957.

Two months after they met, Judy married Romoff. "I always tell him I got free vocal lessons that way," she laughed. She tried hard to be a housewife as well as an actress, doing the shopping, cooking, housework. "My husband and I go to the theater once a week," she said. "That's a rule in our house—once a week the theater. Do you know, we've seen *Pajama Game* 17 times!"

From Copa Girl, Judy branched out and began doing a single act at such New York nightclubs as Bill Miller's Riviera and Le Ruban Blue, where *Variety* was not overly impressed with her, feeling she needed more polish. She did bit parts on live TV in New York, and a few tiny, lost-to-posterity film walk-ons, which she later played down. "I did 'em for 20th Century-Fox when I was 16, and Universal-International a few years ago. But please don't ask me for the names of the pictures." The closest Judy got to dropping a real hint about her early film work was noting that an actress named Peggy Allen played her mother in one movie.

Judy appeared for 13 weeks on *The Milton Berle Show*; she turned up on Eddie Cantor's *Colgate Comedy Hour*, and Jimmy Durante's *All-Star Revue*. But her first big break came from an unlikely source. The popular kiddie show *Howdy Doody* featured a puppet character named Princess Summerfall Winterspring. In 1952, it was decided to replace the puppet with a live actress, and auditions were called. Producer Roger Muir claimed he was amazed at the resemblance between Judy Tyler and the puppet—a rather backhanded compliment at best (like most ventriloquist dummies, Princess Summerfall Winterspring was pretty terrifying looking). "And Judy could dance, and she had a delightful voice, and could sing wonderfully," recalled Muir. "She was hired immediately."

Judy spent three years decked out in the Princess' buckskin suit and braided wig, becoming the darling of the pre-school set—and not only them. "It does surprise me to get so many letters from fathers and older brothers of kids who watch the show," she told *Pictorial Review* in 1953. "There must be a lot of them, judging from the number of letters I get from grown men watching *Howdy Doody* regularly. But they're really all nice letters," she added hastily, "and very sanitary, not at all like the letters I received when I danced at the Copa."

Judy's grown-up singing and acting career was beginning to stagnate when another break came her way in 1955. Reginald Hammerstein, brother of Broadway producer Oscar, spotted Judy on Sid Caesar's *Caesar's Hour* and thought she'd be perfect for the role of the sweet-natured prostitute in the upcoming Rodgers and Hammerstein musical *Pipe Dream*, based on a John Steinbeck novel. She was called in to audition, but things did not go well: she belted out several brassy show tunes in her clarion voice, totally wrong for the part. At a second callback, director Harold Clurman told Judy to forget the theater and sing intimately to her accompanist (her husband, Colin Romoff). Her quiet, touching rendition of "Lost in His Arms" won her the part.

The publicity storm hit, with headlines like "Great Day's Comin' for Judy," "Pipe Dreams for Judy," "Rodgers and Hammerstein Find Another Cinderella." She was Broadway's media darling of 1955. "This part is what I've been working for all my life," she enthused. "You can't imagine, I can't imagine—a starring role, and in a Rodgers and Hammerstein show. Imagine! *Me!*" *Pipe Dream* ran at the Shubert Theater from late 1955 through summer 1956, but it was not the critical or popular hit hoped for. But Judy got her second wind, and it gave her the momentum to take her career up another notch. *Howdy Doody* was a thing of the past (Princess Summerfall Winterspring as a Steinbeck hooker?), but she kept busy through the mid-1950s: club and cabaret dates, TV appearances. She sang on Ed Sullivan's *Toast of the Town* in 1955 and '56, acted in a 1955 episode of *The Elgin Hour*, a dramatic anthology series, and filmed a *Perry Mason Show* segment ("The Case of the Fan Dancer's Horse") that did not air till after her death, in December 1957.

Then, finally, films. Judy was cast in her first starring role, in a film unpromisingly (but descriptively) titled *Bop Girl Goes Calypso* (1957). Produced by the low-budget Bel Air studios but released though United Artists, it was directed by neophyte Howard W. Koch, who went on to produce such hits as *The Manchurian Candidate*, *The Odd Couple* and *Ghost*. *Bop Girl Goes Calypso* is everything its name implies. The plot concerns a stuffy young statistician (Bobby Troup, later a busy television actor) who believes that the rock 'n' roll fad is on its way out, to be replaced by Calypso music (which was, actually, enjoying a brief vogue at the time).

Judy portrayed Jo Thomas, a nightclub singer who is dubious of the professor's findings but is won over by his applause-o-meter and wooden personality, and, well, "goes Calypso." It was a very silly movie, but Judy was irresistible and belted out a few sort-of-rock and pseudo-Calypso numbers with verve and energy. Her voice was

Bop Girl, in the process of going Calypso.

a strong Broadway belt, not appropriate for either of the film's musical genres, but she was riveting nonetheless.

Judy was the only cast member who stood out (other than the crabby club owner played by George O'Hanlon, looking and sounding exactly like cartoon character George Jetson, whose voice he provided from the 1960s through the 1980s). Bel Air couldn't afford big-name groups, and had to content itself with the likes of The Goofers, who managed to be both creepy and depressing. The only real Calypso star in it was Lord Flea (Jamaican singer/composer Norman Thomas), who did himself proud—sadly, he, like Judy, was dead by the end of the 1950s.

By this time, Judy's marriage to Colin Romoff had ended amicably, and she married television actor Gregory LaFayette (whose age was variously given as 19 or 24). The two wed on March 17, 1957, at Miami's Balmoral Hotel, with singer Patti Page serving as matron of honor. Judy was in Florida playing club dates between films— she never stopped working for a moment. Back in New York, she and LaFayette rented an apartment at 158 West 44th Street, right in the heart of the theater district (and, no doubt, kept up the play-going habit of her first marriage).

Judy's showing in *Bop Girl* was good enough for MGM to sign her as Elvis Presley's leading lady in his third film, *Jailhouse Rock* (1957). She portrayed Peggy van Alden, a record promoter who discovers and nurtures musical ex-con Vince Everett (Elvis). He rockets to stardom, eventually signing with the unfortunately named Climax Studios. Vince, of course, gets a swelled head; personal and professional mix-ups ensue. It's a cute little film with few pretensions and, unfortunately, only one good song (the title number). Elvis, still in his gee-whiz country boy mode, comes off well, as does Judy.

But this must have been a hugely frustrating project for the hard-working and ambitious actress: Judy, doubtless signed because of her prowess in musical comedy, did not get to sing one note in *Jailhouse Rock*. Maybe the producers didn't want to waste screentime on anyone's singing but the star's; or Judy's Broadway voice did not fit well with Elvis' rockabilly style. Whatever the reason, Peggy van Alden was a role any competent little starlet could have played. If Judy is remembered at all today, it's as an "Elvis girl," but *Jailhouse Rock* must have felt like a high-profile waste of time.

Although she came off like a perky ingénue onscreen, there was a streak of steely ambition in Judy worthy of Eve Harrington. "I detest people who are always taking credit for me," she told reporter Earl Wilson. "If anybody's responsible for me, it's me! I've broken down more doors in New York City than anybody in this room, I'm here to bet. I have the distinction in my agency of getting any job I auditioned for." Indeed, director Harold Clurman noted that "she is a supremely confident girl, and life seems to have been easy for her."

After completing *Jailhouse Rock* in the summer of 1957 (the film was released in November), Judy and her husband enjoyed a brief honeymoon in Laramie, Wyoming. Judy had signed a contract to appear on the CBS game show *Pantomime Quiz*, and had to be back in New York by the fall. Traveling with their poodle, Hamlet, and a kitten Judy had bought to give to her agent, they decided on a leisurely drive east, rather than take a plane with two small animals. On July 3, they were driving on US 30 through Billy the Kid, Wyoming, when a car pulled suddenly onto the road from the parking lot of an antiques store. LaFayette swerved to avoid it, and smashed headlong into another car in the oncoming lane.

Judy Tyler died instantly; one Presley biographer claimed she'd been "cut in half," though no newspapers at the time indicated anything so dramatic. Gregory LaFayette died later in a hospital; also killed were Donald Jones (a passenger in the other car), and Judy's dog and cat. To make matters even more depressing, looters stole LaFayette's wallet and Judy's cash, furs and jewelry from the wreck. An old family friend, Detective Charles Littman, managed to track down and recover Judy's belongings, though not the cash.

Elvis Presley was shaken by the news, telling reporters that "all of us boys really loved that girl. She meant a lot to all of us. I don't believe I can stand to see the movie we made together, now." Judy was laid out at the famed Campbell's Funeral Church in New York; her ashes were buried in Ferncliff Cemetery in Hartsdale, New York; her husband was buried in his hometown of Hopewell Junction, New York.

Judy's two films were released, enjoyed and pretty much forgotten. A number of other film starlets of the mid-1950s went on to careers big and small: Jayne Mansfield, Shirley Jones, Joan Collins, Audrey Hepburn. With the 1960s, some continued their upward trajectory and others faded away, while Judy Tyler, the "Cinderella Girl" of 1955, was completely forgotten by all but her family and friends.

Lupe Velez

The life of Lupe Velez has every element that biographers adore: scandal, lots of sex, a dramatic death. She was also one of her era's great beauties, a talented dramatic and comic actress and—in the words of Ann Miller—"an absolutely charming, nice lady."

The early life of Guadelupe Velez de Villalobos is somewhat shrouded by mystery and fan-magazine stories. She was born in San Luis de Potosi, Mexico, on July 18 of either 1908 or 1909; her mother has been described as everything from an opera singer to a prostitute; her father may (or may not) have been in the Mexican army. Regardless, the girl in her teens found herself working as a department-store salesgirl in Mexico City, singing and dancing in cabarets at night.

She emigrated north to Hollywood in 1927, where she found work as a bit player in silent films (with Charley Chase in *What Women Did for Me* and with Laurel and Hardy in *Sailors, Beware!*) and onstage at the Music Box Revue Theater. Then success came, suddenly and unexpectedly, when Douglas Fairbanks chose the unknown Lupe as his leading lady in *The Gaucho* (1927). Playing the fiery "mountain girl," Lupe became a hot young competitor to the exotic Greta Garbo and Dolores Del Rio, but also found herself typecast for life. Signed by Fairbanks' United Artists, she went on to more dramatic roles (some on loan-out): in *Stand and Deliver* (1928) and four 1929 films, *Lady of the Pavements, Wolf Song, Where East is East* and *Tiger Rose*. It was an impressive year. In *Lady of the Pavements* she was directed by D.W. Griffith, and in *Where East is West* she costarred with Lon Chaney. Critics and fans were impressed,

Hollywood's most sizzling couple, Gary Cooper and Lupe Velez, in 1929.

and Lupe's accent didn't slow her down when talkies arrived.

Lupe Velez almost immediately made herself known as the town's premiere party girl, no small accomplishment when one considers the competition—compared with her, Clara Bow was a recluse. Lupe didn't need drugs or alcohol to stimulate her rowdiness; she carried on in nightclubs, chattered and flirted through parties, and screamed through her beloved boxing matches, to the delight and horror of Hollywood society.

She also embarked on a series of high-profile love affairs. Lupe counted among her conquests—some less serious than others— John Gilbert, Randolph Scott, Douglas Fairbanks, Tom Mix, Charlie Chaplin, Russ Columbo, Victor Fleming, and Jack Dempsey. But the love of her life may have been Gary Cooper, whom she met when the two costarred in *Wolf Song* (1929). The romance lasted through many noisy breakups and reconciliations, before Cooper married Sandra Shaw in 1933. It seems the objections of Cooper's strait-laced parents overcame his affection for Lupe (his marriage to Shaw lasted, through many other affairs, till his death in 1961). Almost immediately after her final split with Cooper, Lupe married for the first (and only) time, to swimmer and Tarzan star Johnny Weissmuller (it was his third—of six—marriages). Though stormy from the start, the marriage lasted six years, till their divorce in 1939.

Meanwhile, her career continued its upward climb through the early talkie years. She costarred with Edward G. Robinson in *East is West* (in a Chinese role, 1930), and with stage great Nance O'Neil in *Resurrection* (and its Spanish-language version, both 1930). She made the umpteenth version of *The Squaw Man* (with Warner Baxter), and appeared with the odd duo of opera star Lawrence Tibbett and Jimmy Durante in *Cuban Love Song*.

It wasn't till 1932 that RKO had the brainstorm of putting Lupe Velez in a comedy. *The Half-Naked Truth*, costarring Lee Tracy, cast Lupe as a cooch dancer propelled to stardom by her manic press agent. Somehow, out of nowhere, Lupe gave a brilliant, wild, over-the-top comic performance, and "the poor man's Dolores Del Rio" suddenly became "the Mexican Jean Harlow." Lupe continued in that lighter vein with *Hot Pepper* (1933, with Edmund Lowe and Victor McLaglen), and in a cameo in the all-star *Mr. Broadway*,

Lupe Velez, 1932.

hosted by future TV emcee Ed Sullivan. She also hit Broadway for the first time, in the 1932 Ziegfeld revue *Hot-Cha!*, costarring Bert Lahr.

Her last big-budget dramatic role was in MGM's bizarre *Laughing Boy* (1934), which cast Lupe and fellow Mexican Ramon Novarro as American Indians. It was a turgid, overblown melodrama and did not sit at all well with audiences, despite the stars' best efforts (Novarro's unfortunate Prince Valiant wig didn't help matters any).

After that, it was back to comedy, for pretty much the rest of Lupe's career. She spent much of 1933 and '34 in the arms of Jimmy Durante, first in the Broadway musical revue *Strike Me Pink* (1933), in which she sang and/or danced to "A Bit of Temperament," "An Old Hollywood Custom," "Love and Rhythm" and several other numbers. She and Durante also costarred onscreen in United Artists' *Palooka*, MGM's *Hollywood Party*, and RKO's *Strictly Dynamite* (all 1934). All three were brainless and very enjoyable. *Palooka* introduced Durante's theme song, "Inka Dinka Doo," and Lupe played a radio star in *Strictly Dynamite*. But it's *Hollywood*

Party—sort of a showbiz *Dinner at Eight* parody—that provides some of Lupe Velez's best onscreen moments. Playing The Jaguar Woman, onscreen love interest to Durante's Schnarzan, she engages in an egg fight with Laurel and Hardy that is a masterpiece of understated slapstick.

By now Lupe was no longer a threat to Del Rio and Garbo—she was typed as a B-actress. She toured in vaudeville, and briefly moved to England in 1935 to appear in a revue and three films (including *Stardust*, 1936, with expatriate Ben Lyon). On her return to the US, she appeared in *High Flyers* (1937), the last costarring vehicle of the comedy team Wheeler and Woolsey before Robert Woolsey's death. A hugely amusing little musical comedy, it featured Margaret Dumont, a kleptomaniacal dog named Squeezy, and Lupe doing spot-on imitations of such stars as Dolores Del Rio and Simone Simon. She then returned for her third and final Broadway show, Shuberts' *You Never Know* (1938), with music and lyrics by Cole Porter, costarring Clifton Webb, Libby Holman, Rex O'Malley and Toby Wing. Even with those names behind it, the show lasted less than 100 performances.

In 1938 she returned to her homeland to film the Spanish-language *La Zandunga*, a dramatic romance. (Dolores Del Rio, Ramon Novarro, Antonio Moreno and Gilbert Roland would also make Spanish-language films during career slumps, finding more varied, deeper roles than in the US.)

Lupe found—for better or worse—her role of a lifetime in 1939, in RKO's *The Girl from Mexico*. She played the high-spirited Carmelita Fuentes, who marries US ad man Dennis Lindsay, to the horror of his snooty family. It was the beginning of a seven-film, four-year series of "Mexican Spitfire" movies, all costarring vaudeville comic Leon Errol as both Lindsay's Uncle Matt and the lookalike Lord Epping (a series of pleasant but colorless leading men played Carmelita's husband: Donald Woods, Charles "Buddy" Rogers, Walter Reed). The films pretty much wrote themselves: Carmelita gets her husband into some kind of mess, and Uncle Matt bails them out by impersonating Lord Epping, with much slapstick and many appalled dowagers snorting "Well, I *never!*" She was like Lucy Ricardo, with Ricky Ricardo's accent. The films never got much better, but they provided Lupe with a steady paycheck, all the way

Lupe in *Mexican Spitfire Out West*, 1940.

through the last, *Mexican Spitfire's Blessed Event* (1943).

Lupe was not otherwise idle during these years, appearing in half-a-dozen non-*Spitfire* films—she costarred in John Barrymore's last film, the strange, rather sad comedy *Playmates* (1941), was

Eddie Albert's baseball widow in *Ladies' Day* (1943), and played a dual role in the no-star *Red-Head from Manhattan* (1943). She *was* a redhead by that time, having lightened her hair in the early 1940s.

In the spring of 1944 she returned to Mexico one last time, in an effort to stimulate her flagging dramatic skills. In her first dramatic lead in years, she starred in a Spanish-language version of Zola's tragedy *Nana*. It looked as though Lupe, at the height of her beauty in her mid-thirties, might be opting for a lower-wattage, lower-profile career with brighter opportunities to develop as a serious actress in foreign films. But she would be dead by year's end.

Lupe's year-long affair with Viennese-born actor Harald Ramond resulted in pregnancy. Ramond refused to marry her, and Lupe refused to have an abortion. An illegitimate baby would have ruined her career—this was years before Ingrid Bergman's runaway romance with Roberto Rossellini, and not everyone could blithely finesse a baby as did Loretta Young with Clark Gable's offspring. On the night of December 13, 1944, Lupe took an overdose of Seconal. She left a note explaining her actions in no uncertain terms, blaming Ramond and asking her housekeeper to look after her dogs, Chips and Chops.

Lupe Velez's reputation was further tarnished by a ludicrous rumor—one of Hollywood's most infamous and oft-repeated urban legends—claiming that she drowned in her toilet while vomiting her sleeping pills. Not only was this version of her death never rumored till Kenneth Anger's *Hollywood Babylon* printed it in 1959, but it was physically impossible. The only way Lupe could have drowned in her toilet was if her maid held her upside-down and dunked her. Lupe's death was sad and senseless enough; Kenneth Anger succeeded in making her a posthumous joke, as well.

Alice White

Few actresses have generated as much industry hostility as blonde, goggle-eyed starlet Alice White, whose brief career as a late 1920s Jazz Baby ended in anonymity and personal disaster. Only then was Hollywood willing to forgive Alice for her too-sudden rise to the top.

Alice was born in Paterson, New Jersey, on August 28, somewhere between 1904 and 1907. Her mother died when Alice was a baby, so she and her maternal grandmother took off for Los Angeles. She attended Hollywood High School (her classmates included Joel McCrea and Mary Brian), and studied shorthand at a secretarial school. Her early jobs included office work at The Writer's Club and as a script girl for directors Roy William Neill and Josef von Sternberg. "After two weeks [von Sternberg] told me I was an excellent script girl," Alice recalled, "but that I didn't have the temperament for this business. For $18 a week he wanted temperament. So I got temperamental!" Unsurprisingly, that job didn't last long, and soon she was working for Charles Chaplin and at First National.

It was there that Alice got her first on-camera experience. One press release said that she was shoved in front of a camera to test a new lens; she herself admitted that she'd been pushing for acting jobs ever since crashing the studios. Finally, First National's John Francis Dillon gave her a small role in the Milton Sills film *The Sea Tiger* (1927).

At this time, Alice still had brown hair and looked rather like a second-string Clara Bow. Her big eyes, round face and curvy figure helped get her roles, but Alice was still very much untrained as an

Cute as a button: Alice White, ca. 1929.

actress. Enthusiastic and ambitious (a little too much so for some of her coworkers), she worked her way through a number of late silent films. In 1927, Alice had small roles in *American Beauty* (with Billie Dove) and *Breakfast at Sunrise* (with Constance Talmadge); she played Adraste, "a Greek flapper," in *The Private Life of Helen of Troy*, and supported Dorothy Davenport Reid in *The Satin Woman*. By 1928 her star was beginning to rise, and Alice was attracting notice. Her roles were getting bigger, though she was still a fresh-as-paint starlet: *The Big Noise, Three-Ring Marriage, The Mad Hour, Harold Teen*. That same year, she played the sensible Dorothy Shaw to Ruth Taylor's Lorelei Lee in *Gentlemen Prefer Blondes* (though, in retrospect, Alice seems born for the starring role).

Her first real showcase was as Dixie Dugan in *Show Girl* (1928), a pallid, silent adaptation of J.P. McEvoy's hilariously acidic novel. Alice's big year was 1929, during the hectic change-over from silents to talkies. It was then that she was discovered by First National's 29-year-old director Mervyn LeRoy, then married to actress Edna Murphy. LeRoy, who went on to direct and/or produce such classics as *Little Caesar, Gold Diggers of 1933, The Wizard of Oz, Mister Roberts,* and *The Bad Seed,* fell head over heels for Alice. He'd noticed her in his production of *Harold Teen,* and by now had enough pull to develop her as his own star.

Alice, by now a blonde, was star-billed in four 1929 films, three of them directed by LeRoy. The titles tell the stories: *Broadway Babies* ("Incandescent with It!" according to its ads), *Hot Stuff, Naughty Baby,* and *The Girl from Woolworth's* (the last directed by William Beaudine). She also made a few appearances in Warner Brothers' *Show of Shows* revue that year. In her starring films, Alice played the jazzy, dance-mad shopgirl who found fame, love or both through her brilliant talent and sparkling personality. The problem was, Alice White only possessed one of these attributes, and it wasn't brilliant talent. As Richard Barrios says in his delightful book *A Song in the Dark,* "Alice was unwisely cast as a first-rate singer and dancer, even when she was invariably outshone by her costars."

Her 1929 films did well enough at the box office, as musicals were all the rage; and Alice had, to be fair, some points in her favor. She was cute as a button and obviously enthusiastic. While one winced at her clunky dancing and whisper-thin singing, it was impossible to actually dislike the fluffy-bunny girl on the screen. Still, Mervyn LeRoy misread the signals and went on to star Alice in two more films, in 1930: *Playing Around* and *Show Girl in Hollywood.* This last film is pretty much unwatchable today, and again fares badly compared to the terrific J.C. McEvoy book (*Hollywood Girl*) on which it was based. Blanche Sweet, as a

A tougher, harder Alice in *Employees' Entrance*, 1933.

"washed-up" Hollywood star (Sweet was all of 34), stole the film from poor Alice.

Audiences and critics alike were beginning to complain that fun was fun, but Alice White was just not star material. Her films began to slide at the box office, and Mervyn LeRoy gave up (he soon went on to perform a much more successful star-making miracle with Ginger Rogers—that association was too much for his wife, who divorced him in 1933). Within the Hollywood community, it was whispered that Alice White had slept her way to success, while more talented starlets languished. True or not, these rumors did not lend Alice any good will when she needed it the most.

She made three more films for First National before her contract ended: *Sweet Mama* (1930, with David Manners), *The Widow from Chicago* (1930, with Neil Hamilton and Edward G. Robinson), and *The Naughty Flirt* (1931, with Myrna Loy). And then Alice's day as a star—so brief—was over. She was top-billed in one last film, Columbia's *Sweethearts on Parade* (1930), and played second-lead to silent-film star Aileen Pringle in the low-budget thriller *Murder at Midnight* (1931); then, she dropped out of sight.

With her film career apparently over, Alice set out to learn her trade. She spent the next two years touring in vaudeville, also appearing in a west coast production of *Dinner at Eight*. "I never wanted to be built up as a second Clara Bow," she told an interviewer in 1932. Of her derailed career, she said, "I had a misunderstanding with my producers and decided to make this personal appearance tour so I could find out for myself if I had a fan following. Now I'm satisfied that I have."

Alice hoped for the lead role in *Red-Headed Woman*, but that went to Jean Harlow. Not helping Alice's career was the fact that she was often confused by fans (and casting directors) with contemporary wise-cracking blondes Marjorie White (a brilliant song-and-dance gal who died in a car accident in 1935) and Thelma White (best-known today for *Reefer Madness*). Alice's next public appearance was in a real-life sordid sex scandal in 1933. She was beaten by her sometime boyfriend, British actor Jack Warburton, who was himself attacked in revenge by two men hired by Alice's friend Sy Bartlett. It all ended up in court, with Alice testifying that Warburton "beat me up all over the street and grabbed me by my hair. It's a wonder I didn't die." Alice later married her hero Bartlett, a screenwriter (the marriage ended in divorce in 1937; afterward, she briefly wed screenwriter Jack Roberts).

But if Alice's personal life was in a shambles, her career began getting back on track. Indeed, it got on the track it should have been on in the first place: Alice White became a delightful character actress, playing the sort of hard-boiled molls Iris Adrian and Pert Kelton excelled at. Her comeback was in *Employees' Entrance* (1933), where she stood out superbly in a smallish role. Hollywood sat up and took notice. Alice was cast in three more 1933 films: *King for a Night, Picture Snatcher* (a great James Cagney vehicle) and *Luxury Liner*. The same critics who had savaged her in 1930 rediscovered her as a talented supporting actress.

She played supporting roles in five 1934 films, including *Jimmy the Gent* (again with Cagney), *The Gift of Gab* (with Edmund Lowe) and *A Very Honorable Guy* (with Joe E. Brown). Things began to slow down again; she appeared in only one 1935 film, Warner Brothers' *Sweet Music*, starring Rudy Vallee. Alice took off for London to appear in a stage play, but it was soon reported that she was in a nursing home recuperating from a "nervous collapse." Back in the States, she was greeted with smaller roles in smaller films: *The Big City* (1937), *Annabel Takes a Tour* (1938) and the poverty-row *King of the Newsboys* and *Telephone Operator* (both 1938).

She appeared in a stage version of *Hi Diddle Diddle* in 1937, then pretty much retired from public life. She told a reporter that "I never made a great deal of money, and I lost a lot on the stock market, but I'm not destitute. Strangely enough, I don't miss the hoopla and popularity of being a star. But I do miss the loot." Alice's last three films—in which she had small roles—were *The Night of January 16th* (1941), *Girls' Town* (1942) and the Joan Crawford melodrama *Flamingo Road* (1949). By this time Alice was a slim, petite and still pretty redhead. "I think a woman looks kinda silly as a blonde when she gets to be my age," she said.

The 1950s did not begin promisingly for Alice, who found herself embroiled in another sex scandal, this one a mate-swapping alimony lawsuit. Alice sued husband no. 2, Jack Roberts, for back alimony, and showed up in court accompanied by husband no. 3, William Hinshaw. Roberts appeared—to the delight of reporters—accompanied by his current lover, who happened to be Hinshaw's ex-wife. A shouting match ensued, and press coverage was unflattering to all involved. Things did not improve: in 1957 Alice fell off a backyard ladder while holding gardening shears, and was nearly blinded. "Fortunately, I had a loyal bunch of friends who took care of me," she said.

She made a few appearances on local TV in Los Angeles, but by the 1960s Alice was back to her first job, working as a secretary. Of the current crop of film stars, Alice complimented Joanne Woodward and Marilyn Monroe, but complained that "they've gone too far in seeking sex movies . . . I think the public is tiring of that. I believe they're ready for more comedies." When a young friend saw an Alice White film on TV and commented on her "Marilyn Monroe walk," Alice snapped, "I did it first—that's an *Alice White* walk!"

By the time she died at her home of a stroke on February 19, 1983, both Alice's early career as a Jazz Baby and her later success as a character actress were pretty much forgotten. Obituaries were affectionate but brief, and many writers felt obliged to explain who she was to readers unfamiliar with her brief but dazzling career.

Notes & Acknowledgments

These articles were originally written between 1992 and 2004 and appeared in *Classic Images* and *Films of the Golden Age*. I have carefully re-edited, re-researched and re-written all of them, using whatever new information has since come to light. There are no footnotes because the vast majority of the information came from the files of The Billy Rose Collection at the New York Public Library, Lincoln Center. As for all my books, this library—and its wonderful, helpful staff—was a treasure trove of books, magazines, scrapbooks, folders packed with newspaper articles, correspondence, photos.

Any additional information is credited within the articles, or comes from the books listed in the bibliography (also the obits of the more recently deceased, largely from the *New York Times* and the *Telegraph*).

I'd like to thank the following people for invaluable information used in these articles: Kevin Brownlow, Herbie Buck, Taylor Coffman, Olivia De Havilland, Victoria Demchick, Susan Buchanan Dillon, William Drew, Barbara Dell Glass, Bradley Kuiper, Richard Lamparski, Donna Lee, Howard Lee Levine, Randal Malone, William J. Mann, the late Ann Miller, Stephen "Tad" O'Brien, the late Anita Page, James Robert Parish, Peter Plant, the late Michael Powazinik, the late Sylvia Sidney, Lauretta Slike, Bettina Uhlich, Michael Winterstein, the late Yvonne Wood, James Zeruk, Jr.

I'd also like to thank the good folks at the Straight Dope, Daughters of Naldi and Silver Screen Oasis message boards for their advice, contact information and great leads.

My hat is off to my amazing copy editor and fact checker, Richard Kukan, who transformed my garbled, incoherent ramblings into the spiffy document you see before you.

And, of course, Bob King and the *Classic Images/Films of the Golden Age* staff, for asking for these articles and publishing them over the past decade and a half!

Bibliography

Allgood, Jill. *Bebe and Ben: Bebe Daniels and Ben Lyon*. London: Robert Hale, 1975.

Aros. *Renate Müller: Ihr Werden und Wirken*. Berlin: Verlag Scherl, 1932.

Bach, Steven. *Marlene Dietrich: Life and Legend*. New York: William Morrow, 1992.

Barrios, Richard. *A Song in the Dark: The Birth of the Musical Film*. New York: Oxford University Press, 1995.

Bennett, Joan: *The Bennett Playbill*. Chicago: Holt, Rinehart and Winston, 1970.

Burke, Billie, and Cameron Shipp. *With a Feather On My Nose*. New York: Appleton-Century-Crofts, 1949.

Burke, Billie, and Cameron Shipp. *With Powder On My Nose*. New York: Coward-McCann, 1959.

Carey, Gary. *Judy Holliday: An Intimate Life Story*. New York: Seaview Books, 1982.

Clements, R.E. *Queen of America? The Case of Renate Müller*. London: John Gifford Ltd., 1944.

Daniels, Bebe, and Ben Lyon. *Life with the Lyons: The Autobiography of Bebe Daniels & Ben Lyon.* London: Odhams, 1953.

Fairbanks, Douglas, Jr. *Salad Days.* New York: Doubleday, 1988.

Fowler, Gene. *Schnozzola: The Story of Jimmy Durante.* New York: Viking, 1951.

Gil-Montero, Martha. *Brazilian Bombshell: The Biography of Carmen Miranda.* New York: Donald Fine, 1989.

Guiles, Fred Lawrence. *Norma Jean: The Life of Marilyn Monroe.* New York: McGraw-Hill, 1969.

Harris, Warren G. *The Other Marilyn: A Biography of Marilyn Miller.* New York: Arbor House Pub Co., 1985.

Hayter-Menzies, Grant. *Charlotte Greenwood: The Life and Career of the Comic Star of Vaudeville, Radio, and Film.* Jefferson, NC: McFarland & Company, 2007.

Holtzman, Will. *Judy Holliday.* New York: G. P. Putnam's Sons, 1982.

Joyce, Peggy Hopkins. *Men, Marriage and Me.* New York: Macaulay Company, 1930.

Kanfer, Stefan. *Groucho: The Life and Times of Julius Henry Marx.* New York: Alfred A. Knopf, 2003.

Kellow, Brian. *The Bennetts: An Acting Family.* Lexington: University Press of Kentucky, 2004.

Kennedy, Matthew. *Joan Blondell: A Life Between Takes.* Jackson: University Press of Mississippi, 2007.

King, Greg. *Sharon Tate and the Manson Murders*. Fort Lee, NJ: Barricade Books, 2000.

Klöckner-Draga, Uwe. *Renate Müller, Ihr Leben ein Drahtseilakt*. Bayreuth: Verlag Kern, 2006.

Lambert, Gavin. *Norma Shearer*. New York: Alfred A. Knopf, 1990.

Mansfield, Jayne and Mickey Hargitay. *Jayne Mansfield's Wild, Wild World*. Los Angeles: Holloway House 1963.

Marshall, Michael. *Top Hat and Tails: The Story of Jack Buchanan*. London: Elm Tree Books, 1978.

McGee, Tom. *Betty Grable: The Girl with the Million Dollar Legs*. Vestal, NY: Vestal Press, 1995.

Moore, Colleen. *Silent Star*. New York: Doubleday and Co., 1968.

Newquist, Roy. *Conversations with Joan Crawford*. Secaucus, NJ: Citadel Press, 1980.

Oakie, Jack. *Jack Oakie's Double Takes*. San Francisco: Strawberry Hill Press, 1980.

Oller, John. *Jean Arthur: The Actress Nobody Knew*. New York: Limelight Editions, 1997.

Robbins, Jhan. *Inka Dinka Doo: The Life of Jimmy Durante*. New York: Paragon House, 1991.

Rosenblum, Constance. *Gold Digger: The Outrageous Life and Times of Peggy Hopkins Joyce*. New York: Henry Holt and Company, 2000.

Saxton, Martha. *Jayne Mansfield and the American Fifties*. Boston: Houghton Mifflin. 1975.

Shipman, David. *The Great Movie Stars: The Golden Years.* London: MacDonald, 1989.

Shipman, David. *The Great Movie Stars: The International Years.* Boston: Little Brown & Co., 1995.

Swenson, Karen. *Greta Garbo: A Life Apart.* New York: Scriber's, 1997.

Wagenknecht, Edward. *Marilyn Monroe: A Composite View.* Philadelphia: Chilton Book Company, 1969.

Index

LaVergne, TN USA
21 September 2009
158404LV00004B/40/P